James Gatto

Frenchtown

A Semi-Fictional Memoir

Cover Photography:
@Sergey - stock.adobe.com
©Olexandr - stock.adobe.com

Book Design: Tricia Miller/MillerWorks

PAU 4-059-469

Dedicated to Joanne, Tommy, John, Patsy, and to all the other characters who live in my memory and in my imagination.

Thanks, guys!

Contents

A Note from the Author

Some months after my wife passed away, I was contacted by a former college classmate. He was one of a few I had hoped to reconnect with at our 50th college reunion. My wife's passing just a few months before the reunion precluded my attending. He suggested that we could gather periodically in zoom meetings, and that, because we all wrote as a pastime, perhaps we could share some of what we had written or were currently writing. I wrote what became the first chapter of *Frenchtown* for one of our early zoom gatherings, and the rest, as they say, is history.

Frenchtown started out a performance piece. I wanted it to be read on a stage to a live audience. And so I wrote … and wrote … and wrote some more. However, once I hit the six hour mark, I knew that *Frenchtown* would never be performed live, especially because I was still writing with no apparent end in sight.

I think that it was Mike Lomonico, one of my fellow "Old Stags" along with Byron Collins, Doug Johnson, and Mike Shiels, who first suggested that Frenchtown could be performed as a podcast. That way, the story would still have a performance component.

I auditioned six couples. A former student of mine, Daina Shatz, and her husband, Jeffrey Anbinder, were chosen to bring *Frenchtown* to life. Working with them over a period of months was a gift. The quality of their performances speaks for itself. Virtually everyone who took the time to listen has remarked on the "professionalism" of the presentation. That is owed to Daina and Jeff, who were ably supported by David Keith, who proved himself an expert technical director. The final podcast component was the introductory and play-out music, which was performed by Lisa "Spike" Norman. (The *Frenchtown* soundtrack and more is available at https://bluedogaudiopro.com/.) To date, I'm proud to say that the Frenchtown podcast is approaching two thousand listens.

Podcasts are not everyone's cup of tea. I can understand that. I think that's especially true of "story" podcasts, where you pretty much need to stay engaged with what you're hearing in order to maintain consistency. Story podcasts are good commute fodder, especially if you own a Tesla, which I don't. Listening at home, however, usually means that you're doing ten other things all at the same time, so it's easy for an audio story to just become another distraction which can easily get lost in the shuffle. And so, Frenchtown is now a novel.

I want to take a moment to acknowledge some of those who helped along the way. Kathy Keith was my associate producer. She was one of two people who steadfastly encouraged me and held my hand during the entire process. The other person was Lorraine Nelson who read and commented on every page. I may well have given up along the way except for her ability to motivate me to stick with it. If Stephanie Levine goes blind from all the punctuation editing and spell checking she did, I'm responsible. She was, and is, an expert grammarian. Elaine Bessette was another motivation resource. Our relationship as writers has been almost symbiotic. She was encouraging my writing while I was encouraging hers. Her book, *Twisted Fairy Tales* is a hoot. I consider myself lucky to own an autographed copy. Tricia Miller acted as editor and prepared the digital manuscript for printing. She did an incredible job of post-production. Finally, I'd like to acknowledge my family's continuing support. Thanks to Carolyn and Rick, Kathryn and Emily, Jeanette and Ruth, and, most of all, to Madeline.

Frenchtown is mostly a work of fiction. I say "mostly" because some of the places are (or were) real, and the people and events are loosely based on people I knew and things we did. I purposely avoided introspection when I was writing *Frenchtown*, afraid that the emotional repercussions would slow my process, perhaps even end it altogether. Introspection, for me, came only recently, when I returned to the original, pre-podcast narrative. I surprised myself when I realized that I hadn't read *Frenchtown*, as a first-time reader would, in several years. It was a revelation. This was especially true of the earlier chapters.

I've worked as a private tutor for a number of years. When a prospective client contacts me, I always suggest that we initiate contact via a zoom consultation. Part of the process that allows me to get to know a student comes in the form of a battery of questions. For example, I always ask: "What is the last movie you watched, in a theater, on TV, or online? What is your all-time favorite movie? What TV shows do you try never to miss? What was your favorite story growing up?"

I ask these questions because I've always believed that you can learn a lot about a person if you know what stories influenced them. The stories that influenced me were those movies I watched as a child. If you're new to Frenchtown, by the way, they're described in detail in Chapter 3, "The Strand." The stories that informed my view of the world and shaped my personality were right there on the bigger-than-life black and white screen. I am a product of that storytelling, and so, in turn, is my own storytelling. The fact that I'm still profoundly influenced by those formative experiences is the "revelation" I speak of. It's nice to know, at my advanced age, that I'm still learning about myself. I have a decorative tile hanging in my kitchen. In it, a little gnome with a red hat is peaking out from behind a tree, one of many trees in a painted forest. That gnome reminds me every day, that no matter whom you're writing about, you're really always writing about yourself.

A technical note. I decided to handle the dialog in Frenchtown in a somewhat unconventional way. Longer dialog exchanges between two characters is presented in a "play script" fashion. By this, I mean that the character's name, followed by a colon, will introduce what the character says. My intention was to streamline the traditional "he said/she said" interruptions. I interrupt this form of dialog, on only a few occasions, to describe actions that are relevant to what is happening at the time.

Shorter dialog exchanges are presented more conventionally.

Prologue

You're probably wondering about the name, aren't you?

Well, the first thing you need to know is that Frenchtown wasn't a town at all. It was a working class neighborhood on the west bank of the Connecticut River, halfway between Hartford and Springfield, which existed to serve what was then the largest rug and carpet factory in the world, Bigelow-Sanford.

The second thing you need to know about Frenchtown is that nobody French lived there. Instead, the neighborhood was almost exclusively first and second-generation Italian and Polish. The final thing you need to know is that Frenchtown was as much a state of mind as a place, but more about that later.

My earliest memories of family are fleeting and indistinct. I remember shoveled paths of snow where the bordering banks were taller than I was. I remember shooting sucker-tipped arrows at a picture of a deer, which my grandfather had painted on a sheet of metal and attached to the side of our house. And I remember dipping an old brush into a pail filled with water and then "painting" our house. It always looked great until the water dried, then you'd have to paint it again.

And I remember my grandfather helping me build a plastic model of a World War II fighter plane while I had the measles. These memories are like Kodak black and white snapshots of a time long past-just fleeting images. My first concrete memory is of something that happened in kindergarten.

PART 1

NORTH SCHOOL

Ding Dong Dead

Thompsonville hosted two elementary schools, North School and South School. The names speak for themselves. Frenchtownies opted for tradition in lieu of invention. Both were neighborhood schools in the truest sense. There were no school buses. You walked to and from, and if you lived close enough to one school or the other, you walked home for lunch. There was no parking lot, so teachers parked their cars on the streets. I learned this in third grade. Until then, I assumed that my teachers lived in the school. Why wouldn't I? After all, they were always there when I arrived in the morning, and they were still there when I left in the afternoon. I think I envisaged a kind of academic communal lifestyle. I remember that I had crushes on my first and second grade teachers. My second grade teacher, in fact, married in the spring of that school year. She went from Miss (insert unspellable Italian name here) to Mrs. Devine. This left me devastated but even more determined to eventually claim her for myself. My third, fourth, and fifth grade teachers were crones, my sixth grade teacher a man.

I've always ascribed to the adage: "First impressions last." Do you remember your first impression of school? What about your first day of school? Do you remember your first day? By this I mean *public* school because there were no nursery schools or private pre-schools in Frenchtown. Nobody could have afforded them. My education began in kindergarten. And, no, I don't remember my first day either. My first impression, however, is of a shortened day, in fact, the last day before the start of Christmas vacation.

Our kindergarten teacher was Miss Sullivan, an aging spinster, whose older sister, also an aged spinster named Miss Sullivan, was the principal. I'm sure it was a joyous time for us. When you're five or six years old, those last few days before Santa's visit have your sugarplums doing jitterbugs. All of the talk was about what we were hoping Santa would leave under our trees. Only a class Grinch would question how Santa could come down our chimneys when most chimneys in Frenchtown terminated not in fireplaces but in furnaces.

Our classroom had a high tin ceiling with suspended light fixtures. I mention this because I remember those warm incandescent lights which cast a warm glow even on dark winter days. I've spent most of my working life in rooms lit exclusively by fluorescent lights, and I hate their cold, lifeless pallor. The tall windows of our classroom were decorated with cut-out, asymmetrical paper snowflakes, and thalidomide snowmen. Just below the windows was a rank of radiators which sometimes hissed and gurgled. The radiators were capped with metal covers which acted as shelves for classroom supplies. Our favorite activity involved rigid cardboard box tops which were covered in brightly covered wrapping paper. They were stored open end up and contained wooden blocks in various shapes and sizes, all painted in primary colors. Red and green construction paper garlands and Santa Claus cut-outs gave the room a particularly festive atmosphere.

While we were singing "I'm a Little Teapot" for the third or fourth time (we liked acting it out), Miss Sullivan's playing slowed and then stopped altogether.

Our normal routine was to start each day with "good morning" songs, which Miss Sullivan pounded out on an ancient upright piano painted institutional green. We would then bring the boxes of colored blocks to our desks where we played independently while Miss Sullivan hovered nearby to act as supervisor/counselor/referee. While we were singing "I'm a Little Teapot" for the third or fourth time (we liked acting it out), Miss Sullivan's playing slowed and then stopped altogether. As she slowed, Miss Sullivan gradually lowered her head closer and closer to the keyboard. She stopped playing completely when her head came to rest on the keys. It was turned sideways, and her eyes were closed. We finished the song without accompaniment and then waited for "Jingle Bells" or "Santa Claus is Comin' to Town," but bells didn't jingle and Saint Nick was apparently running late. Although no one spoke, I think it's fair to say that we all assumed that Miss Sullivan had simply fallen asleep, hopefully after staying up late to help Santa wrap presents for all of us. After a few moments of silence, we turned as one to look at Joanne Shultz, who was both the smartest kid in the class, and, coincidentally, that week's "Class Leader" (we had a different one every week. Joanne looked as puzzled as everyone else for a moment, but then she regained her composure and took control proclaiming, "All right, let's play with blocks." And we did so with gusto.

Indeterminate time passed during which the suspension of adult supervision allowed for minor liberties to be taken while Miss Sullivan napped. A few students sat next to friends and worked jointly on block projects, Natalie Vancini visited each table to criticize works in progress and offer her suggestions for improvement, Tommy Ferraro tried to distract certain girls (the ones he liked) so that Johnny Damian could steal some of their blocks—preferably the red ones, Joanne Shultz and Marie Molinski made a list of the boys in class they hated and ranked the names from most hated to least hated, Mary Bourke told Bobby Kasazska that they should get married but Carol Armenio interrupted the proposal to say that she and Bobby were already engaged, Cha Cha Rinaldi somehow fashioned a replica of a suspension bridge out of blocks (a favorite Cha Cha Rinaldi pastime), while Patsy Russo surreptitiously ate clay (a favorite Patsy Russo pastime).

Suddenly, the classroom door opened, and an officious 6th grade "milk money" girl entered. She looked around the room and finally spied Miss Sullivan at the piano. She approached respectfully and waited. She cleared her throat twice. When she didn't receive a response, she very reluctantly tapped Miss Sullivan on the shoulder—no response. She tapped harder—no response. She poked—no response. She poked harder. Her poke became a push. At that, Miss Sullivan slowly slumped to the left. Like an old building imploding in slow motion, she slid off the piano stool and onto the floor.

Miss Milk Money screamed loud and long and bolted from the room hysterically, spraying nickels in all directions. Johnny scooped them up. Some of the girls (and a few boys) started to cry. I could see the bottom of Miss Sullivan's slip protruding out from under her skirt. All I can think of was something I once heard my Aunt Sarah say to her sister, my Aunt Mary, when her slip was showing. She said, "It's snowing down south." As this was said in July, I didn't understand it, but I remember Aunt Mary then adjusted her dress and the snow stopped falling.

Soon we heard footsteps approaching at a gallop. The first to enter was Mr. Knight, North School's grandfatherly custodian, who took one look at Miss Sullivan snowing down south and said, "Oh, shit."

And that is my first impression of public school.

Catechism Class

Catechism Class met once weekly after the regular school day had ended. Everyone in my second-grade class was Catholic (as far as I knew everyone in the civilized world was Catholic). So every Monday afternoon we traveled in convoy from public to parochial, from material to spiritual, from sublime to ridiculous. En route we passed Vesci's Bike Shop, Caronna's Market, Scavatto's Pharmacy, Molinski's Flower Shop, Alaimo's Package Store, Gatto's Music, etc., aka Thompsonville's Stations of the Cross, until we arrived at our own private Golgotha, St Patrick's Church School.

The church school was one of three buildings that made up the St Patrick's trinity. The others were the church itself, whose architecture could best be described as Early Grotesque, the Rectory (ditto), and the Sisters of Mercy Convent. A funny thing about the convent is that in all the years I walked, bicycled, and later drove by the convent, I never saw a nun enter or leave the building. My grade school self eventually concluded that nuns practiced Holy Teleportation.

Our classroom was on the second floor. It had a distinct old school building smell which was unmistakable, a combination of overheated radiators, pencil shavings, chalk dust, and vintage nun.

The double doors opened on a wide staircase, the wooden stair treads worn smooth by the shoes of thousands of children, some walking into bondage while others acted more like Egyptian slaves jubilantly fleeing the Pharaoh. Full-time St Patrick's students (we called them "lifers") would thunder down one side, their day ended, while we laboriously climbed the other. At the top of the stairs, a good sister imposed order by wielding a yardstick like a traffic wand and endlessly intoning "stay to the right, stay to the right." As the two groups passed, they (the lifers) would sometimes give us questions to ask in class which they assured us would put us in the good graces of our nun/teachers. I remember suggestions like "Ask her what does self-abuse mean and should you do it," "Ask her if Jesus was a Catholic," "Ask her if nuns go on dates with priests," "Ask her if Limbo is a place, or a dance, or both." St Patrick's students were really evil.

Our class "textbook" was the Baltimore Catechism. I've hated Maryland ever since. The catechism was divided into chapters, and each chapter consisted of a series of questions and answers. We were expected to memorize the answers and to respond from memory when called on—but only for certain chapters. The remaining, more interesting chapters were reserved for older students who were preparing for high end sacraments. Still, the index was titillating. I saw chapter titles that used words like "sacrifice" (remember Jungle Jim movies where a virgin was always going to be sacrificed to appease some bloodthirsty god), penance (which I knew meant punishment), temporal punishment, which someone said was punishment to your head, and extreme unction. Whatever that meant it was "extreme" so it demanded attention.

I never saw a nun enter or leave the building. My grade school self eventually concluded that nuns practiced Holy Teleportation.

If you answered a catechism question correctly, you were rewarded with a "Saint Card"—picture baseball cards with saints instead of ballplayers. On the face of each card was a painting of a saint doing something beatific, while the back of each card highlighted the saint's "stats" i.e. the saint's life, his wondrous deeds, and why he became a saint, which was usually by dying in some gruesome (but always inventive) way. Also like baseball cards, there were no suits or denominations so we invented our own. I mean, come on, everybody knew that a St Michael (I loved his sword!) was more valuable than a St Francis (too many squirrels and bunnies) and, needless to say, a Virgin Mary was more valuable than Mary Magdalene, because, after all, the Virgin Mary was a virgin, whatever that was.

The Jesus cards, a whole series which recorded every aspect of his life and death, were the most prized except for the very hard to get Father, Son, and Holy Ghost cards, which one of the older kids dubbed the Sacred Trifecta. I didn't know what that meant, but I thought it might have something to do with church bingo which was every Wednesday.

Patsy was shaped like a fire hydrant, had a round, angelic face, curly Medusa hair, and was a total anarchist.

The class consisted of Sister Kerosina asking us to recite the answers to catechism questions from the previous week. Then she'd talk about the subject of the current week's chapter, during which we'd carve dirty words into the old wooden desktops. The lesson concluded with her reciting the questions and telling us to memorize the answers for the next class meeting.

Sometimes the class ended a little early. She couldn't dismiss us before time because some kids would have parents or older siblings waiting to escort them home, especially during the winter when it would start getting dark pretty early. That's when she would say our favorite five words: "Do you have any questions?" And, *voila*!, Patsy Russo took center stage.

I mentioned Patsy some time ago. The last time you saw him he was surreptitiously eating clay while Miss Sullivan was somewhere between rigor and mortis. Patsy was shaped like a fire hydrant, had a round, angelic face, curly Medusa hair, and was a total anarchist.

I distinctly remember that the first time I saw him he was fighting an older, larger fourth grader. The dispute was over the ownership of a green marble. You might think this trivial, but back then no two marbles were alike. They had individuality which gave them character. They had unique colors and swirls, very unlike the current cats' eyes imposters with their generic plastic centers embedded in clear glass. I once had a friend who dropped a tab of acid and spent hours just staring at the swirls in one of those old school marbles, all the while intoning, "the colors, the colors."

The fourth grader, who was clearly stronger than Patsy, put him in a head lock, and we figured it was over, but Patsy countered by punching him in the jewels. When he staggered, Patsy grabbed the marble, held it up like a trophy for all assembled to admire, and promptly swallowed it. Even the fourth grader, still gasping and holding his crotch, seemed impressed. Then Patsy ran like hell. I decided, at that very moment, that Patsy was someone worth knowing.

I caught up with him in the cemetery. Anytime you needed to hide from somebody, including parents, the cemetery was a sure thing. Sometimes we just visited because it was low-hanging forbidden fruit. Younger kids were fascinated by the morbid significance of the gravestones, the earthen mounds, and especially those little locked buildings where coffins were stored when the ground was frozen. Middle school kids went there to smoke cigarettes they had stolen from their parents and to plot world domination; high schoolers went there to make out.

On Mortality

Most children first confront mortality through the death of a parent or grandparent, or, in my case, through the untimely demise of Fritz the Turtle. I inherited Fritz, along with his name, from a friend whose family was moving out of state. He didn't want Fritz to have to form a new circle of friends, so he left him in my care. Fritz met his end at the hands (the foot actually) of our mailman who left poor Fritz even closer to the ground than he normally was. Still, it was a bloodless, gutless end, with Fritz somewhat unnaturally compressed. His funeral was dignified; protocol was observed. We buried him in a Band-Aid can, but we took the band aids out first because they weren't going to do Fritz any good.

Funny thing about death: it's pretty final, though some religions consider it more like a cosmic graduation ceremony. I mean death is what the French would call a *raison d'etre* where religion is concerned, don't you think? If we live moral lives, then paradise awaits. Now, some would say that, historically, this concept of delayed gratification came about as a way for oppressors to ensure their own comfort and profitability by continually imposing hardships on the oppressed, i.e. the powerless Plebes propped up the powerful Patricians who promised the powerless Plebes a powerful post vita paradise (and not by a dashboard light). Wasn't it Karl Marx who said (I'm paraphrasing here), "Religion is the opiate of the masses?" I'm pretty sure that's what he meant. That moment in the arena when you're about to turn into lion chow is the perfect time to get those holy pheromones cranked up.

What bothers me most is the "Get 'em while they're young" indoctrination, best represented by Sister Kerosina first introducing us to things like the Immaculate Conception, this before I knew what "conception" meant, and "immaculate" was a word used in TV commercials to hock cleansers. Patsy concluded that Mr. Clean was Jesus' father. The rest of us thought it was St Joseph.

Patsy Russo was Irish/Italian, or, if you grew up in Frenchtown as I did, Italian/Irish. J.K. Rowling would probably have called him a Mudblood (like Hermione), and that pretty well describes how he was thought of and treated by most of the racial/ethnic purists in my neighborhood. Between his genetic profile and his appearance, he didn't really have much going for him. On top of that, he had a lisp. Well, to be fair, it wasn't actually a lisp. I once mimicked him to a speech major I much later dated in college, and she described his impediment as a tongue thrust. She and I did a lot of tongue thrusting of our own, but that's another story. As a result, Patsy's given name, Patrick, came out "Patwick," which is why his mother started calling him "Patty," but that sounded too girly, so "Patty" eventually evolved into "Patsy," or, as he used to say it, "Pathsy," but I always called him Patsy. Confused? You had to be there. What really set him apart (and made me want to be his friend) was that he was both very bright and a dedicated anarchist.

Back to catechism class. Here's Patsy's m.o. where the good sister was concerned. I'll interpret for you.

Sister Kerosina: *We seem to have a few minutes to spare. Why don't you get started on your homework for next week's class. Do you have any questions?*

Patsy: *Thister! Thister!*

S.K.: *Yes, Mr. Russo.*

Patsy: *Thister, my mother's got a crutch at home on the table with the baby Jesus and everybody and…*

S.K.: *I think you mean a crèche, Mr. Russo, not a crutch.*

First he baits the hook.

Patsy: *uh…okay…you're right Thister, her crutch is in the bathroom, but what I mean is about all the animals.*

S.K.: *What about them?*

Then he casts the line.

Patsy: *Well I understand about the camels because it was in the desert and that's how the Wise Men got there, right?*

S.K.: *Very good, Mr. Russo. Yes, they followed the star to find Baby Jesus and to bring gifts.*

Patsy: *Yeah, and that's why there's a sheep and a cow and a donkey.*

S.K.: *Very good again, Patsy.*

She had switched to his first name. He was getting closer!

S.K.: *There was no room at the inn so the Virgin Mary gave birth to Baby Jesus in a manger.*

Patsy: *But what about the squirrels and bunnies, Thister? They don't have squirrels and bunnies in the desert, do they?*

S.K.: *Well, not normally, no, but this was a very special occasion, a miracle, and with a miracle all things are possible.*

Patsy: *Even a monkey?*

S.K.: *There's a monkey?*

Patsy: *Yeah. My sister put a monkey in there.*

And the fish takes the bait.

S.K.: *Well, God created all animals, so I suppose a monkey could have been there if He willed it.*

He reels her in.

Patsy: *Who? The monkey?*

S.K.: *No, Mr. Russo, God. Now does anybody else have a question?*

You could tell from the change in Sister Kerosina's posture that she was becoming increasingly uncomfortable. She may even have begun to wonder if Patsy was playing her. He was.

Patsy: *Thister! Thister!*

S.K.: *I've answered your question, Mr. Russo, now let's give someone else a chance.*

No other hands went up. We were enjoying this—all of us. Remember that we were the class that had the reputation of killing its kindergarten teacher.

S.K.: *All right, Mr. Russo, proceed with your question, but make it quick because we're almost out of time.*

Patsy: *Yes, Thister. Thister, I was watching this program on TV about the war* (WW II—remember that the war ended in 1945 and this is the mid-50's) *and I saw how the Japs believed their emperor was their god.*

S.K.: *They were heathens, Mr. Russo. There is only one true God.*

Patsy: *Yes, Thister, thavages. But their emperor told his pilots to crash their planes into American ships. They were called Kamakathies. And he told them that if they killed Americans that way they'd go to heaven and they believed him because they thought he was God. So are they in heaven now Thister?*

S.K.: *Absolutely not, because their emperor was never a god.*

Patsy: *But Thister, they thought he was, so it wasn't their fault. Is there a Jap heaven Thister? And if you commit a sin but you don't know it's a sin when you commit it, then is it still a sin?*

S.K.: *I think that Father Benedict could explain it to you better Mr. Russo because we're now out of time. Stop in his office on the way out.*

Patsy: *But Thister…*

S.K.: *Go to his office now, Mr. Russo.*

And with the words "go to his office" Patsy (and the class) knew he'd won. He never went to Father Benedict's office by the way. He took a victory lap around the church parking lot instead. Patsy was a master.

Bat Day

The Youth Center was just a short walk from my house. In fact, Thompsonville's entire commercial and municipal center was just a short walk from my house. The town had grown up to service the immigrant population that worked in The Mill, specifically the Bigelow-Sanford Carpet Company—then the largest rug manufacturer in the world. The Youth Center building was a brownstone monstrosity with a public gymnasium and a small Police Station on the first floor, along with a grouping of administrative offices and a large, open game room on the second. The game room hosted pool tables, ping pong, table hockey, etc. and an area was also set aside for crafts-mostly of the macaroni glued to paper plates variety. Thompsonville didn't have need for much law enforcement, hence the token police station. Frenchtown was known to police itself: that is, the Italian/Polish population dispensed its own form of justice quickly, efficiently, and often brutally.

An annual summer highlight was the Youth Center/St Patrick's Church co-sponsored trip to Yankee Stadium. We looked forward to this event with great anticipation, so I'm surprised that I don't recall these trips in greater detail. I remember that we traveled in a convoy on school buses, that it was always unbearably hot, and that after the first 30-45 minutes of travel during which we sang songs, played games, and showed off our Yankee attire, the trip became interminable. My memories of times spent in the stadium are equally vague. I know that our seats were set well back from the field, and that whenever something momentous happened (which wasn't near often enough) everyone stood and cheered. The adults in front of us blocked our view so we could only applaud their upper backs. I also remember spending much time in the concourse which was usually more interesting than what was happening on the playing field. The smell of grilling hot dogs, relish, mustard and chopped onions is somehow both unique and unforgettable. On rare occasions I'll catch a whiff at carnivals or outdoor gatherings and, if I close my eyes, I'm right back in the Yankee Stadium concourse ridiculing Johnny Pelligrino for putting ketchup on his hot dog.

The real attraction to this trip wasn't the journey to get there, or the ballgame, or even the hot dog smell. It was the prize waiting for each of us on arrival. Can you imagine Thompsonville's civic and religious leaders even hatching the following idea? "*Hey, I know! Let's round up a whole lot of these bored, summer-stupefied, testosterone-fueled fun bags, cram them onto hot, sweaty, stinky buses for five or six hours until their natural pre-teen energy is ready to incandesce, then, and here's the best part, we'll make sure each and every one is given a weapon. They'll love us. What can possibly go wrong?"* Welcome to Yankee Stadium Bat Day.

On Bat Day, every child below the age of whatever was given a miniature Louisville Slugger. They were about 12 inches long, made of pine and branded with the manufacturer's logo, and monogrammed with the name of a team member. The Mickey Mantles and Yogi Berras were the most desirable, the bats with pitchers' names the least so. Much trading and bartering ensued. Patsy usually made out well by daring somebody that he could perform a feat of outrageous gustatory talent to win his desired bat and then doing it. Somehow I usually ended up with a Bobby Richardson, a second baseman, not the most glamorous position to play. I always tried to trade up to a Hank Bauer for three reasons: first, it was an easy trade to make (they were about equal in status), second, because I liked the name "Hank," and third, because he played right field. Right fielders were never the strongest batters on the team, but they often had to execute longer throws than anyone else, and I had a strong throwing arm, so Hank and I were brothers (in arms), yuck, yuck. The second reason, his name, was actually the most important where I was concerned, because you acquired your bat's player's name and pseudo-identity for the next couple of weeks. So I temporarily became Hank, a name I aspired to as the epitome of tobacco chewing nicotine spitting, beer swilling masculinity. For a short time I swaggered and spat a lot, even in the house-when no one was looking of course. Phil Rizzuto lived next door, Enos Slaughter down the street, and Mickey and Yogi both lived one street over on Russell Ave.

Whenever something momentous happened, everybody stood and cheered. The adults who sat in front of us blocked our view, so we could only applaud their upper backs.

Another way of trading up bat-wise was to flip for your bat of choice. Remember when I mentioned Saints Cards? Back then, there were cards for everything. In addition to Saints cards and baseball cards, there were also "flags of the world" cards. (Ask me to describe the original flag of Yugoslavia; go ahead, I dare you), fire engine cards (I always liked the pumpers better than the hook and ladders), airplane cards, (still my favorites) and famous authors' cards (BORING!), etc. Here's how flipping worked. Say I would offer to flip for someone else's bat. If I won the flip, then he would have to exchange his bat for mine. If I lost, he walked away with two bats. The stakes were high. If he accepted the challenge, he flipped first.

He held the card horizontally at the center of its top edge. Some guys felt there was an advantage to looking at the face of the card when you flipped, some preferred to see the card's back. When ready, he would push the card forward and down so that it turned horizontally end over end until it landed face up or down. Then I flipped. If I, as the challenger, then matched his flip, I won, and he would have to exchange his bat for mine. If I failed… well, let's just say that coming home batless on Yankee Stadium bat day was absolutely mortifying.

Bats became the weapon of choice until they inevitably broke, usually while being wielded in combat, said combat being popularized, of course, by the bats themselves. The more the population of surviving bat-day bats whittled down (pun alert), the more they increased in value. The population of welts, bumps, and bruises decreased proportionally. We weren't usually all that attracted to physical violence, but the bats made it both inevitable and almost irresistible-at least for a time. However, Frenchtown was very much defined by what some would call a "mill town mentality" and Italians, in particular, are not exactly known for settling disputes with quiet, deliberative negotiation. All in all, it was a pretty tough place to grow up.

Bats became the weapon of choice until they inevitably broke, usually while being wielded in combat, said combat being popularized, of course, by the bats themselves.

THE MILL

My Grandfather

August 7, 2:17 a.m. Step outside. It's two o'clock in the morning and the cast iron railings on the back steps are still warm from the past day's sun. Twelve hours from now you won't want to touch them at all. It was 97 today, and tomorrow will be the same, and the day after that, and the day after that, and…. You can see the humidity; the air is saturated, almost hard to breathe in fact. You have a clear view all the way across the town center to St Patrick's. You know it's there, but you can't see it, because there's just too much moisture in the air. The sky is cloudless, but there are no stars. The moon is a fuzzy crescent. The few lit store signs sport colorful neon halos: Nowak's Pharmacy in blue, Western Auto in white, The Strand Theater in pink. The sweat-fog reeks of damp vegetation. Tomatoes and peppers are ripe in the garden, but you have to harvest before 7:00 a.m., and, even at that hour of the morning, you know it means you'll be starting a long day smelling pretty ripe yourself. Mosquitoes are starting to pay you attention. You feel them, but you cannot hear them. If someone were speaking to you from just a couple of feet away, you probably wouldn't hear them either. This is because the windows in the loom buildings are wide open to catch a breath of air, and the noise is deafening. Each loom, and there are dozens, consists of hundreds of small metal parts performing numerous mechanical tasks, and each moving part makes a sound, and, collectively, these sounds grow into a cacophony choir. The third shift workers communicate only with hand signals.

The unintended consequence of living with factory white noise was volume. People, even in the most casual or personal of conversations, spoke more loudly than normal; televisions needed to be turned up so that seniors could hear soap opera dialog; music was played loudly on home stereos and on car radios; even the sound system in The Strand Theater was cranked, but this white noise was the price of a steady job. This was the sound of Thompsonville's prosperity.

Thompsonville was the heart of Enfield, and Frenchtown was the heart of Thompsonville, and The Bigelow-Sanford Rug Company was the heart of Frenchtown. Most of the employees were first-generation immigrants. B-S actively recruited them as a source of cheap labor. I remember hearing that B-S had even advertised in foreign newspapers (Italian and Polish) to build a workforce which kept The Mill running 24/7; three shifts a day, every day except Sunday.

Everything about The Mill was huge. It covered many acres and consisted of over 20 buildings of every size, shape, description, and function. The largest of these buildings housed the looms and shuttles where the weaving took place. Picture two-story brick buildings with flat roofs. The rooms on each level were at least 16 feet high to accommodate the pulley system that powered the machines. Exterior walls featured rows of tall, narrow windows, set in brick, which could be opened to provide ventilation and cooling. There was no air conditioning. Now, imagine these buildings as long as aircraft carriers or Carnival Cruise ships. They were immense. I grew up a few hundred feet from one of these behemoths.

Although the company employed many hundreds, maybe even thousands at its peak, only one person had the run of the place, with access to any room, in any building, at any time of the day or night. Only one person made his own work schedule, determined his own hours on site, was allowed to come and go freely with no explanation necessary, and never, ever punched a time card. And that person was my grandfather.

Three generations under one roof were common in Frenchtown. In addition to my sister, mother, and father, our family also included my father's parents and my grandmother's spinster sister. My father, after being discharged from the navy at the end of WWII, worked as a professional musician and was often touring, so I didn't see much of him. That made my grandfather my principal male influence.

> **Although the company employed many hundreds, maybe even thousands at its peak, only one person had the run of the place, with access to any room, in any building, at any time of the day or night.**

Simply put, grandpa was a mechanical genius. His knowledge, skills, instinct, and intuition regarding machines, how they worked, why they sometimes didn't work, and how to get them working properly again, were so valued by his employers that they just kept out of his way—for over 50 years. He "owned" that place.

He'd arrive every morning around 6:00 and go straight to his office, which was a modified storage room. Shelves and boxes overflowed with equipment, supplies, hand tools, power tools, and hardware of every description. His work benches were cluttered with parts and assemblies, some needing repair, some brand new, and some now broken and no longer repairable but saved to be disassembled for spare parts. To an outsider it was chaos personified, but he could put his hands on anything he might need for a repair in seconds. He'd start each day by looking at his clipboard of work orders. New ones would have been added by second and third shift personnel. Work orders were divided into three categories: urgent, asap, and important (in other words, never going to happen). Then he'd map out his work route for the day from building to building-no point in having to retrace your steps unnecessarily. He'd load up his tool box with whatever tools, hardware, and other equipment he thought he might need for that day's repairs, and he'd set off.

Occasionally I was allowed to spend a few hours with him as he went about his daily routine. I went in with him in the morning, but I'd usually lose interest by lunch time. I enjoyed spending time with him because he'd try to make me feel as though I was actually helping, even though, deep down inside, I knew I actually wasn't. However, what I really reveled in was the degree of respect he was shown by both management and his peers as he went about his daily routine. I took as much pride in that as he did.

I'm pretty sure that part of the reason he loved his job and did it so well is that it provided him with an escape from his own personal Darth Vader, aka his wife, aka my grandmother. Everybody called her "Bossa." And that about summed her up. I remember reading somewhere that Afro-American culture is matriarchal. The same could be said about Italian-American families—at least back then. She ruled with an iron fist. Her word was law.

My Grandmother

My earliest memories have my grandfather, my grandmother, and her sister all working in The Mill. With my father on the road, that left my mother to care for me and my sister. However, musical tastes were changing rapidly in the 50's. Patti Page eventually gave way to Elvis. American music went from "How Much is that Doggie in the Window?" to "Hound Dog" seemingly overnight. My father's work changed commensurately, with the tours lasting longer and covering greater distances. Those changes, in combination with the need to provide a more reliable income for a growing family, eventually led my father to open Gatto's Music Center in the heart of Thompsonville's commercial center. My mother worked there behind the counter mostly selling records, while my father sold and serviced record players, radios, and TV's. My grandmother and her sister left the factory and became full-time babysitters to me and my two-year younger sister.

I remember hearing a saying that pertained to sex: "Women need a reason, men just need a place." This saying, slightly modified, would also pertain to fighting where certain Italian families were concerned: Italians don't need a reason, Italians just need a place. The place, in my family's case, was anywhere on the first floor, always on a Sunday afternoon. The bell for round one more or less coincided with the opening kick-off of the weekly NFL match up. The reasons varied. Often they involved a transgression by some relative. Somebody had said or done something about or to someone else. A codicil to the modified aforesaid adage: Always have an enemy, and, if you don't have one, invent one, because sometimes imagined slights were even juicier than real ones.

DING! And the bobbing and weaving (always in Italian) commenced, soon to be followed by jabs and uppercuts. Verbal punches became the logical escalation. My sister and I usually fled the scene to avoid generational collateral damage. When we were very young, my mother shepherded us upstairs to her room where she played our favorite records (Little Toot!) loudly or read us stories (*The Little Engine that Could*) also loudly. As we grew older, my sister and I learned to sequester ourselves, usually outdoors where the now muffled arguing could often still be heard.

Now I've never been able to speak Italian very well, even though it was the language of choice in our house, but I understood some of what I heard others say. Certain names of relatives came up frequently and heatedly during the Sunday Night (actually afternoon) Fights. My grandfather had three brothers: Tommy, Gerry, and Nicky; and nine sisters: Mary, Sarah, Rose, Angeletta, Josephine, Annie, Katy, Sophie, and Maria. Mary and Sarah (who married brothers Harry and Johnny by the way) and Rose were often targets. "Of what?" You might ask. "No clue." I might answer, but they were the fattest targets.

Now, Bossa, my grandmother, was the grand master of Italian profanity. The more her need to vent, the more linguistically creative she became. Her diatribes usually began with simple name-calling.

My aunt Sarah, for instance, might be called a *strega* (a witch), a *cretina* (a dummy), *deficiente* (simple-minded), a *jabrona* (dumbass), or a *puttana*, *zoccola*, or *troia*, which all mean "whore," but without any sexual connotation. Derogatory Italian names for men were fewer and less descriptive. It was almost as though Bossa considered men such low-hanging fruit when it came to insults that she couldn't be bothered to get too inventive. *Bastardo* was the most common male epithet, along with *stunad* (dummy), *chooch* (jackass), and *testa di cazzo* (shithead), which was often directed at my grandfather. One thing I learned about Italian venting is that you try to mitigate at your own peril. Once Bossa was on a roll, it was best to just let her spew. The tipping point was often her use of *pezzo di merda* (piece of shit). This was about as far as nouns could take her.

One thing I learned about Italian venting is that you try to mitigate at your peril. Once Bossa was on a roll, it was best to just let her spew.

Verb alert! As is true in English (and probably any language for that matter), the "f" word and all of its foreign equivalents rule. She often said *fongool* (fuck you), and *vafongool* (go fuck yourself), but her variation of choice was always *vaffanculo* (go fuck yourself in the ass), this, again, usually directed at my grandfather and/or his kin. On a few, notable occasions, when she felt herself particularly aggrieved, she dragged out her verbal heavyweights. This was when we heard *vaffanculo a chi te morto* (go fuck your dead family members in the ass), or the ultimate: *li morfacci tua, de tuo nonno, de tua madre, e dei tres quattri daa palazzina tua* (go fuck your dead relatives, your grandfather's dead relatives, your grandmother's dead relatives, and the dead relatives of three quarters of your neighborhood). As children, we, my sister and I, were forbidden to use any of these words or expressions. We settled instead for *gogootz*, which is the Italian word for zucchini. Said with the right emphasis, it kind of sounded profane to us.

I started this part of my narrative as a tribute to my grandfather, so it's only fitting that I should return to him as I approach the end. Sometimes when Bossa was approaching a rant climax, other names would float to the surface, names like Phoncina, Chlorinda, Duchina, etc. These names were always shot like arrows of accusation at my grandfather, and Bossa would often accompany them with phrases like "I know," "I know what you're doing," "you don't think I know, but I know," etc. I didn't understand what she meant at first, but eventually I began to catch on to the fact that his occasional forays off factory grounds to Hydack's Hardware weren't always what he made them out to be. Common sense dictated that his need for a couple of 5/16 x 2 inch machine bolts was bogus when he had a neatly labeled jar full of them in his parts cabinet. If I pointed out the obvious, he'd usually mumble something which incorporated the word "metric." It took me a while to grasp the evasion.

In a way, it was a good thing that my grandfather outlived my grandmother. She would have invented a whole new vocabulary if she had seen the number of little old ladies in black dresses who attended his funeral.

Bossa became an invalid sometime later. She lost her right leg above the knee to diabetes. Her sister, my great aunt, lost her left leg below the knee to diabetes two years later. My sister sometimes referred to our home as Stump City.

In a way, it was a good thing that my grandfather outlived my grandmother. She would have invented a whole new vocabulary if she had seen the number of little old ladies in black dresses who attended his funeral. His surviving sisters were mortified, but every man old enough to appreciate the significance of the turnout drank a toast to him that night.

One final thought. I once asked Sister Kerosina what they did with legs that were amputated. Once she was sure it wasn't a trick question, she answered that they were buried in consecrated ground just like intact bodies. Patsy and I once spent a whole afternoon in the cemetery looking for a marker that said "legs," but we never could find one.

THE STRAND THEATER: Part 1

If The Mill was Frenchtown's heart, then The Strand Theater was its soul. To me, it became a celluloid sanctuary. For one thing it was but a short walk from Stump City. Second, it was one of the only buildings in town with air conditioning. Third, it was cheap. Saturday's line-up featured several cartoons, followed by a Three Stooges short, followed by the "kiddie show" feature, which was often a western, but sometimes a Tarzan movie where Johnny Weissmuller wore only a loincloth and said "Umgowa" a lot. Occasionally we were blessed with a sci-fi, which featured a giant radioactively mutated insect which looked and moved like it was constructed of cardboard (it was), followed by a serial (Lost Raider Airmen of the Moon's Treasure or some such.) This was followed by a short travel feature which always ended with the narrator wistfully intoning "and as we bid a sad farewell to beautiful, Bora Bora, Tahiti, Hell's Kitchen, etc.," followed by the two full-length features of the week. This marathon amounted to roughly six hours of air conditioned entertainment for 30 cents. As a bonus, if you hid in the men's room after the entire program ended, you could sneak back into the auditorium for the evening show without having to pay again! Of course the two features were the same ones you'd already seen in the afternoon, but remember that The Strand was Thompsonville's only large air-conditioned building and, sometimes comfort trumped boredom. Ask me to recite the entire dialog from "The High and the Mighty"—that's the film where Duke's a commercial pilot and the plane is in trouble—and stand back. I do a great Robert Newton by the way. He played one of the passengers in the film, but to me he could only ever be Disney's version of Long John Silver. Whenever the stewardess walked down the aisle to make sure everyone's seat belt was fastened, I expected to see a parrot on his shoulder.

If The Mill was Frenchtown's heart, then The Strand Theater was its soul.

Several things made The Strand an important part of my upbringing outside of the obvious convenient, inexpensive escape it provided, the first of which was its architecture. Every factory town had its theater. Windsor Locks had The Rialto, aka The Rathouse, Windsor had The Plaza (there wasn't one), and Thompsonville had The Strand. Some towns even had "legitimate" theaters where plays or concerts were performed. I don't know if that was The Strand's genesis. The exterior was faintly art deco, so I suspect The Strand came later, probably in the 30's. There was a lobby with a concession stand; candy cost 6 cents for a regular bar, 11 cents for an oversize one. The seats were dark blue, deeply upholstered, and, by then, a little threadbare. The smell of the theater was a combination of must, popcorn, and b.o, but, to me, it was the fragrance that dreams were made on, not "of." Shakespeare never said "dreams are made of." Sam Spade said that in The Maltese Falcon—pardon the digression. There was no balcony. To me, the wonder of The Strand was the ceiling. In the center was a large recessed circle, and painted inside the circle were constellations with little light bulbs strategically placed to represent the principal stars of each. My favorite was Orion with his three-starred belt and his dagger. Scorpio, with his claws and his stinger, was pretty cool too, as was Taurus with his horns, and all this in a kind of permanent twilight. Wondrous!

Most films were still in black and white back then, and I liked that. In fact it was the metaphorical black and white of movies that I liked most of all. Films back then had a moral clarity that infused my concept of what the world was, or at least of what the world should be.

I still struggle with that issue. Are there any moral absolutes in this world? Is truth conditional? Air-conditional? (yuk! yuk!) Is it subjective? Is there such a thing as karma? And, if so, is "what goes around, comes around" our best hope? Is it our only hope given that many of us no longer believe that justice will be administered in the afterlife? What about irony? Is irony karma in action?

I couldn't be a cop, a defense lawyer, or a judge. If I were a judge, I'd be prone to ask questions before sentencing like, *"Have you always been this stupid?,"* or *"So how many times exactly did your mother drop you on your head?"* I might be even worse as a defense lawyer: *"Your honor, this asshole has no redeeming qualities whatsoever, lock him up with the rest of the tattoo crazies"* or *"Your honor, does this state still have the death penalty? It does? Great! Dust off Ol' Sparky!"*

Films back then had a moral clarity that infused my concept of what the world was, or at least of what the world should be.

Life was so much easier in The Strand. There was little nuance. It was easy to identify the good guys. They had names like Brad, Joe, and Johnny. They were always humble, modest, and respectful. They upheld the rule of law. If they were hurt, the injuries were never lethal; they healed quickly, completely, and bloodlessly. Women were young, pretty, and virtuous. They had names like Daisy, Donna, and Diana. Doris Day was the forever virgin—probably still is for that matter. You could kiss a woman—chastely. If you wanted tongue, then you'd better have an engagement ring handy. And babies? Well, we knew they didn't come from storks. Nobody had even seen a stork to begin with, much less one transporting a baby to beaming, expectant parents. Raise your hand if you've ever seen a stork. So where did babies come from? More immaculate conceptions? Mr. Clean strikes again!

My mother once tried to explain to me where babies came from. I remember that she drew a picture on the back of an envelope. There was this oval-shaped thing with an opening on one end. Inside was an amorphous blob. She said that was me. When I asked her how I got inside the oval thing, she drew a small worm-like tube where the opening was and said that was how I both got in and got out. It looked too small for an entrance or an exit, but I needed time to contemplate the mysteries of life, so I didn't ask any more questions just then. Soon after, I duplicated the drawing for Patsy who said that it reminded him of a peach cut in half with me as the pit. Patsy said that babies came from sex, but he didn't know how exactly. His bedroom was right next to his parents, and sometimes when his dad came home from having a few too many beers at The Ringside he'd leave their bedroom door open and Patsy would hear all this grunting and moaning. Then his dad would yell, "He shoots! He scores!" Then he would start snoring. So naturally we concluded that sex had something to do with a man and a woman making goofy noises and then yelling crazy things. We decided to ask Sister Kerosina about it the next time we had catechism.

War films were never screened as kiddie show features, but they were certainly popular with adult audiences back in the 1950's, so if you stayed past the kiddie show, which many didn't, you sometimes got to see one. Most World War II films were about fighting the Japanese, not the Nazis, Why was that? After all, the Nazis had perpetrated the Holocaust, whatever that was. I think it was probably because the Nazis, out of uniform, were indistinguishable from the rest of us; cruel, yes; arrogant, yes; supercilious, yes; but otherwise, just like us. With the Japanese, however, you added a racial dimension. Even in black and white, you knew that their skin tone leaned yellow. Then there was their buck teeth and soda pop bottle glasses, and the way they would grin maliciously while machine gunning an American airman descending helplessly in his parachute. Pearl Harbor was a manifestation of their cheat-to-win philosophy.

Westerns were war films set in the Old West. You had the same "good guys wore white hats/bad guys wore black hats" stereotypes, and if the bad guys happened to be Indians, then you even had the racial component with red skin substituting for yellow skin. Westerns, unlike war stories, featured beautiful women who could represent morality and/or immorality. The moral woman was the wholesome "school marm" type, while the immoral woman was usually the saloon girl who sometimes hid a heart of gold behind seductive clothing and exaggerated make-up, aka a "painted" woman. In more contemplative westerns (yes, there were a few), both women loved the hero, and his choice to marry the school marm type showed him turning his back on moral uncertainty once and for all. The saloon girl type, in these circumstances, relinquished her claim reluctantly, but with a certain degree of acceptance that even she had preserved the moral balance.

I found that science fiction and horror movies somehow led me back to the question of religion.

In science fiction movies, war stories set in a potential, although improbable present or future, science was often represented by older, often eccentric, professorial men who were usually ignored by authorities, but who were often believed by young, handsome reporters. It helped that the Professor Irwin Corey types usually had beautiful daughters. I found that science fiction and horror movies somehow led me back to the question of religion. If I came home frightened by what I'd seen, I was reassured that the supernatural in any form wasn't real. It couldn't be, because there was no proof that monsters from the deep or creatures from outer space existed. If I said that Patsy's dad claimed that he saw a ghost hovering in the cemetery (probably after another night boozing at The Ringside), I was told that his story was "anecdotal"—there was "no verifiable proof," but if I pressed the issue by saying that baby Jesus being born through immaculate conception had to be anecdotal too, I was metaphorically crucified by a stare from my grandmother that would incinerate wallpaper, accompanied by mutterings from her sister of how deficient my mother had been in parenting me. But I still don't get how some people can believe in God, practice religion, and deny the existence of the supernatural. I mean, in my book, religion and the supernatural just go hand-in-hand, like peanut butter and jelly.

Almost all the protagonists in those old films were men; women were, at best, sidekicks, and, at worst, distractions, though sometimes useful in the sense that they could nurse the wounded hero back to health so that he could continue the good fight. I remember having a terrible crush on Ann Robinson who played the scientist's daughter in *War of the Worlds,* and on Julie Adams, the *Creature from the Black Lagoon* lady. Both women were pretty, wholesome, caring, unintentionally sexy, and great screamers. Given the opportunity, I would gratefully have married either. That way I could grunt, she could moan, and then we'd both yell, "He shoots! He Scores!" simultaneously.

THE STRAND THEATER: Part 2

In some ways, that old movie house was a school for me, and the people who ran it were my teachers. I learned life lessons from it, from them, and of course from the movies I watched. The theater was managed by Mr. Anderson, middle-aged, balding, a personification of what I would call worn dignity. In other words, he was a human embodiment of the theater he managed. Remember those commercially produced Christmas stockings that popped up in stores every year? They were a couple of feet long, and their red mesh let you see the collection of toys and candies inside. They weren't cheap, and to a five-year-old kid they were awesome. Well, on the Saturday before Christmas, the Strand, in the guise of Mr. Anderson, hosted a Christmas party for kids 12 and under. Admission was free, and each kid got one of those stockings. EACH KID! The line was around the block, but no one went home empty handed. Just one restriction: you had to be from the neighborhood, and we enforced that vigorously. Mr. Anderson was the spirit of Christmas to me—and he still is. He taught me the importance of good will and the value of generosity.

Then there was Miss Driscoll. From her I learned the importance of fantasizing. She sat in the ticket booth which was next to the lobby doors. She was a reasonably attractive middle-aged woman with huge bazookas (our slang for large breasts). In other words, her chest looked like the grill on a '56 Cadillac. She often wore blouses where there was a clasp at the neck, then an opening of roughly four inches which displayed her ample cleavage, and then a row of vertical buttons down to the promised land. Those four inches gave life purpose where I was concerned. The taller I grew, the more clearly I could view those divine globes. I wanted to just cliff dive into that soft valley and never come up for air again. I knew instinctively that she was a great screamer. Patsy wore his father's elevator shoes.

What happened on the Strand's screen was often less interesting than what happened at the foot of the Strand's screen. This was especially true if you were sitting through the double feature for a second time, which brings me to George Riley. George was the usher. He wore a uniform, was armed with a flashlight, and, as my father used to say, "George's elevator didn't go to the top floor." In retrospect, I think George was probably somewhere on the spectrum.

He had a horrible job. We knew he was powerless. The strongest action he could take was to stand at the end of our misbehaving row and catch us in his flashlight's beam. Now you might think we'd be chagrined, embarrassed, even humiliated. NAH!! The spotlight made us celebrities to our peers, and we took full advantage of the drama potential. However, we never degraded

George. In fact, we often inflated his authority to exaggerate threat. If George caught you in his beam, he'd kick you out. He wouldn't let you back in for a month. HE'D TELL YOUR PARENTS!! Of course, George wouldn't ever think to do any of those things, but it was important for us to believe that he would, otherwise there would have been no consequences to our misbehavior—and hadn't the Nuns taught us that actions always had consequences? Remember what I said about Italians—if they don't have an enemy, they invent one.

What happened on the Strand's screen was often less interesting than what happened at the foot of the Strand's screen.

Now everything I've said about George held true for all but one of us—Patsy. George and Patsy shared a misbegotten kinship; they were both victimized for appearance and behavior. In Patsy's case, as I've already mentioned, he was short, round, with Medusa hair and a tongue thrust. George was thin, balding, and what people back then called "simple." He was one of those guys who looks and acts like he's in his late 40s when he was probably still in his mid-20s. He didn't wear clothes; they just sort of hung on his slight frame. On top of that, his posture was poor; he didn't really walk so much as skulk, which made him look sneaky. George was sad, later pathetic. You knew that being an usher tapped his full potential. We called him "Lonesome George" after the alter-ego of a 1950's comedian. As far as Patsy was concerned, George was a moving target, literally, not figuratively.

THE STRAND THEATER: Part 3

We were at our most inventive when two conditions were met. The first was that a heat wave had driven us to seek refuge in The Strand for several consecutive days, and the second was that both features which we watched repeatedly on those consecutive days were of no interest to us whatsoever. A good example of such films was *A Face in the Crowd*, which depicts the rise and fall of a rural crooner, as played by a pre-Mayberry RFD Andy Griffith. Aunt Bee probably became senile, and Opie must have turned to heroin to escape the stifling reality after Barney passed away. To us, this movie had no saving graces whatsoever, so we resorted to treasure diving. Now, obviously, when I say "treasure" I'm not referring to scattered gold doubloons or chests spilling over with all manner of diamonds, emeralds, and rubies. The only chests spilling over at The Strand belonged to Miss

Driscoll in the ticket booth. Be still my heart. By treasure, I'm referring instead to discarded candy and popcorn boxes which littered the floor of the Strand in great abundance. I remember that we began treasure diving by competing with each other for who could collect the greatest number of empty Milk Duds, or Black Crows, or Jujubes, or Dots boxes in the shortest time. Crawling on hands and knees from the beginning to the end of seemingly countless rows of seats was dirty but satisfying work. I'm sure George must have been befuddled by the fact that he could sometimes hear us scuttling but often didn't catch sight of us for long periods of time. We didn't come up for air very often. The problem with that particular pursuit was, of course, the "now what?" factor. We needed something more.

Just as we were taught that cigarette smoking would invariably lead to marijuana smoking, which would lead to coke snorting, which would lead to heroin shooting, we logically progressed from candy box collecting to popcorn box collecting. You could buy a simple "dry" box of popcorn for 15 cents, but "buttered" aka, wet popcorn, was 25 cents. (I put "buttered" in quotes because it wasn't butter at all.) Dry popcorn came in collapsible square cardboard containers which were wider at the top to allow for groping in the dark, and then tapered near the bottom to fit better in your hand. Wet popcorn came in wax-coated, tapered cardboard cylinders. Empty wet popcorn boxes were of no interest beyond stacking them to see whose pile was tallest—again the "now what?" factor. But empty dry popcorn boxes opened up a whole world of possibilities, once Patsy discovered that a collapsed box, skillfully aimed, made a great Frisbee substitute. Enter Lonesome George.

Now I'm sure that an aeronautical engineer or a professor of physics could calculate all the variables involved in popcorn box assassination (weight and greasiness of box, strength and determination of tosser, height and speed of skulking target, etc.) so that a formula could be devised to accurately map the trajectory of the cardboard missile. Patsy didn't possess a degree or a formula, but he was still a master. He'd wing one at Lonesome George and then immediately scramble on hands and knees to another location. When George shined his flashlight where Patsy had been, one of us would let fly from behind him. When he turned in that direction, Patsy would cut loose from his new location. Now, keep in mind that this is happening in a darkened theater where a movie is being projected, and a few people are bonafide ticket holders there to watch—but, fortunately, just a few. On special occasions, George got a "salvo," that was four or five boxes winging simultaneously from different directions. Cruel? Yes, but comedy often is, besides we never aimed for his face

Now if you'll join me and Mr. Peabody in his Wayback Machine, I'll ask him to put it in "forward" and move us forward a few years in time. The

Strand, like most small town neighborhood theaters, went into a prolonged decline mostly as a result of the boob tube in our living rooms, which I can't condemn too much because selling and repairing them represented a sizable portion of my parents' income. The theater's downward trajectory only accelerated when it became a porno house showing X-rated movies, mostly to guys who wore long winter coats even during August heatwaves.

Eventually it closed, but, remarkably, it still exists. Every seven or eight years someone will come along with a proposal to re-open it as a neighborhood arts center or a performance venue, or a cultural attraction of some sort. When that happens, a story will appear in local papers, often accompanied by a contemporary photograph of the interior which remains very much a time capsule. It's all still there: the screen, the seats, maybe even a stray popcorn box or two. Most important to me, the circular recess in the ceiling is still there with its painted constellations. Orion still brandishes his mighty sword, and Scorpio still threatens with her deadly stinger. But the lights that represented their stars are gone now. The bulbs eventually burned out and no one bothered to replace them.

> **On special occasions George got a salvo, which was four or five boxes winging simultaneously from different directions. Cruel? Yes, but comedy often is, besides we never aimed for his face.**

For years after the theater closed up, I'd sometimes see Lonesome George walking around Thompsonville—I don't think he could ever get a driver's license. He'd often be talking into a hand-held walkie-talkie with a long, telescoping antenna. He'd be talking at full volume and carrying on an intense conversation. We, me, my family, my friends, my hometown, we knew, all of us, there was no one on the other end, but we never let on. None of us.

THE STRAND THEATER: Part 4

Now, if I ask Mr. Peabody to move us further ahead into the future (but we're still in the past mind you), I'll show you why I believe in circumstance but not serendipity. What's the difference you say? Circumstance suggests design, karma if you like. Serendipity is simply random—big difference.

When I was away in college, Patsy enlisted and ended up in Vietnam. We wrote back and forth a few times, but our lives were so different by then that we really didn't have much to tell each other once we got past the reminiscences. I remember that he said he was considering the military as a possible career choice. He said that he liked the army; that is, he liked how structured everything was, but that he really hated Southeast Asia. Eventually the letters tapered off to nothing. Some months later, my mother told me that she'd heard from someone who came in my parents' store that Patsy had been wounded in combat. A short article about him appeared in *The Thompsonville Press* soon after. She clipped it and saved it for me. It didn't really tell you much, just that his wounds had been serious and that he'd been sent to an Army hospital in Japan to recuperate. Eventually the whole story came out about how the Vietcong overran his outpost, and he'd taken a bullet in the head. It may even have been friendly fire. Either nobody knew, or no one was saying. I wrote, but he never responded. I eventually spoke to someone who knew his Mom. She was telling people that Patsy would be a long time recuperating because he had to learn how to pretty much do everything for himself all over again. She also said he'd never truly be Patsy again. Patsy finally came home after over a year in hospital. With his physical limitations and his mental challenges, he couldn't live at home ("at least not at first" they said) without a full time attendant. The army didn't offer to pay for that, and Patsy's parents certainly couldn't afford one. Instead, the government paid for his keep in Parkview Plantation, which, while it billed itself as a "comprehensive rehabilitation facility," was actually just a glorified convalescent home, i.e., a place where people waited to die.

I visited Parkview Patsy (his name for himself) whenever I was home from college. I found it to be incredibly difficult to see him like that, but I tried to hide my dismay and discomfort.

I visited Parkview Patsy (his name for himself) whenever I was home from college. I found it to be incredibly difficult to see him like that, but I tried to hide my dismay and discomfort. Patsy saw through that pretty quickly. It made him appreciate my visits even more. He'd usually be in a wheelchair, propped up and stabilized by pillows, and waiting for me in the lobby where the TV played loudly and the smell of stale urine wasn't quite so strong. His lower body was often covered by a quilt crafted by one of the residents because Patsy often complained about his legs and feet being cold. His Medusa hair was long gone thanks to U.S. Army barbers, and the scar on the left side of his head stood out prominently. The right side of his mouth drooped a bit which made him sound drunk when he spoke. He joked about that. When a nurse brought him his meds he'd order another screwdriver. He salivated freely; sometimes he drooled uncontrollably. His right arm and hand were often spasmodic. We'd talk for a half hour or so, and then he'd start to tire. On one of my first visits I offered to wheel him back to his room. He gratefully accepted. Once there, I offered to help get him from the wheelchair to his bed, but he said it would probably be better to let an attendant do it, so he pushed a call button attached to his bed frame. I turned on his TV while we waited and was looking for a program I thought he might enjoy when the attendant walked in. It was George Riley, aka Lonesome George. Remember what I said about circumstance?

Patsy and George greeted each other, and then George strained to lift Patsy from the chair to the edge of his bed. I offered to help as Patsy clearly outweighed George by 50 pounds or more but George said "not necessary." Once George had made him comfortable, Patsy asked George if he remembered me. I felt pretty embarrassed right then. George looked at me for the longest 10 seconds of my life and then said flatly "yes, I remember." I started to verbally stumble myself into an apology, but George cut me off with an abrupt "history" and he then left. Patsy then explained to me that George had only been working at the Parkview for a couple of weeks. He got the job through some kind of foundation whose name I don't recall, but I know "disadvantaged" was included in the title. They dropped him off in the morning and picked him up in a van when his shift ended. I asked Patsy if he thought George held a grudge. He said he didn't know, but that George hadn't demonstrated any animosity so far.

I made a point of visiting Patsy whenever I was home through college and graduate school, on holidays and during semester breaks. He remained much the same during those years, neither improving nor declining. At some point he must have accepted that the Parkview had become his permanent residence. We didn't talk about it. What was there to say?

While Patsy himself didn't change, his relationship with George did. Over time, they became casual friends, and, later, even close friends. George started finding ways to spend more time with Patsy while on duty. He even came in to visit Patsy on his days off, and he often stayed after his shift to watch TV with Patsy or to play cards or board games. They both liked playing Sorry. George then bicycled home alone in the dark, sometimes on snow covered streets. I almost always saw George when I visited Patsy, though my visits became less and less common when I finished school and started working. Then came marriage. Then came children. But I always made a point of visiting Parkview Patsy at Christmas, bringing a small gift, at first just for Patsy, but later for George as well (he loved Planters Mixed Nuts). George had set up a small, artificial Christmas tree for Patsy next to his bed, where Patsy could turn the lights on and off with a rocker switch. The tree's base was covered with a white towel with the "Property of Parkview Plantation" stencil hidden by artificial snow, which looked and smelled suspiciously like Ivory Soap Flakes. Nestled in the "snow" were wrapped gifts with labels which said "From George to Patsy" and "From Patsy to George."

> **Patsy's mom and dad insisted that George stand in the receiving line. He did. In fact, he wore the best clothes he owned: his usher's uniform.**

Shortly after the birth of my first child, I visited Patsy to show him some photos and to ask if he would be an "extended" godfather to Brendon, my son. He seemed to like that idea. I was surprised to see that he had lost weight since my last visit and seemed noticeably less coordinated in both movement and speech. I pretended not to notice, but I could never fool Patsy. Anyhow, neither of us spoke about it until I was leaving. We said our goodbyes and wished each other a Merry Christmas. My habit when I reached the door of his room was to turn to give him a quick goodbye wave. Before I started my turn, he said "hey." When I turned back, he said "Parkinson's," then he turned on his side away from me.

The disease worked its will on Patsy quickly and mercilessly. I saw him only twice more. Each time he was more frail. Each time he was less aware of me and of his surroundings. During those final stages George became virtually a personal nurse to Patsy. He fed him every day, bathed him with a sponge, helped him brush his teeth, and when Patsy became incontinent, George took care of that too.

Patsy died when Brendon was almost two years old. George was asked to be a pallbearer, but he was too frail himself to carry the weight of a coffin, so he demurred. I'm sure that part of the reason was also that George didn't own a dark suit and certainly couldn't afford to buy one. I had a word with Patsy's parents about that, and his Mom spoke to George, but George was too proud to accept that kind of offer. Still, both Patsy's Mom and Dad insisted that George stand in the receiving line, and he did. In fact, he wore the best clothes he owned: his usher's uniform. Nobody said a word about that. In Frenchtown we knew how to show respect. George stopped working at the Parkview soon after. He couldn't bear being in the place without Patsy. I heard from someone that he became very reclusive, rarely stepping outside his little subsidized apartment. He passed less than a year after Patsy. He just wasted away to nothing. He didn't so much die, as he willed himself to stop living. Some people said he died of a stroke, some said he starved himself to death, but I knew the truth. George simply died of a broken heart.

George taught me forgiveness. George taught me charity. George taught me love.

On Love of Movies / On Love in Movies

Bernstein: *"A fellow will remember a lot of things you wouldn›t think he' d remember. You take me. One day, back in 1896, I was crossing over to Jersey on the ferry, and as we pulled out, there was another ferry pulling in, and on it there was a girl waiting to get off. A white dress she had on. She was carrying a white parasol. I only saw her for one second. She didn't see me at all, but I' ll bet a month hasn't gone by since that I haven't thought of that girl."*

This monologue is one of my favorites. I call it the "white parasol" monologue. It's from the movie *Citizen Kane*. Bernstein, a friend and business associate of the late Charles Foster Kane, is being interviewed by a reporter who needs to generate copy for Kane's obituary. The discussion of Bernstein's memories of his early days with Kane expands as Thompson, the reporter, ruminates about memory in general, and as Bernstein recalls this memory in particular. The actor, Everett Sloane, delivers it masterfully, with just the right amount of wistfulness. It could so easily have become maudlin, but he doesn't let it. It's one of the great romantic speeches from Hollywood's "Golden Age."

As a child, love, to me, was something that happened between a handsome man and a pretty woman on a big screen in a darkened theater. The celluloid relationship often started off contentiously, but it gradually evolved to a stage of mutual interest and admiration as the two parties joined forces to meet some shared challenge. Mutual interest then led to genuine attraction, eventually to declarations of undying affection, a ring, a wedding, and marital bliss. Moaning and thrashing in the bedroom weren't in the script, nor were poopy diapers. Dialog wise, the relationship's progression went something like this:

SCENE 3

She: *He's my idea of nothing, Father. His horse has better manners, and it's better looking too.*

He: *She's a spoiled brat, Sheriff. Say, you're a square guy. How could you raise a daughter like that anyway?*

Father: *She gets it from her mother.*

SCENE 27

She: *If we don't switch those train tracks right quick and reroute the express, it'll plow into the derailed circus car and kill all the performers!*

He: *Don't worry. I'll save the clowns.*

She: *Do you think you can?*

He: *I have to!*

She: *Be careful, Tex.*

He: *Don't worry. I'll come back to you.*

She: (sighs)

SCENE 43

He: *You know, a feller can get awful lonely out there on the prairie where the only light comes from the stars, just him and his horse and some coyotes a'howlin' off in the distance.*

She: *It sounds so peaceful though; I think I'd love it.*

He: *Yeah, it's peaceful all right. The sky is so clear, you'd think you could just reach up and pluck those stars out of the sky like little diamonds.*

She: (lost in a reverie) *Like diamonds.*

He: *Yeah, diamonds, like this one here in this ring that I been a'hidin' between my toes in my smelly old cowboy boot that I ain't taken off since we left town last week.*

She: *Oh Tex. It's beautiful. And it smells so ripe.*

I love movie dialog.

I'm pretty sure that pedestals were invented for women like that, and I was always too happy to put them up there. After all, their "screen" lips were bigger than I was! I mean, they were always so beautifully coiffed, so exquisitely made up, so attractively dressed, so perfectly spoken. And, on top of that, you always knew from the very first moment that he set eyes on her, or her on him, that they'd end up riding off into the sunset together. Their future together was preordained by the "Standards and Practices" branch of The Hayes office which reflected the mores and morals of the time. Sure, there would be ups and downs before commitment became final and irrevocable. Boy meets girl, boy loses girl, boy gets girl. Right? Except in a war movie perhaps where the studio system was selling the Bijou audience on the need for sacrifice. Then it was: boy meets girl, boy loses girl, boy gets girl, boy gets killed, but so bravely, a bittersweet ending for certain, but one in which democracy would be preserved for unborn generations.

I had serial crushes: Maureen O'Hara, Paulette Goddard, Myrna Loy, Olivia de Havilland, Ingrid Bergman, Rhonda Fleming, Ann Sheridan, Rita Heyworth; the list goes on and on. One thing that all had in common, is that the leading man always won his lady's love by performing a service which benefited her. For example, he would risk everything to save her from a burning building, a volcanic eruption, stampeding cattle, rampaging horses, rampaging sharks, rampaging giant mutated insects, lightning strikes, hurricane force winds, tidal waves, death by drowning, suffocating, falling from great heights, falling from ungreat heights but on poison-tipped stakes; Hollywood screenwriters went to great lengths to invent novel threats. But what I learned from all this, is that love can be won by service. Years later I would learn that this was a founding principle of the courtly love tradition which began in France during the Middle Ages and eventually spread to England.

It would have been impossible for me to understand why that notion, that being loved requires service, resonated with me so much back then. However, it didn't just infuse my youth; it infused my life. It still does. I think perhaps I now finally understand why.

For one, those movie goddesses were disposable, as also were the coifs, the make-up, the costumes, and even the words they memorized and recited so earnestly. I understood that those movies were fabrications, that they ceased to exist (or should) when the house lights came on and Lonesome George would go aisle-by-aisle collecting left behind trash. I think I always knew the reality, but chose the fantasy instead, because it allowed me to role play by substituting myself as the leading man. And why not? He was taller than me, better looking, smarter, wittier, braver, more "er" everything when compared to me. If I could be all those "er"s, then I could get the girl too. I'm sure that every child goes through a stage like this. So why didn't I grow out of it?

I think the answer lies in something I've already said. I grew up in a house where displays of emotion, especially if they were meant as expressions of love, were discouraged. I never could express love because I never saw love expressed. It's like John, my friend who grew up without a father. How could he be expected to be a good father if he'd never had a father (or a father figure for that matter) to model on? The Hollywood vision I had of what love should be stood in sharp contrast to what I saw and heard at home. My father never showed convincing affection. I don't even know if he ever felt it. Maybe. My mother, because she never got affection, never gave affection. Maybe this was all occasioned by the fact that three generations lived under the same roof.

Whatever the cause, love simply never lived in that Frenchtown house. But it lived right down the street in The Strand, usually in black and white, but sometimes even in glorious Technicolor. I never learned how to express love, but I did learn, from movies, that love could be expressed through service to a beloved. And so that's what I've always done: expressed affection by serving, by which I mean being complimentary, being considerate, and being generous. The problem that I've sometimes encountered while wearing this halo, however, comes with those who suspect ulterior motives when compliments, consideration, and generosity are extended, especially if I expect a modicum of reciprocation in return. When there is no reciprocation, I'm sometimes left feeling foolish for having "gone the extra mile" and created unrealistic expectations of return.

So, you might ask, "How has this 'Strand love' worked out?" "It depends," he answered, "mostly on the object of my then affection." Some people like the idea of perching on a pedestal, but not many and not for long, because they recognize that their own imperfections will soon make their pedestal teeter.

Some don't get it. Some get it but just don't like it. And some particularly don't like it because they misread its intention. Can you blame them? I don't. It's kind of an unusual motivation for wanting to just do something good or nice. Some people try to assign an ulterior motive to simple generosity. Does that say more about them than about me? Maybe. I don't know. Either way, I know that I own it, but The Strand owns it too.

So what about Bernstein's "white parasol" monologue? I mentioned it because something similar has happened to me twice. The first time was between my freshman and sophomore years of high school. My parents, like Tommy's, had bought a cottage on Cape Cod which we (all three generations) visited frequently during summer months. One night in particular stands out. I remember that it was dark, not twilight, and we were driving down Main Street in Hyannis. I don't remember why or who was in the car outside of my father, who was driving. I was in the front, passenger seat with the window rolled down and my right arm propped on the car door.

Main Street Hyannis in high summer was like a carnival midway. Rubberneckers, mixed with tourists and shoppers, overflowed the sidewalks onto both sides of the street. Every store was open and ablaze with lights. Some shops extended their wares right out onto the sidewalk on rolling display racks; the more seasonal the shop, (t-shirts, beach wear, bathing suits, straw hats, ocean-themed souvenirs, etc.), the more extravagant the lighting and the colorful inventory. It was a celebratory atmosphere. People were on vacation, and they were clearly taking full advantage of both the balmy summer weather and of the moment.

Main Street was dissected in two places by crossing streets. We were stopped by a red light at the first, Ocean Avenue. I looked out the open window to the people standing on the corner to my immediate right. Foot traffic had paused to allow for crossing cars. There, only a few feet away, was a family grouping. Father was tall, handsome, deeply tanned, and wearing a jacket and tie. The jacket was a classic blue blazer. He wore it with white slacks, a white shirt, and a dark red tie. Mom, who sported salon-fresh hair and freckles, wore a simple, form fitting beige shift which showcased her figure, but in a sophisticated sexy kind of way. Daughter, about my age, was mind-numbingly pretty. She was slim, had long blond hair that flowed down to her shoulders which were covered by a thin, white cardigan. Her dress was pale pink. It was what people in Frenchtown would call a "party dress." In a sea of primary color t-shirts, cut-offs and sandals, the family radiated class like heat. Her limpid, blue eyes stared directly into mine for exactly two seconds, and I dove in head first. Then, the light changed and we resumed or slow crawl down Main Street, which, to me, had suddenly become garish and tawdry.

I remember that mental snapshot to this day. Who were these people? Where were they from? Had they just been to dinner at a high end restaurant? There were a few in Hyannis. Where were they going? Where are they now? I'll never know, but the girl in the pink party dress haunts me to this day. She was my first "white parasol" moment.

Years later, when I was on tour with a band, we played a five-day residency in Las Vegas. We performed in the Golden Nugget Casino Ballroom, and it was a sell-out each night. The tables closest to the stage always went to high rollers and whales; a whale was a high roller on steroids. One particular table, slightly off to the side, stood out because it sat just two but was only ever occupied by one, a very pretty lady. She always wore a blue dress, always sat alone nursing a martini, and always got up and left when the band's closing theme began. She was there every night, she wore a different blue dress each night, and she always left before any of us could get to her. None of us knew her. One of the other guys in the band, Gene Roland, even wrote a song about her, called "Blue Ghost." You'll find it on an album from the early 60's entitled "Adventures in Blues." I always wondered if she was the girl in the pink dress, grown a little older, checking up on me, or perhaps there to remind me of who she once was, and of whom I still am.

I said that I had two "white parasol" moments in my life. The second involved a young woman in a black dress with a white collar. But that's a story for another time.

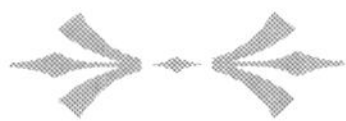

HIGGINS SCHOOL: Part 1
The Land of Tween

Here's what I think should happen when we finish elementary school. We should receive a golden round-trip ticket to a land called Tween, which I believe actually exists on the side of the moon which we never see from Earth. We would exit the elementary school building on the last day of classes and step immediately onto a ramp sloping upward into a cavernous spaceship with the words "Tween Ark" painted on the sides in huge letters and a picture of Richard Branson. Sister Kerosina would be standing there with her yardstick intoning, "Keep to the right, keep to the right." Once you entered Tween Ark, you remembered nothing. You simply disappeared from Earth for two or three years. Nobody questioned your absence; in fact, they were happy to see you go—even your parents!

When you returned from Tween, you had passed from childhood to young adulthood, ready to start freshman year of high school. But you remembered nothing about those lost years in between, because there wasn't anything worth remembering. Also, there was the Purgatron, a huge machine that you had to walk through to exit the ark on your return. The Purgatron erased everything: things that you had said or done that you wished you hadn't, inappropriate and ill-timed body noises, loss of coordination in limbs during particularly awkward growth spurts, bubonic plague-quality acne, hormonal body odors associated with both solid body parts and orifices, bad teeth, bad hair, all things braces, etc, etc.... Gone! All gone. Sounds good, doesn't it? All aboard!

A.D. Higgins Junior High was small as compared to middle schools today, which are more like puberty factories. Higgins School was a simple two-story, rectangular building with seven or eight classrooms on each floor, a small "cafetorium" which served triple duty as a cafeteria, an auditorium, and a gym, and a library about the size of two regular classrooms combined. That was it. That was A.D. Higgins. Oh, and it had both a baseball diamond and a soccer/football field in the back. North School had been right at the end of my street, whereas Higgins was about a four-block walk. I could have ridden a bus to Higgins if I wanted. It would have picked me up right in front of my second home, the Strand Theater, but that wouldn't have been cool. And being cool was very important. We dressed cool, we talked cool, we walked cool, we even thought cool. We were obsessed with cool.

Cool is/was like pornography. You couldn't define cool if you tried, but you all recognized it when you saw it or heard it or felt it. Sometimes it was easier to describe cool by what it wasn't. For example, cool was not going to see movies with your best buds just to crawl around on a sticky floor in order to collect empty popcorn boxes to wing at Lonesome George. Cool was not being seen walking with your younger sister unless necessity dictated, and if it did, she had to walk about ten feet behind. Cool was never wearing shorts no matter how hot it was. Cool was not having a lunch box, unless it was one of those nondescript "working man" types. Cool was no longer watching The Mickey Mouse Club unless you were doing it only to keep tabs on Annette's progression from girlhood to womanhood. Cool was James Dean. Cool was a windbreaker with a turned-up collar. Cool was jeans. Cool was smoking. Cool was all about attitude. You get the picture.

> **Cool is/was like pornography. You couldn't define cool if you tried, but you all recognized it when you saw it or heard it or felt it.**

Being in grade 7-1L was definitely not cool, but that's where I was. Grades were numbered from 7-1 to 7-8, except for 7-1L. Just as it was obvious to everyone that 7-4 was for the "brainiacs," it was also obvious that 7-1L was not. We couldn't figure out the rankings for the other seventh grade classrooms, but the "L" in 7-1L seemed pretty ominous—low? lousy? losers? Our homeroom teacher was Mrs. Sharp, an older gray-haired woman with wire rim glasses. I'm pretty sure she was on Prozac or some equivalent of the time. She was always chipper in the morning when we had her for homeroom and then for English during first period. After English we headed off to our other classes. Moving to a different class at the end of each period was a novelty at first, but we soon realized that it only gave us multiple opportunities to be bored for shorter lengths of time rather than one sustained period of boredom in the same room. We came back to homeroom to get our lunches and then headed down to the cafetorium. Meanwhile, three hours had passed during which time Mrs. Sharp had transformed from Glinda to Gorgon. Whatever she was on had clearly worn off. But only until after lunch when she escorted us back to homeroom so that we could pick up our books for afternoon classes. A quick swig or snort of something in a ladies' room stall during lunch break had again clearly worked its magic. We saw her for the last time each day when we again returned to homeroom and waited to be called to buses. By then, she was re-gorgonized.

My father found out that the "L" in 7-1L actually was a stand-in for "U" as in underachievers. I'll bet most of the class had ADHD to one degree or another, but that acronym didn't exist back then, so neither did the condition.

It was just easier to describe us as "easily distracted," "unmotivated," or "underachievers." At least I had Patsy with me and two other friends, Tommy and John. They went through North School with me, but it wasn't until Higgins that we started hanging out together. We were the original "Fab Four," of 7-1L anyway. More about them in a minute.

Now, I don't remember much about my classes. Mrs. O'Leary taught music. I remember her because she was almost bald with little wisps of badly dyed red hair. It looked orange. She sticks in my mind because my dad told me that her husband was a sailor aboard the *Indianapolis* who died when the ship was torpedoed near the end of the war. Remember the speech that Quint gives in the movie *Jaws* about the *Indianapolis*? The one about how many of the sailors who survived the sinking were eaten by sharks? Mrs. O'Leary's husband was one. It's a good thing the movie came out long after junior high, because I know for sure Patsy wouldn't have been able to resist softly humming the shark music (dum-*dum*-dum-*dum*, dum-*dum*-dum-*dum*) whenever he'd pass Mrs. O'Leary in the hallway.

Mr. Marshall was our science teacher. I remember him as tall and slim, with hair that stood straight up like a starched blonde brush. I sometimes wonder if Jim Henson was in our class, because Mr. Marshall, as I remember him, looked like the muppet named Beaker. Ironically, the only thing I remember him actually saying to us was about hair. He was teaching us about puberty. I assume that teachers back then had to be very careful about what they said about subjects like puberty or reproduction. I mean Sister Kerosina might have been eavesdropping from the coatroom, ready to bulldoze her way into the class, waving her Baltimore Catechism around and yelling "Immaculate Conception!" as loudly as she could.

Anyhow, what Mr. Marshall said was,

"Some of you have probably noticed that hair is growing where you've never had hair before." (Yes, we had noticed). *"That's a sign that you're going through puberty. God* (it was okay to say 'God' in public schools back then) *and nature want you to grow hair in those places. The hair is there to protect you."*

And I was thinking "what is hair growing on my nuts going to protect me from? too much sun? a well-placed kick?" (sometimes referred to as Frenchtown Foreplay). I didn't get it, but I wasn't about to ask about it. No one did. Anyhow, God and nature apparently now no longer deem it necessary to protect my head.

The other seventh grade teacher who stands out in memory is Miss Driscoll—yes, the same Miss Driscoll from the Strand ticket booth. Serendipity strikes again! We learned from Joanne Shultz (Remember her? She was class leader when our kindergarten teacher, Miss Sullivan, went belly-up) that Miss Driscoll was working the ticket booth as a part-time job to pay for education classes so that she could get teacher certification. So, there she was with her twins, who Patsy promptly named "Left" and "Right," teaching us about ancient Rome. And, to give her credit beyond God and nature, she was pretty good at it. One of the eighth graders told Tommy to ask her about the four Roman emperors: Caesar, Squeezer, Humper, and Dumper. We suspected that these names were somehow inappropriate, because he was the same St Patrick's Church School lifer who told us to ask Sister Kerosina what self-abuse was and should we practice it. I have since concluded that learning how not to be victimized by older people is a sign of increasing maturity.

Tommy Ferraro lived down closer to the cemetery and the river. His house was newer and nicer than everyone else's. His dad was the State Labor Commissioner, so he was probably pulling in a good salary. Tommy's mom kept house and gave piano lessons. Women did stuff like that back then. She was tall and slim, while Tommy's dad could best be described as "petite." Tommy took after his dad. He was just small, but every part of him that was small was in proportion to his overall smallness. In fact, sometimes when you glanced at him, your first impression was that he was farther away than he actually was. Tom wasn't all that smart academically, but he was both clever and witty. He could come up with funny stuff at will. I remember we had the radio on once, and this song came on that was popular right then. It was an instrumental, a tango called "Jealousy." One of us immediately went to change stations to find a Dion or Del Shannon tune, but before that happened Tommy started singing:

"Leprosy
It's crawling all over me.
There goes my eyeball into your hi-ball.
Kiss me quick,
I'm losing my upper lip…"

That's all I can remember, but that was typical Tommy. He could just pull stuff like that out of thin air.

John Damian was an odd duck. For one thing, he was older than the rest of us by one year. That was because he and his mother had moved around a lot, so he was held back a year when they first moved to Thompsonville. They rented the second floor of a house across from Tommy. He never talked about his dad. I seem to remember something about him being career military. I know that his mom didn't wear a wedding ring, and John said that sometimes guys she met at work took her out on dates. John was a little taller than me and

Patsy, and taller still than Tommy—hell, everybody was taller than Tommy. Outside of his age and not having a father, John fit right in, but I always felt that John considered himself somehow inferior for having only one parent. We never felt that way about him, but I think he may have felt that way about himself. Like Tommy and me, John was an only child. Well, to be fair, Tommy and I both had younger sisters, but girls, especially little girls, didn't count. The thing is that John liked to steal stuff—shoplift I mean. And he was really good at it. Sometimes he'd steal stuff just to prove that he could, and then throw it away. Sometimes he'd steal stuff to give to us as gifts. Sometimes he'd steal stuff even though he had enough allowance money to buy it, and if you asked him why, he'd just say, "I don't know." I don't think he ever got caught. Like I said, John was an odd duck. Then again, we were all odd ducks, except for Joanne that is.

Geography, along with a dearth of other girls in her age group, brought her into our little circle; that, and the fact that Joanne was easy to like; she fit in comfortably. We didn't even think of her as a girl.

Joanne Shultz was different. She was Tommy's next door neighbor. She was in the "brainiac" class at school, so we didn't see much of her there, but she often hung out with us outside of school. She was tall and gangly sort of in a "track star" kind of way. Geography, along with a dearth of other girls in her age group, brought her into our little circle; that, and the fact that Joanne was easy to like; she fit in comfortably. We didn't even think of her as a girl. However, it was clear to everyone that Joanne was not only smarter than we were but also considerably more mature. Even Patsy eventually stopped trying to impress her with his "fart at will" prowess.

Now, this is going to get a little uncomfortable for a minute.

I remember that it was spring, and we, the Fab Four, were sitting on the cement patio that Tommy's kitchen door opened on to. There was an umbrella table and folding chairs on the patio which faced the side of Joanne's house. One of us, John I think, had found a box of these cigar shaped things on the top shelf of his mother's closet. He knew that she sometimes hid open packs of cigarettes up there, and once in a while he'd sneak one. Anyhow, he'd brought one of these "cigars" over to show us. It was labeled Tampax. This, of course, led to a lively group discussion of women's periods. We'd heard of them, but the whole subject seemed off limits, because even girls talked to each other about them in a kind of whispered code. Still, we all knew something, but not one of us knew everything. Somebody (it might have been me) wondered aloud if we could get the real scoop from Joanne. That, of course, led to another lively discussion, which finally brought us to the conclusion that we could ask her about it, but it would have to be done in a tactful way. Patsy, reluctantly, promised not to speak. The rest of us swore to a man not to get smutty. So the next time we were together (the five of us, that is) we asked. It came out something like this:

What's a period?

Do all girls and ladies have periods?

Why do they get periods?

What can they do (or not do) when they have periods?

Can they play sports? Can they swim?

Somebody'd heard a rumor that they couldn't swim for an hour after eating lunch or something.

How often do periods happen?

And then the obvious clincher from me:

Do you have periods?

Joanne answered all of those questions in a sober, dignified way, all except the last. I can still see her expression. She's right there in front of me. And I can see it change from quiet dignity to confusion, to anger, to sadness. A line had been crossed. A chasm had opened up; a divide that could never again be spanned by simple childhood camaraderie. She started to tear up, then her face contorted and she was crying; then she was sobbing and running for home calling for her mom. I can hear her sobbing and calling right now.

We felt awful about that, but we really couldn't understand what we'd done wrong. Still, we knew we'd done something wrong, so we went into the cemetery and stole some flowers, the ones that were still relatively fresh from recent burials, and we brought them to her door. They made me ring the bell, because I had asked the "bad" question. Mrs. Shultz came to the door, and we fell all over each other with apologies. She said that Joanne wasn't feeling very well, but she'd be sure to give her the flowers and tell her how sorry we were. We told her that if it made Joanne feel any better, we'd call ourselves the Fab Four plus One from now on. She smiled enigmatically and closed the door. Joanne came over the next day to hang with us after school. We were a pretty subdued group. Nobody mentioned what had happened the day before. In fact, I don't think anyone ever mentioned what happened that day. Life went on, but something had changed. It was never quite the same after that.

You know there's a poem called "The Rhyme of the Ancient Mariner" about this old sailor who had once done a terrible thing on an ocean voyage. God punished him by making him relive the sin by telling the story repeatedly to people who might benefit from it and not make the same mistake he did. That was his penance, you see, to relive his guilt over and over by telling the story. Those few seconds when Joanne's face changed—they haunt me. I never meant to hurt or embarrass her, but I did. Sometimes I do that. And it always seems like a girl or a woman is on the receiving end. Coincidence? I hope so. Serendipity? I hope not. It's one of my great failings. I acknowledge that. And if Joanne were here in front of me, right here, right now, I'd say, "I'm sorry" again, until the next time.

I can't remember much else about seventh grade. Must be the fault of the Purgatron. Outside of what I've already said, it just feels like an extension of elementary school in a different building, along with the acquisitions of new friends like John and Tommy, some new teachers, changing classes for each subject, and, most importantly, the quest for cool. Eighth grade, however, was a whole new ballgame in three respects: drums, girls, and it was also my final year of childhood.

HIGGINS SCHOOL: Part 2
Becoming a Chick Magnet

My father worked as a professional musician, a drummer, before the war, and after the war, and during my first few years of life. He played mostly big band music which was popular at the time but starting to lose its audience to new musical styles. Ironically, my mother's brother did the same, played drums in a big band, but he and my father didn't know of each other when they were both working. The point is that I was probably genetically predisposed to be a drummer as well. When my father stopped playing professionally, he zippered the drums up in their canvas covers, and they took up residence in our garage where they gathered dust for years.

Inevitably I decided to take the drums down off the garage shelves in order to unzip the covers. The drum "shells" were covered with a glued linoleum type material in a "black marine pearl" pattern. Fabulous! And all the hardware was chrome-plated. They were beautiful. It was love at first sight. My grandfather helped me carry everything downstairs to our cellar. He also helped me to set them up. My dad didn't have a driver's license when he first started playing gigs, so my grandfather would drop him off, help him set up, and then later pick him up to return home. My grandfather was once a roadie! Who knew?

My father showed me how to hold the sticks. He had little time for more as the TV side of his business had really taken off. There was talk about my taking drum lessons, but he (and everyone else for that matter) thought I'd lose interest quickly. However, playing the drums came naturally to me so I didn't. By the time the subject of taking lessons came up again, I was already well along in perfecting my mistakes. So in lieu of lessons, my father set up a "play along" sound system so that I could learn to copy the masters by listening to them on records then trying to replicate what I was hearing. I played what I heard on those big band recordings; I learned from the best. Of course there were downsides like never learning to read music for instance, but for a kid with ADHD it was perfect, especially as the kid in question had developed a growing interest in girls.

There was talk about my taking drum lessons, but he (and everyone else for that matter) thought I'd lose interest quickly. However, playing the drums came naturally to me so I didn't.

Now if I were to ask you what musical instrument would most likely turn a boy, who was average in size, looks and intelligence, into a chick magnet, you'd most likely say guitar, specifically "electric" guitar. And you'd be right. But the electric guitar didn't reign as the king of pop music instruments until the early-to-mid 60's with the British Invasion (The Beatles, the Stones, The Kinks, The Who, etc.). Before the guitar ruled, the drums ruled. So that was it. I was ready to enter Chick Magnet Land!

Of course, doing so was complicated by having the drums in my parents' cellar. I gave serious thought to putting up a string or two of Christmas lights to create ambiance, but that was cheesy even for me. Instead, I hung some posters of singers which I got from my parents' music store on the cellar walls (fyi, nothing sticks to cement for more than a day). However, being surrounded by larger-than-life images of Connie Francis, Tommy Sands, and Pat Boone didn't exactly create a Studio 54 vibe. I started buying magazines like Downbeat and Metronome so that I could cut out ads which pictured my drum idols sitting behind or standing next to their Slingerland and Ludwig drum sets. The clippings helped a little, but a six-inch Buddy Rich was no contest next to a two-foot Perry Como. Still, I beavered away at playing, sweating profusely, burning up countless calories; two hours a day and more of concrete cacophony. My grandmother and her sister started to look like those World War I shell shock victims you sometimes saw in old newsreels, staggering around and then staring off blankly into space. I needed a break, my big break, and it finally came in the form of a Junior High talent show.

I probably wouldn't have done it except at the urging of Tommy, John, and Joanne. Patsy enjoyed the "car wreck" potential of watching me crash and burn in public, but I didn't take his attitude personally. Together we canvassed the competition. Some was formidable: a girl playing classical piano, a baton twirler, a guy making his science project paper maché volcano erupt: some not so much: another guy showing off his airplane model collection (which were skillfully assembled but none of them flew, and what good is an airplane that doesn't fly?), a girl showing how to bake brownies in one of those "Little Homemaker" plastic ovens (they took forever!), and another girl reciting a poem called "Hiawatha" by Henry Wadsworth Longfellow—BORING. When the others offered to help me set the drums up for the show, I was sold. I had roadies! Chick Magnet Land awaited.

After consulting with my posse, it was decided that I would play along to "Hawaiian War Chant," a popular big band drum solo vehicle of the time. Several recordings were available to choose from. I decided on one by a British band called The Ted Heath Orchestra, mainly because it showcased my "Drum God," Ronnie Verrell. The plan was to bring Tommy's portable record player along and put the microphone right up against its three-inch speaker so that I could hear it, along with everyone else, and play along. Then, when it got to the drum solo part, Tommy would lift the needle off the disc and it would be just me. I started preparing myself psychologically by tucking a pair of drumsticks into my belt 24/7. They were positioned right about where my right-side pocket was and extended down to about my knee. This "look" required an uncomfortably tight belt (I had to give up eating for a couple of weeks), but it saved me the embarrassment of having the sticks slip out and land on the ground; definitely not chick-magnet cool. It also meant that I couldn't completely flex my right knee when I walked. I ended up looking like a character on a 50's western series named Chester who faked a limp to draw attention away from the horses who were better actors than he was.

The big night finally arrived. Each one of us carried a drum set component from my house to the school. My father would have driven them and us, but Patsy begged to be seen carrying the bass drum; so, we walked instead. It was determined that I would go on after intermission so that the audience wouldn't have to wait around for us to set up. Do I really have to tell you how nervous I was? I didn't think so. My parents sat toward the back as per my request. I don't remember much about the first act; the baton twirler twirled, the brownies baked, the volcano erupted. When the lights went on for intermission, everybody headed for the PTO refreshment tables, including my roadies! Joanne took control and rounded everyone up. Patsy stuffed his face, and John stole ice cream for later. Anyhow, everything was set up in due course. Tommy headed to the side of the stage with his record player and the album. An announcement was made that Act 2 would be starting in a minute or two, and people started to head back to their seats. When everyone had settled, the cafetorium overhead lights were turned off leaving the drum set looking pretty darn impressive up there on the stage all lit up by a couple of spotlights that looked fresh off of Noah's Ark. The master of ceremonies, Mr. Salomone, the vice principal or principal vice depending on whom you asked, introduced me. Patsy, seizing a "too good to miss" opportunity, jumped up onto the stage, yanked the microphone out of Mr. Salomone's hand, took a bow, and carried the mic over to the side of the stage where Tommy waited.

When everyone had settled, the cafetorium overhead lights were turned off leaving the drum set looking pretty darn impressive up there on the stage all lit up by a couple of spotlights that looked fresh off of Noah's Ark.

Now you're probably expecting me to tell you that we had brought the wrong album, or that the record player's batteries died, or that Tommy dragged the needle across the record when he went to lift it, creating that horrible "fingernails-on-chalkboard" noise, but none of that happened. The music started—the right music—and we could all hear it just fine. We got to the solo part, Tommy lifted the needle, and then it was all up to me. Now, I'd love to tell you that it was the greatest drum solo I had ever played, but it wasn't. It was okay though, about average where my drum solos were concerned, but that was good enough. The one moment that really stands out came when I dropped a stick. I don't even know how it happened. One second it was there and the next it just wasn't. Now I had other sticks. They were tucked into a piece of hardware on the side of my bass drum so I could easily have just reached for an extra and continued. But I didn't. I froze. I just sat there staring at the rogue stick as it slowly rolled about five feet away and then finally settled.

Patsy saved me. He sensed what was happening, rushed out onto the stage in full view of the audience, picked up the happy wanderer, handed it to me, looked me right in the eye and said "keep going," bowed to the audience (again), and rushed off stage. And I did. I kept going. I finished the solo with my musical coup de grace, a fast, loud flourish, where I wailed on everything I could reach and walked off. I know there was applause—none louder than from the side of the stage where my roadies waited. That was the only applause that counted anyway. Then it was quickly back on stage to remove the drum set so that a pair of seventh grade twin sisters in cute "farm girl" outfits could sing "A Bushel and a Peck." When the talent show finally ended, a prize (just one) was given out to the winner: the baton twirler. My posse said that I was robbed, but she was actually pretty good. Maybe if I hadn't dropped that stupid stick….

I finished the solo with my musical coup de grace, a fast, loud flourish, where I wailed on everything I could reach and walked off.

Anyhow, I didn't win, but I still felt like a winner. I was now a chick magnet. A couple of younger girls even asked me to autograph their programs. But, you know, in hindsight, I now realize that the really important part of that whole experience came in the space of just a few seconds when Patsy handed me the stick, and our eyes met, and he said "keep going" and then he turned to the audience and took a bow.

HIGGINS SCHOOL: Part 3
Fred Upstairs

If the talent show is an indelible memory of my seventh grade year, the eighth-grade semi-formal dance serves a similar purpose for my final year in Higgins School. My eighth-grade homeroom was in Room 8-7, proof positive that higher numbers didn't equate to greater academic achievement as my 8-7 class was virtually identical to my 7-1L class with one difference: we had gone from novice underachiever status in seventh grade to veteran underachiever status in eighth. Our homeroom teacher Mr. Leo Lepre, affectionately nicknamed Leo the Leper by Tommy, (of course) was kind and encouraging, especially when it came to doling out extra credit for creative writing. I remember taking full advantage of this policy, but I can only recall one submission, a short science fiction story called "The Monster with One Green Eye." It had something to do with a spaceship that had crashed into a lake late at night and immediately sunk to the bottom. Its sole occupant (the monster) had survived unscathed and began venturing forth under cover of darkness to explore the nearby lakeside cabins. Naturally these cabins were occupied by beautiful young women who closely resembled Ann Robinson in *The War of the Worlds* and Julie Adams in *The Creature from the Black Lagoon*. I don't remember anything else about the story. If I had to guess, I probably cast myself as a young kid, ignored and underestimated by these nubile goddesses and their studly suitors, who ultimately rode to their rescue through a combination of courage and ingenuity to save them from a horny Cyclops wannabee alien. A very different green eyed monster made an appearance, however, at the semi-formal dance.

My parent's store in Thompsonville was almost directly across the street from Chriton's Card and Gift Shop. Mrs Chriton was an older lady who sold cards, gift wrap, party supplies and stationery. Her son, Donald, was an accomplished dancer who eventually went on to make quite a name for himself as the lead dancer and choreographer on the Carol Burnett Show—possibly the only Thompsonvillian to make it big in the business of show. Anyway, long before he achieved that level of recognition, Don offered dance classes in rented spaces; ballroom and "contemporary dance stylings" for the adults and tap for the "juniors" aka us. He also offered classes during the lead-up to spring social events such as the eighth-grade semi-formal and the high school junior and senior proms. My mother went across the street for mid-morning coffee with Doris (Mrs Chriton) every day. You now know where I'm going with this, so I'll cut to the chase.

The classes were held in the junior high cafetorium. My pleas to be excluded went unheard. My grandfather found my distress amusing. Tommy was "volunteered" by his mother, but John said it was too uncool, which was probably an excuse for the fact that his mom couldn't afford it, and Patsy insisted that he already knew how to dance from watching Connecticut Bandstand on afternoon TV.

So, there I was, along with Tommy, on a Tuesday night ranged along one wall along with a group of other miserable-looking boys staring across an open space at an even larger group of equally miserable-looking girls ranged along an opposite wall. Don Chriton stood in between the two reluctant groups in a social "no man's land." I know you've heard the expression "misery loves company." Well, our collective misery bonded me to other boys, some of whom I didn't even know, and others whom I did know but would just as soon not have. I'm sure it was the same for the girls.

So, Mr. Don (as he liked to be called) greeted us and started pairing us up by size. Girls outnumbered boys, so we ended up with some boy-girl couples and a lot of girl-girl combos. He spaced us out in no man's land and demonstrated the box step with a tall, solo girl. Then he had us all try it while he walked around giving each pair some individualized instruction. Diminutive Tommy got paired up with petite Carlene Casserella, so they made a good pair (fyi they're still a good pair, three diminutive boys and five petite girls later). It started for them as love at first sight and it still is.

Mr. Don had paired me up with a pretty blond-haired girl from the brainiac class named Priscilla Marlow whom I knew a little. So we talked and made robotic boxes while Mr. Don coached. Priscilla was nice, easy to talk to, and easy on the eyes. I, of course, was a chick magnet so we made a good pair. The only problem was that Priscilla had no sense of rhythm whatsoever.

Priscilla was nice, easy to talk to, and easy on the eyes. I, of course, was a chick magnet so we made a good pair. The only problem was that Priscilla had no sense of rhythm whatsoever.

I found this out when Mr. Don put on a record and started us box stepping to music by calling out "forward, side, together, back, side, together, etc." Priscilla was taking piano lessons so you'd think she'd have a sense of time, but I had been told even before meeting her that piano students and their teachers are not just arhythmic, they're actively anti-rhythmic. This is because keeping consistent time and tempo interferes with their being able to play the right notes in the right sequence with the right fingering. When playing Beethoven's Moonlight Sonata, for instance, a piano student's accomplishment was only measured by how well she played all the notes on the sheet music exactly as printed, even if her version started as a trot and ended as a gallop.

Anyway, Priscilla was nice so I tried to help her out and we managed, sort of. Mr. Don then showed us how to turn as we did the box step. This was accomplished by taking certain steps at 45 degree angles instead of just straight ahead. So now we looked like drunk robots. He put on some music and before you knew, it we were dancing to the Tennessee Waltz. Mr. Don had cleverly timed this to happen when parents were arriving to take us home. The "ooo's" and "ahhh's" from moms insured us that we'd all be back next week, and we were. Over the next few weeks, we perfected box stepping, both straight and curved, along with the cha-cha, which was basically a box step for stutterers, and the jitterbug. John didn't say much about this "dance stuff" because it was still uncool in his eyes; Patsy started calling me Fred Upstairs.

HIGGINS SCHOOL: Part 4

D Day

I don't remember ever formally inviting Priscilla to the semi-formal. We had remained dance partners during all of the lessons, so I think we both assumed that we'd go together and we did. Like most eighth-grade boys, personal grooming wasn't high on my list. This changed dramatically during the run-up to the dance. Clothes were washed and pressed, my one suit jacket was sent to the cleaners, a new clip-on tie was purchased, etc. My mom even went next door to Spaulding Florist and picked out a wrist corsage for me to give Priscilla. I think one of the laws of the universe is that mothers find events of this kind a whole lot more important than their sons do. And mine did. On D (dance) Day, I was allowed to use my father's electric razor. The result was some face fuzz, but if there were whiskers mixed in, they were well hidden. I was then liberally doused with Aqua Velva and told to get dressed and brush my teeth. The D Day picture taking then began. My mother took photos, my grandmother took photos, and her sister took photos. My father didn't take photos; he dragged out his Super 8 movie camera instead. I was posed indoors and outdoors until embarrassment became humiliation. I'll bet Mr. Kodak cleaned up on D Days back then. My mother backed us out of the driveway, then pulled in again so that I could retrieve Priscilla's corsage from the refrigerator. As we pulled back into the driveway, I was greeted by the sight of my grandmother and her sister piling into the back of my grandfather's old Chevy, each one with camera in hand. I gave my mother a panicked look, and she just shrugged her shoulders; her way of saying "not guilty." And so, we were finally off; Prince Charming in his royal carriage, a 1956 Dodge Polara wagon, followed closely by his entourage in a black '49 Chevy.

I think one of the laws of the universe is that mothers find events of this kind a whole lot more important than their sons do. And mine did.

The picture-taking reached frenzy proportions at Priscilla's house. Her mother took photos, my mother took photos, my grandmother took photos, her sister took photos, Priscilla's mother took photos, her grandmother took photos, the neighbors took photos, a photographer from *Life Magazine* probably took photos, and, just to make sure nothing was missed, my father and Priscilla's father recorded everything for posterity on dueling Super 8's—a true Kodak bacchanal. Priscilla looked very nice in a pink party dress and matching corsage (my mother had called her mother). After what seemed like forever, we were finally allowed to make our way to the school cafetorium which, we were assured, would be unrecognizable, having been magically transformed into the semi formal's theme, Neptune's Underwater Kingdom.

If you're expecting sarcasm, you're going to be disappointed. Yes, of course it was cheesy, but sometimes even cheesy requires creativity and hard work, and Neptune's Underwater Kingdom had clearly required a lot of both to achieve its own unique level of cheesydom. The cafetorium was transformed by green light bulbs in the overhead fixtures, and blue helium filled balloons held in place by white ribbons tied to bricks wrapped in tin foil that sat on the floor and as centerpieces on tables. Said tables were covered by paper tablecloths with a seahorse and shells motif. The paper plates and cups matched the tablecloths. There were even cardboard palm trees that looked a bit worn, probably from repeated use, but we didn't care. A bubble making machine that may have been borrowed from *The Lawrence Welk Show* furthered the ambiance. A wooden chair covered in dark green velveteen doubled as Neptune's Throne. And punch was served with fruit garnishes held together by little plastic tridents. All of the dance class kids were there along with a good many other eighth graders. The music was a combination of old and new but definitely with a nautical theme: "Old Cape Cod," "Ebb Tide," "Beyond the Sea," "Slow Boat to China," "Harbor Lights," etc.

The first half hour or so was mostly taken up with mingling and very little dancing. Some couples arrived fashionably late. At least that was the impression they wanted to create. I think it probably had more to do with stopping by grandma's house on the way to the school, so that they could hear things like, "look how big you got" and "you look so grown up" and "it just seems like yesterday I was changing your dirty diaper"—just the kind of mental picture you wanted to share with your date.

Mr. Don made a guest appearance all spiffed up. All the dance class kids gravitated toward him. One of the chaperones announced that he'd agreed to judge a jitterbug dance contest. So, we all hit the floor and showed off our best moves dancing to The Hucklebuck while Mr. Don and his partner (Mr. Larry) weaved in and out among couples. When one of them tapped you or your partner on the shoulder, you had to walk off the floor and stand on the sidelines. In just a few minutes the Hucklebuckers were whittled down to three couples, Tommy and Carlene, Priscilla and me, and Dave and Marsha, who had also been in our dance class. I had a sinking feeling as Mr. Larry approached Priscilla from behind, but I wasn't really surprised when he tapped her shoulder. She had all the right moves, but at all the wrong times. David and Marsha were eliminated next, leaving Tommy and Carlene the winners. I was happy at the outcome, although I know Priscilla was quite disappointed, but I figured that if it couldn't be us, I was glad it was them.

Anyhow, everybody seemed to be having a reasonably good time until one particular couple walked in, and the room suddenly got noticeably quiet. It was Johnny Damian, looking very handsome in jacket and tie, and on his arm was Joanne Shultz. She was stunning. She wore a cream-colored satin blouse and a floor length tight, deep red velvet skirt with a slit up the side from here to forever, revealing perfect nylon stockinged legs. In just a few seconds, every girl in that room wanted to be her, and every boy wanted to be him—including me. Time stopped. The green-eyed monster was very much alive and kicking in that room, and I don't mean the one I had written about for extra credit. Once the initial shock had worn off, the mingling and dancing gradually picked up, but I think every girl in that room made a point during the dance to compliment Joanne on her dress, her hair, her make-up, her date, etc. And she held court like the queen she was. And to think this was the tomboy I'd hung out with. We'd ridden bikes together, climbed trees together, built a fort together, shared sodas and hot dogs with each other… and now? Wow! I still think of Priscilla as a girl, but from that moment on, Joanne was a woman!

I had a sinking feeling as Mr. Larry approached Priscilla from behind, but I wasn't really surprised when he tapped her shoulder. She had all the right moves, but at all the wrong times.

My reverie was broken by an announcement that King Neptune himself was about to hold court. The music stopped abruptly, and in marched the king, attended by two younger girls wearing what appeared to be Arabian Nights style costumes. The king was resplendent in a long purple robe with a matching belt and necklace made of strung together clam shells. He carried a large, gold, plastic trident. He had a long green "seaweed" beard, which looked like it might have been crocheted, and a huge plastic crown festooned with more of the same stuff. But you couldn't disguise the hair. It was Patsy. I felt hurt that he and John had kept their plans for the dance such successful secrets. I suppose that I wanted the Fab 4 to just go on unchanged forever, especially after the talent show where all of us seemed to be unified by a common cause. But then it occurred to me that the "common cause" was to give me a moment. And they did. And I had it. But now it was their turn, Tommy and John and Joanne and Patsy. Now it was their moment.

Once seated, he untied a scroll and read it. The minute he started with the words, "Let it be known of all assembled herein…," we knew that it had been written by Mr. Lepre. The "thee's" and "thou's" were a dead giveaway. It was a proclamation granting all of us citizenship of "his" underwater kingdom and making us all his subjects. When he finished, he stood up on the chair and made each couple come forward so that he could dub them "Neptunians." We all took part (the chaperones saw to that), and he touched each of us lightly on the shoulder, solemnly intoning the words, "You are now Neptunians." He almost gagged when John and Joanne took their places in front of him, but he then delivered his blessing with aplomb.

When I think back on my "Tween Ark" years, I'm grateful to have forgotten much of the awkwardness that's normally associated with puberty. Thank God for the Purgetron! But there are certain lessons that I can now acknowledge with gratitude. For one, I learned that girls are more than just wannabe guys. There's a line spoken by one of the actors in the movie *Some Like It Hot*. That's the film where two struggling musicians in roaring 20's Chicago inadvertently witness a gangland murder and disguise themselves as females in order to join an all-girl orchestra which is going on tour. One of the guys says, "My God, Jerry, it's a whole different sex!" My junior high years, in particular the backyard incident with Joanne and her transformation at the dance, taught me that lesson in spades. Girls/women are indeed "a whole different sex." Another thing I learned is that acting "cool" is a costume, like when Patsy dressed up as King Neptune. You can wear it for a while if it suits you, but it doesn't change who you are when you take it off, so taking it too seriously is foolish. It's artifice, nothing more.

Finally, I learned that every young person needs a "thing" to define himself to himself, and to the world at large. My thing was playing the drums. Tommy's thing became evident shortly thereafter. It took a bit longer for the others.

TOMMY'S THING

Whoosh and Boom

Tommy was living proof of the paradox that big things sometimes come in small packages. In fact, his size would always present something of a contradiction, starting with his birth at a whopping 10 pounds, 3 ounces.

This was quite a curiosity, given that his dad stood only at five foot eight inches, with his mom at least six inches shorter. You can imagine the good-natured ribbing that both parents got. The gibes, although well intentioned, started to wear after a while, but they gradually diminished as Tommy got older and started school. It was clear by then that he would follow his parents and go from being a small child to a small adult. Tom's Dad, who was known for his frugality, saw an upside to this; he almost always took advantage of "children five and under admitted free" types of opportunities. However, although it may have saved the Ferraro family a few dollars here and there, it certainly did nothing for "Little Tommy's" self-image. It seemed he would always be the last to be chosen when a group of boys chose sides for a baseball game or to play volleyball in the park. He even began to accept mascot status as his fate. That is, until the Saint Calogero festival during the summer between his seventh and eighth grade.

> **Nothing could be more fun than loading up on cotton candy, soda, and fried dough, followed by a ride on the pukes-a-lot, violently voiding, and then starting the cycle all over again.**

La Festa, as it was known locally, was always held between the first and second weekends in July. It began on the first Sunday with a high mass in St Patrick's Church. A life-size painted statue of Frenchtown's patron saint was added to the more familiar cast of characters, who held sway for the rest of the year (Jesus, St Joseph, the Virgin Mary, etc.). The carnival opened that afternoon and stayed open until the following Sunday night. It was encamped at Mount Carmel in North Thompsonville. While there is a Biblical connection to the name, the Mount Carmel of La Festa was decidedly secular, consisting of a brick building with a large, empty field alongside. The field served as a venue for local softball leagues, and the bar on the first floor of the Mount Carmel building served 25 cent drafts and 60 cent mixed drinks to Mount Carmel Society members. You could become a member by contributing a one-time fee of two dollars and signing a book just inside the door. A second floor multi-function space was also available to members for weddings, anniversaries, family gatherings, wakes, etc.

The carnival, with its neon lights, merry-go-round calliope music, and the aroma of all foods friable from the vendors and cooking tent, was a magnet for Frenchtownies of all ages, especially the kids who were drawn like moths to a flame. Many families even postponed scheduling family vacation outings and trips until after La Festa. There were hoop toss games, balloon and dart games, a shooting gallery, wheels of chance, dime toss games (land a dime on a painted circle and win a prize), skeet-ball, a water gun horse race game, and on and on. There were rides like the Ferris wheel, the whip, the scrambler, the tilt-a-whirl, and a ride the kids dubbed the "pukes-a-lot," which consisted of a long-pivoted arm with "rocket ships" at each end. The arm see-sawed up and down as it rotated while the rocket ships spun; hence the name. Nothing could be more fun than loading up on cotton candy, soda, and fried dough, followed by a ride on the pukes-a-lot, voiding, and then starting the cycle all over again. Add to the atmosphere the merry-go-round calliope, piped in Dean Martin and Al Martino Italian-American favorites, the bells, the yells, the screams and a local band of teens who ascribed to the old musical adage: "if you can't play good, play loud," and you had a feast for both stomachs and senses.

Tommy loved it all—every little bit. He, John, and Joanne were even allowed to walk there and back escorted by Joanne's older sister, Alicia, and her boyfriend, Wally. It was almost a mile, but through neighborhoods pronounced "safe," so Alicia and Wally cut the "small fry" loose as soon as they had gone far enough to be out of parental supervision sight. Once there on the grounds of the "consecrated carnival," Joanne usually peeled off to join other pre-teen "hens," and John usually headed out on a five-finger discount shopping expedition to see how many stuffed animals he could liberate, rather than win. That left Tommy to entertain himself with a pocketful of change.

One night in particular, as the carnival was approaching its ten o'clock curfew, Tommy wandered over to a roped-off section behind the tents. There he met "Buddy Pyro, the Master of Disaster." At least that was how Bud Partucci billed himself on the painted side of his small trailer. It was adorned with a larger-than-life Bud in a tuxedo replete with top hat and white gloves, each hand grasping bunches of lit firecrackers and rockets, a maniacal grin, and a huge mushroom cloud forming a dramatic, ominous backdrop. In reality, Bud wasn't much larger than Tommy, 50ish, balding, smelling like he could use a shower, and chain smoking Lucky Strikes. He was unpacking what appeared to be baseballs and softballs wrapped in tissue paper, except that each "ball" had a protruding wick about three inches long. When Tommy asked if he could watch, Bud, grateful for the momentary notoriety, agreed. He explained to Tommy that fireworks weren't launched by rockets as the public generally assumed, but they were actually lowered into mortars, metal cylinders of different sizes he called "cans," and "ground-launched" when he lit their wicks. Tommy saw a lot of Chinese characters on the packaging, but each "work" as Bud called them also had an English name like chrysanthemum, peony, diadem, willow, rings, etc. By the time Bud finished explaining how works differed by name, Father Benedict came on the sound system to announce the end of the day's activities, to thank everyone for turning out, to remind them that the carnival would reopen the next day at 3:00, and to give a blessing. When the prayer ended, Bud went to work lighting the fuses with a glowing cigar. Tommy was in heaven. The thump and whoosh of each work, not to mention the smell of black powder, sulfur, and saltpeter, the sparks and glowing trails were all intoxicating. The crowning glory came when Bud looked around to make sure they were unobserved and handed the stogie to Tommy, pointed at a wick, and said, "there, light that one." Tommy did, and his brain exploded along with the work. He stared at Bud with glassy eyes. Bud said, "Better than sex, ain't it?" Tommy nodded eagerly, although he wasn't in much of a position to compare the two.

Tommy was in heaven. The thump and whoosh of each work, not to mention the smell of black powder, sulfur, and saltpeter, the sparks and glowing trails were all intoxicating.

Tommy became Bud's shadow for the remaining nights of La Festa. He learned all about how to put on a "whoosh and boom" show as Bud called it. He learned all about works and cans, screamers and whistlers, dubs, duds and flubs, snakes, bow ties, how to load, how to prime, and how to charge, all while helping Bud set up before and clean up after. Although no one would ever mistake Bud for a stockbroker or a lawyer, he was, in his own way, very professional when it came to how he did what he did. Safety was everything; he never took a shortcut, and he double checked everything. He told Tommy that he both knew and knew of too many guys like himself who couldn't count to ten using their fingers because they were missing too many. Some even lost whole hands; some lost eyes.

He also explained how a good display was more than just shooting off works at random and saving a few for a grand finale. According to Bud, a good display controlled a rube's (a rube was a patron) eyes without the rube even knowing it. For instance, you start a display with some ground effects like volcanoes to get the rube looking down. Volcanoes were cone-shaped works that shot colorful sparks up three or four feet. Then you progress to skeletal wooden frames called "dead men," with attachment points at eye level for Saint Catherine wheels which spun like crazy, creating an enormous circle of colored sparks. Now the rube's eyes were angled up about 20 degrees above eye level. Then you hit him with low aerials to raise the angle to 30 degrees, then mid-level aerials to reach 45 degrees, and finally "heavies" to get the angle up to 60 degrees, where the "ooh's" and "ahhhs" really got cranking. Once you got a rube to that point, you could take him wherever you wanted, 30 degrees, 60, 45, back to 60, then down to 30 again, and the rubes would follow like sheep. "Better than sex," old Bud would say, "better than sex."

On La Festa's final night, Bud set off a special display with works he'd kept in reserve for the occasion. The display was longer, larger, higher, and louder than anything he'd done up to now, and it culminated in a special work called "Mother of Millions," which made the Deathstar exploding look and sound like a cherry bomb. The ground literally shook, and the flash was virtually thermo-nuclear. Babies cried, little girls (and a few boys) wet themselves, an older woman fainted, old men sporting VFW caps compared it to aerial bombardment, Father Benedict, his arms outstretched, shouted "*a mirac*!," and Sister Kerosina thought she might have orgasmed, proving Bud's adage "better than sex."

Even before Tommy and Bud parted ways and Al Martino sang "Al Di La" for the final time, Tommy was devising a plan.

Tommy saw a market for his newfound expertise in the form of house parties, weddings, anniversaries, birthdays, graduations, first communions, coming-out parties; in short, social occasions of every shape and size. He knew from his own upbringing that next to eating and fighting, Italian-Americans loved fireworks most of all. So, he knew he had an audience if allowed to perform his magic, and if he could acquire product. For this he looked to Bud. The arrangement was this: Tommy would front the money, Bud would buy the product, Tommy would book the gigs, then they'd put on the show together and split the profit evenly. Bud's half of the partnership would be silent; the face on the business was Tommy's and his alone. Little Tommy Ferraro was now Big Tommy Nitro.

Selling this concept to his parents was no easy task. His father was skeptical; his mother was dead set against it. The one thing Tommy had going for him was his cousins, his mom's sister's sons. They were generally boorish and boastful, each one an overachiever, each "full of himself" as Tommy's dad would say. Lawrence, aka Larry, was an accomplished track and field athlete with a cupboard full of cups and medals. The Pan-Italian Games were his showcase, and there was talk about the Olympics. George was the scholar in the family with perfect scores on his SATs. A range of scholarships from some of America's best colleges were at his disposal. Finally, Mark was set to assume control of the family business, a prosperous lumberyard and building supply company, where he already supervised employees who were more than twice his age. Each of the boys wore the nicest clothes, ate the best food, and drove his own late-model car. "Not new," their father would proudly say, "but 'newish'. After all, we don't want to spoil them." This pronouncement was always accompanied by winks and backslaps delivered to the listener.

Tommy used his cousins to make his case. Each one of them had his own "thing." Tommy didn't have a "thing." Tommy needed a "thing." Big Tommy Nitro could be his "thing." Tommy's proposal was followed with what seemed to him to be an interminable period of discussion and deliberation. His parents met Bud (Tommy subtly suggested that he shower first), who told them that he was impressed by Tommy's maturity and his entrepreneurial spirit. Bud liked Tommy, but he also liked the "ca-ching" sound a cash register makes. Tommy's parents were impressed by Bud's professional demeanor and by the fact that he had treated Tommy "parentally," as his mom put it. That was followed a week later by a field trip to Bud's cabin, where, because it was a bit off the beaten path, Tommy and Bud could demonstrate safe pyrotechnic practices without attracting unwanted attention. But what ultimately sold Tommy's mom was the Ferraro's attendance at cousin George's (he was the scholar) graduation party, which was professionally catered and featured a live band and an open bar. Tommy's mom and her sister had always been unspoken rivals, so when George's Mom revealed that "St." George had been granted a full scholarship to Trinity College in Hartford, Tommy's Mom countered with a knee-jerk response about her own son's start-up business. And before you could say "whoosh-boom," Big Tommy Nitro was in business.

Tommy didn't have a "thing." Tommy needed a "thing." Big Tommy Nitro could be his "thing."

Business cards were printed along with posters and fliers, where a blank space was left for Tommy to marker in the dates, time, and location of his next gig. He even took out ads in the St. Calogero Society Newsletter, the Mount Carmel Bulletin, and, most importantly, The St. Patrick's Church and Church School Reminder, where Tommy added the word "devotional" to the printed copy. The centerpiece of each poster and flier was a black and white photo of Tommy's face, wearing his best "power" expression superimposed over a drawing he'd copied from one of those Charles Atlas comic book ads showing a strongman's physique, to which Tommy added lightning bolts clutched in both hands.

Unfortunately, Tommy's venture suffered to some degree from poor timing. It was the end of July before Tommy got the green light from his parents and mid-August before Tommy started his publicity blitz. His first big gig finally came at the St Patrick's Fall Festival which was staged over Labor Day Weekend in the parking lot just outside the church school. It was sort of La Festa lite with fewer rides, games, and concessions. To enhance the autumnal vibe, scarecrows, jack o' lanterns, black stuffed cats, and ghosts were offered as prizes, a "haunted house" (which was basically a truck trailer with spooky music and creepy black light paintings inside) was added to the small group of rides, and corn on the cob, clam chowder, and Indian Pudding were added to the traditional burgers, dogs, and fries menu. Tommy's part of the show went quite well, thanks largely to Bud's behind the scenes know-how and some perfect weather. He managed, mostly through family, friends, and relatives, to book additional gigs at two county fairs, three weddings, and a department store grand opening. By then, the market for "whoosh and boom" shows was beginning to "season out." Tommy did one last big gig at a Halloween fest sponsored by St. Stephen's Catholic Church, just across the border in Massachusetts, and that, as they say, was that.

He and Bud packed everything up in Bud's trailer. They then met to make sure expenses had been covered and that they had divided the proceeds fairly. Bud was happy and said that he was sure they'd do even better next season, which, in New England, started up again in May. In the meantime, Bud would be heading south to the Carolina's, Georgia, and Florida where the demand for his services would continue. He promised to keep in touch with postcards, but they both knew he wouldn't. And he didn't. As for Big Tommy Nitro—well, although his season had ended, his reputation was made, especially where his peers were concerned, and that, of course, was what mattered most of all. From now on he was Tommy Ferraro. The "little" was gone once and for all in everyone's mind, including his own. And that, Tommy concluded, really was better than sex. At least for now.

JOANNE'S THING

"Girl, You'll Be a Woman Soon"

Say the word "sleek" out loud to yourself. Now say the word out loud again, but this time elongate the "ee" sound. What comes to mind? What mental picture forms? Some animals are sleek, a cheetah, for instance, or a weasel. Can you picture a fat ferret? I didn't think so. "Sleek" is just one of those words where meaning and sound combine and then complement each other. Do you know any people who are genuinely sleek? Certainly it's becoming harder and harder to find them, although they certainly stand out much more than they would have even a decade ago. I think that being sleek probably was always more important to women than to men, maybe because it gave them so many fashion options. You've all seen models strutting along fashion show runways. Now those women are sleek.

Joanne was sleek. Other girls envied her for it. They would say things like, "Oh, Joey (their just-between-girls nickname for her) you're so lucky. You can wear anything, and it always looks good on you." The problem was that Joanne didn't want to be sleek; Joanne hated sleek. Joanne wanted to look more like Joanne than Joey, but her body seemed oblivious in that regard. And her lack of curves served to create the impression in many that she was a tomboy, which she was, but mostly because others expected her to be. Yes, she was athletic. She played "boy sports" like baseball and basketball and was respected for her skill in both. She excelled at track and field competitions and won ribbons and medals which she had once displayed proudly but now hid away. She had the legs and stamina of a long distance runner but didn't like long distance running and the loneliness that defined it. She especially hated that some kids still referred to her as "Stick" or "The Stick." She could thank her mother for that. Back in first grade around the holidays, her teacher, Mrs. Lyons, concerned that Joanne and her class were still traumatized by events one year before when Santa had permanently spirited away their kindergarten teacher to the North Pole, hit upon the idea of a Christmas Costume Party to entertain and distract the troops. She needn't have bothered, because the troops had only the vaguest memories of Miss Sullivan's dying swan act, the milk money girl's screams or Mr. Knight's "shit." In any case, the party was on and first grade mothers did their best to humiliate their children, all in the Christmas spirit. Joanne's Mom, capitalizing on Joanne's slim build, constructed a cardboard peppermint stick with an open bottom for legs, armholes for arms, eye holes for—well, you get it—and a curved top which leaned left and caused Joanne to walk in left-handed circles when she wasn't correcting for her list. From that time forward Joanne was "Stick," mostly amongst those few who envied her intelligence which was somewhere between brilliant and genius.

Joanne was sleek. Other girls envied her for it. They would say things like, "Oh, Joey (their just-between-girls nickname for her) you're so lucky. You can wear anything, and it always looks good on you."

Her mother advised patience. She had a "nature will provide" mindset, but, to Joanne, nature didn't seem interested in providing, and Joanne soon decided to take matters into her own hands. She tried eating more in the hope that fat would go to her hips and not to her stomach. However, the fat didn't go to either, and stuffing herself made her feel lazy and lethargic. She tried isometric exercises to fill out her bust, but her breasts remained what guys derisively referred to as "mosquito bites." When her friends went shopping with their mothers for training bras (Patsy called them "slingshots"), she went to Vincent's Shoes to buy a new pair of sneakers. She even began to fear that people would assume that she was experiencing some sort of developmental delay, or that, even worse, she'd turn out to be a lesbian. God forbid! The Fab Four were no help. The one time they'd acknowledged her as a girl was when they'd asked about periods, and she'd gotten all upset because she still hadn't started hers when all of her friends had. Once the dust settled from that, they went right back to treating her like one of the guys.

It would have been nice if Joanne could have looked to her mother for support, but she knew it simply wouldn't be forthcoming. That was because Joanne's grandfather, on her mother's side, was a respected attorney who wanted very much to add "and son" to his shingle and stationery, but Joanne's mom was an only child, and prospects for additional offspring ended with her birth. As a result, Joanne's mom grew up trying to be the boy her father had really wanted. Like Joanne, she excelled equally in athletics and academics and even eventually took her law degree, which was very unusual back "in the day." When her father became a judge, Joanne's mom inherited her grandfather's law practice and even expanded it. People called her "ambitious," and, although it was sometimes meant to be derogatory, she treated it as a compliment. Respect from the public, and especially her peers, was everything to her; motherhood, fashion, and personal appearance took a back seat. Her clothes closet was divided into business suit frump and casual frump, and make-up was restricted to lipstick and a little rouge. This, however, doesn't mean to say that she was neglectful as a wife or a mother. She wasn't. Her husband and her daughter simply didn't engage her in the same way that her profession did. She sometimes felt guilty about that—but not for long. She was just one of those people who was set on dedicating her life to meeting her father's expectations, continuing even after her father's only remaining judgment was the one St. Peter would pass on him.

Joanne had to find support elsewhere. She couldn't look to her dad who was pretty much oblivious to most things female. It's not that she was estranged from him, but intimacy with his daughter (and with his wife for that matter) would never be his strong suit. Their only common ground was

Joanne's athletic accomplishments. Joanne also didn't actively pursue "girly-girl" status as did some of her friends who had developed earlier than she had, but she didn't want to be a gender-neutral sounding board for the fab four where feminine topics were concerned either. She knew they didn't set out to make her feel like that, but she had. She had other girls who were friends, but she didn't have any girlfriends, if that makes any sense. She felt alone, even in company; especially in company. Her salvation finally arrived in a totally unexpected way when John privately asked her if she'd mind meeting with his older sister, Ruth, because "she wants to ask you something."

Ruth Davis was a broad, but a classy one. The difference, according to Ruth, herself, was one of looks and style, and, most importantly, attitude. She abhorred passivity in either gender. She was six years older than John. Each had different fathers; both marriages had failed. They had both spent most of their lives in a single-parent setting. Ruth's dad was a machinist who had died in an industrial accident, while John's dad was career military. Both kids had been raised on a string of Army bases, John from birth and Ruth from the age of eight. Every time their dad was reassigned (which was frequently) Ruth and John would need to play catch-up in a new school. The result for both was a lot of disruption where learning was concerned. Ruth's mom and dad had rented a place in Enfield which was only about three miles from Bradley Field, where he was stationed with the Air National Guard at the time. When he got reassigned, her mom had followed him to his new assignment in Texas where she lived on the base, but they decided to keep paying for Ruth and John to live in the rented house for a while so that "the kids" could at least make it through high school. John had partially overcome the academic handicap, being held back only one year, but Ruth never did. She chose to drop out of high school at the start of what would have been her junior year and completed her learning at Miss Evelyn's School of Fashion, Hairdressing, Cosmetology, Carriage and Deportment. She now worked as a hairdresser, and she was good at making others look their best. Naturally, her expertise extended to herself. Her clothes were provocative but not sexy. Her make-up was impeccable. She wasn't book-smart, but she was street-wise and clever. She'd broken several hearts, but her own was largely unaffected up to now. In short, Ruth was a formidable and desirable young woman with a strong independent streak.

Some months back, Ruth had met and started dating a handsome Greek, named Demetrius, who worked as a butcher in the supermarket his father managed. It wasn't long before they started talking about spending their lives together, but there was a complication. Demetrius' parents were from the old country, which meant that Demetrius had to get his father's blessing before proceeding, which was only right because the young couple had to turn to his parents to foot the bill for the wedding and reception, Ruth's mom not being able to contribute much more than a wedding present. Demetrius' father said that he wouldn't give money or his blessing until he could tell his friends, and, more importantly, his relatives, that his future daughter-in-law had at least graduated from high school. And that's what Ruth wanted to talk to Joanne about. Ruth wanted Joanne to tutor her for the G.E.D.

The meeting took place at John's house where Ruth explained her circumstances. She also explained that it just made sense that she should ask Joanne for help as they already knew each other casually, being virtual neighbors, and because Joanne had already built a reputation as an exceptional scholar, especially where math and science were concerned (the areas where Ruth felt most deficient), and that their meetings could be conducted with discretion as Demetrius would simply break both arms of anyone of Joanne's or John's friends who couldn't keep their mouths shut. Naturally, Joanne was rather reticent, but when Ruth showed her some books about the G.E.D. that John had liberated from the library, Joanne was much reassured. Still, she explained that she would test Ruth frequently on GED-equivalent materials to insure her progress, and she would tell Ruth immediately if she (Joanne) felt that she had taken Ruth as far as she could. She also made it clear that she couldn't guarantee results, because she could only control the teaching end and not the learning part. Ruth accepted that. When it came to the subject of payment, rather than negotiate dollars and cents, Joanne proposed that Ruth teach her, in return, about how she could become more womanly in dress, appearance, and behavior; in other words, how to do more with what she had. Ruth knew she could. And with that, the deal was sealed.

When it came to the subject of payment, rather than negotiate dollars and cents, Joanne proposed that Ruth teach her, in return, about how she could become more womanly in dress, appearance, and behavior; in other words, how to do more with what she had.

They met once a week at Joanne's house. They started with a review of what Ruth had covered in her freshman and sophomore classes, and both were pleasantly surprised at how much Ruth had retained. Also, the fact that Ruth had taken both math and science during those two years and the school system only required three years of each for graduation, meant that Joanne's teaching and Ruth's learning were facilitated even more. Ruth kept her part of the bargain by helping Joanne choose a complimentary foundation and blush, then moving on to "eye enhancement," where they experimented with false lashes, mascara, shadow, liner, etc., etc., etc. Joanne was surprised by the options available and the variety of effects they produced. By the time they were ready to tackle algebra two, they had moved on to hairdressing, and plane geometry opened the door to posture in sitting, standing, and walking. Ruth also helped Joanne to choose a scent and told her never to use the word "perfume," because it would make Joanne sound "common." She called Joanne's choice of scent her "signature." Although they were usually finished and Ruth had left when Joanne's mom came home, outside of a comment about Joanne's room smelling like the cosmetics counter at a Filene's, the attorney showed little interest. And the only time the Fab Four missed Joanne was when they needed somebody to fill out the infield for an impromptu after school baseball game.

By the time they were ready to tackle algebra two, they had moved on to hairdressing, and plane geometry opened the door to posture in sitting, standing, and walking.

When word started to spread about the upcoming dance, Ruth took Joanne on a field trip to The Marnell Shop, Frenchtown's go-to place for proms, weddings, mothers-of-the bride dresses, first communion outfits, etc. While Joanne picked out and tried on several dresses that her mother would certainly have approved, Ruth wasn't satisfied with the admittedly conservative selection. When Joanne hesitated to look elsewhere, Ruth said, "Do you want to be Joey in a party dress or do you want to become Joanne?" That rattled Joanne's cage a little, but she didn't protest when Ruth led her to Chez Lenore. Ruth assured Joanne that Lenore had more fashion sense than Miss Marnell and a more open mind. Joanne remained skeptical.

Lenore Gambrini had an interesting reputation going back to WWII, when it was rumored that she was a "Victory Girl"; that is, one who contributed to the war effort by entertaining the troops when they were home on leave. Whether or not that reputation was deserved could never be proven, because servicemen were frequently known to boast about their conquests, mostly to their fellows, and hometown "plain Janes" saw Lenore as an easy target for jealous snipes when "men in uniform" passed them over.

Lenore, confident of her combined sex appeal and business acumen, simply ignored them, which, of course, infuriated her critics even more, which, of course, was Lenore's intention. Rumors about her possibly prurient interests persisted even to the present, with some even convinced that she had a special backroom where sex toys and dominatrix supplies were displayed. Of course, no one had actually seen it. Although they swore they would never set foot in Chez Lenore, once the bloom was off the rose for many marriages, those same critics would discreetly use the shop's rear entrance to check out Lenore's stock of Frederick's of Hollywood girdles, bustiers, "torpedo tits" bras, crotchless panties, etc., always first having insured that none of the cars in Lenore's parking lot looked familiar. Lenore was always busiest when she opened at 1:00 ("I'll get there before anybody else") or just before she closed at 9:00 ("I'll go now because everybody's probably already left."). Housewives trying to resuscitate their marriages insured Lenore a steady income.

When Ruth pulled into Lenore's parking lot, Joanne almost bolted for home, but Ruth assured her that she did much of her shopping there and knew Lenore well. Ruth led the way in, and sure enough, Lenore greeted her with a hug. Joanne's first impression of Lenore was of a woman her mother would have called "mutton dressed up as lamb." Lenore was no spring chicken, but she dressed, spoke, and, more importantly, acted like a lady twenty years younger. Even Joanne had to give her credit for keeping the years at bay. The only thing that gave Lenore away was the faint odor of Johnson's Baby Powder, which Joanne associated with her grandma.

Ruth explained that they were looking for a dress that would fill Joanne out a bit.

"Enhance her attributes in other words," said Lenore.

"Exactly," Ruth replied, *"but it should be elegant too."*

"Did you bring her heels?" Lenore asked as she started to sort through a rack and pull out several dresses.

"Right here," said Ruth. *"I'm loaning her a pair of mine."*

Ruth produced a pair of black high heels from a bag that Joanne hadn't noticed before. Joanne obediently began trying dresses on, feeling almost surreal about the whole process. Eventually the choice narrowed down to one of Lenore's more conservative outfits: a straight line skirt and a vanilla colored blouse that fit Joanne perfectly, creating just the effect they wanted, and rendered just slightly untraditional by the skirt's wine red color. Both ladies pronounced this outfit "the one." Ruth asked Lenore to put it aside, explaining that they'd be back to pay for it. Then she and Joanne said their goodbyes and thank you's.

After tackling the quadratic equation at their next scheduled session, they tackled the prom dress issue. Joanne was having second thoughts about the choice of colors knowing that most girls would be in pastels.

Ruth: *Look, Joey, I've shown you how to sit in a skirt so that you're not flashing Tom, Dick, and Harry. I've shown you how to stand like a model with one foot slightly in front of the other, and I've shown you how to shift your weight when you walk, so that you don't look like you're getting ready to play third base. The outfit looks amazing on you. It says, 'I'm more than just one of the guys.' Trust me, with that dress, your hair up, and my makeup, you will be stunning, I promise.*

Joanne: *Do I really need to wear high heels? Nobody'll see them.*

Ruth: *Miss Evelyn says that high heels shift your center of gravity so that your chest sticks out in front, and your butt sticks out in back, and that's what we want. We want sleek but not flat. As Lenore said, enhance your attributes, right?*

Joanne: (nods)

Ruth: *Now, tell your mother that we picked out a dress and you need the money to pay for it. If she doesn't like it when you try it on for her, she can always return it and take you shopping herself.*

Joanne: *She never has time.*

Ruth: *I'm counting on that.*

THE BALLAD OF ANGELO AND BOB

Patsy's Inheritance

Patsy's Dad was Angelo. He was loud, self-opinionated, a boozer when he could afford to be, and a talented auto mechanic. He worked for the Porcello brothers who owned a Mobil service center back when "service" consisted of more than a pimply kid behind a counter giving you change for beef jerky; turkey jerky if you were health conscious. Angelo liked the no-strings aspect of working for someone else who made the appointments, ordered the parts Angelo needed, made out the invoices, took payment from customers, etc. Angelo knew that his strength was in dealing with machines, not with people. He also liked that he could often be done for the day by mid-afternoon. That allowed him to cut out early instead of waiting around for late afternoon emergency repairs, which didn't happen too often. He could then choose between spending a couple of hours at The Ringside shooting pool and sucking suds and/or shooting the shit. He could also take in some repair work on the side, which was good money, because he didn't have to give the Porcellos a cut.

Angelo's parents, Patsy's great-grandparents, came to America from the "old country" to work in The Mill which had advertised there for workers. His dad, Tony, made the adjustment to new places and new faces much more easily than his mom, Sophia, did. Tony made new friends easily, but Sophia had left a tight circle of friends and family behind. Every reversal of fortune, no matter how minor, elicited moans and groans from Sophia over how this would never have happened back in her "pieez" (hometown) where everyone was happy, honest, moral, friendly, etc. etc. etc. Oh, how she missed how "the people would sing and dance in the plaza all the time." Tony, who remembered the same "pieez" as mostly rice paddies and a hotbed of fascist nationalism where Mussolini would have been very much at home, labeled Sophia delusional. Angelo's first complete baby sentence was "*Tu se pazzo*"—You are crazy.

Angelo grew up strong and healthy in Frenchtown, and he went through the public school system. Miss Sullivan was his kindergarten teacher! He graduated (just barely) from Enfield High School. His mother helped him find his first job. Sophia knew that Angelo loved to eat, so she figured he'd do well around food. Before you could say "Sophia's second cousin," Angelo was working as a short-order cook at Zippy's diner. He did well there, proving to be both reliable and industrious, and a reasonably good cook as well. Angelo just liked working with his hands. Whether they were wielding knives and spatulas or screwdrivers and wrenches really didn't matter to him. What Angelo didn't like was customers who complained. Push came to shove, sometimes literally, when a dissatisfied diner patron wanted something to be returned to the kitchen. The camel broke his back when a female patron complained that her fish and chips had been fried in rancid oil. Angelo, who had just changed the oil the previous week, knew that it was fresh, but he bit the proverbial bullet, threw out her order, and started over. When her plate was returned to the kitchen a second time, Angelo strode directly to where she was seated and offered to have her inspect his fryolator close up, while still in operation naturally. Thus ended Angelo's culinary career.

Angelo's next job was as a stock boy in the local Sears store. He liked this job for its variety, not of the goods he stocked, but of the departments he visited. One morning he'd be in men's sportswear; that afternoon he'd be in tools and hardware. One day he'd be unpacking and setting up furniture groupings; that afternoon he'd be restocking automotive paint. Angelo did well at Sears for almost a year. His downfall came when he was assigned to do inventory in one of the large basement storage areas, where he was caught by a supervisor taking inventory of Angela from Housewares' intimate apparel. This would normally be treated with a reprimand, but Angela was the store manager's niece, so Angela stayed, but Angelo went.

His downfall came when he was assigned to do inventory in one of the large basement storage areas, where he was caught by a supervisor taking inventory of Angela from Housewares, the store manager's niece.

Angelo got his present job at Porcello's through Vincent Porcello's son, Mickey. He and Angelo were on the basketball team, the Weavers, together in high school and had remained friends after graduation. Soon after he went to work for the Porcello Brothers, Angelo met, courted, and married Carmella Nucio; Patsy came along seven months later.

One morning at Porcellos, Angelo met Bob Smith, who had brought his car in for a brake job. Because he lived alone, Bob had to wait around while Angelo worked on his car. Porcello's had a waiting area, but it was pretty grungy, and the most recent Field and Stream magazine was at least four months old. Bob had made his appointment at 8 a.m., the first of the day, so he was kind of trapped in Porcelloland, because no other businesses within walking distance had opened yet. The appointment dragged on while Bob waited for the brake parts Angelo needed to be delivered by the parts store runner. Angelo, meanwhile, did a couple of oil changes. When Bob called the day before to make the appointment, Mike Porcello, who worked the counter, recorded the make, year, and model of Bob's car, so Mike could have ordered the brake parts there and then, leaving Angelo ready to get to work immediately on Bob's car the next morning. Not ordering the parts until Bob actually showed up for the repair meant that Bob's appointment ran longer, and Brothers Porcello could charge him for additional time while Angelo did the oil changes as well. Vincent Porcello, who thought himself clever, liked to call this practice "double dipping" – get it? oil? dipstick?

Having thoroughly thumbed through the *Field and Stream* and *American Legion* magazines (how many ads for trusses can you look at?), Bob grew restless and decided to ignore the "workplace warnings" and wander into the bays where Angelo had his car up on a lift. Angelo knew that the Porcellos wouldn't approve, but it wasn't his business, so liability wasn't high on his list of concerns; besides, Angelo sometimes liked a little company when he worked. They started to find verbal common ground about last night's Yankees game and the team's chances of getting to the Series. If you were a Yankees fan in the 50's, it was a foregone conclusion that they'd, at the very least, make the play-offs. Their conversation then moved on to other "male safe" subjects, such as cars, the weather, women, TV, beer, and then back to baseball to restart the cycle. At some point Bob asked Angelo if he did any work on the side and whether Angelo knew as much about motorcycles as he did about cars. Angelo said yes to both. When Bob explained exactly where he lived, Angelo knew who he was immediately, because Bob Smith was something of a local legend.

Bob Smith was born with a spoon in his mouth, and it didn't take him long to turn it silver. He was an entrepreneur from the get-go, ferrying groceries from supermarkets directly to the homes of Suffield residents who were either too old to do it themselves or too rich to be bothered. He called his first business B.B.D.'s (Bob's Bicycle Delivery). Within a year he had two other boys working for him and was taking a kickback from the owner of the A&P to steer business his way and away from the other Suffield supermarket, The First National. When he graduated from high school, he was voted "Most Likely to Succeed" by his classmates, roughly 15% who were in his employ by then. There was talk by his parents of his going on to college, but Bob, who at this point was making more money than his father, decided to forego higher education, for the time being at least, instead setting his sights on the one thing in life that he valued most for having profit potential.

It wasn't difficult at all to find out how to make ice cream nor was it difficult to recognize that, marketed properly, ice cream could turn a significant profit. The problem, of course, was that ice cream was considered by most people to be a seasonal treat. After all, who wanted to eat something ice cold during January and February in New England? You want ice cold? Step outside. The solution was in two parts. First, create an indoor space where traditional soda fountain fare could be served; hamburgers, hot dogs, and fries, along with ice cream, so that people could eat in comfort, and, second, expand the range of ice cream flavors beyond the traditional vanilla, chocolate, strawberry trifecta. Thus was born Dutchland Farms, which Bob named for his forbearers. The first restaurant opened in the spring of 1923. As important to the menu was the location. The American public was spending more and more time traveling by automobile. Mr. Ford's creations, thanks to his assembly line innovations, were well-made, reliable, and, most importantly, blue collar affordable. Gas was cheap and roads were improving. America was on the move and Bob Smith was moving with it.

Before long, Bob had renamed his restaurants Bob Smith's Dutchland Farms, and he had eight of them with plans for continued expansion. Bob's D.F.s were all located within three miles of an indoor or outdoor movie theater and stayed open late to accommodate the crowds emptying out of theaters and who weren't yet ready to head home. He also set out to attract the attention of young singles who were beginning to recognize that Dad's Model T, in addition to providing basic transportation, could also serve as a mobile bedroom. Before long, Bob could afford to build one of the largest (and fanciest) homes in Suffield on 26 acres, where he invited his parents to live with him in an expansive in-law arrangement. Included was an "ice cream laboratory" where Bob could experiment with new flavors. For instance, Bob was the first to realize that ice cream didn't need to be soft. He added nuts. Butter Pecan? Bob. Maple Walnut? Bob. Pistachio? That was Bob, with a little assist from some green food coloring.

By the time Howard was first starting to play with his Johnson, Bob Smith had become a very eligible and a very desirable bachelor.

By the time Howard was first starting to play with his Johnson, Bob Smith had become a very eligible and a very desirable bachelor. And Bob did have an eye for the ladies, but he tempered it in order to devote himself to his ever-growing business, and to his other great love: anything on two and four wheels that caught his eye. Bob started to amass an impressive collection of both women and vehicles. The vehicles he housed in several barns that came with the property, the women in several apartments he routinely wrote off as a business expense. Everything was coming up roses for Bob until 1929. Howard Johnsons survived; Bob Smith's Dutchland Farms did not. The difference? Howard Johnson was a great believer in franchising whereas Bob Smith had retained sole ownership, and, as a result, bore the full brunt of the downturn. By the time the country emerged from the Great Depression, Dutchland Farms was a memory.

However, Bob had made more than enough money not only to survive but to continue to indulge himself with cars and babes for years to come. He dabbled in the fledgling airline industry, hobnobbed with the likes of Howard Hughes, before old Howard went batshit crazy, wined and dined some second tier Hollywood starlets, who would only ever be starlets and never stars, and eventually married one named Helen Hewitt. Mr. and Mrs. Smith then indulged in the lifestyle of Suffield landed gentry, where they produced first a boy and then a girl.

When war clouds loomed on the horizon, Bob volunteered his services to Army Field Nutritional Services (AFNS) in the hope that his particular expertise could make some contribution to the cause. He eventually found his way into the Food Packaging Division (FPD) where his knowledge of how best to insulate refrigerated foods was put to good use, and for many foods beyond ice cream. His greatest contribution, however, came in the world of paper straws. The military used millions. Bob knew that the one problem with paper straws was that once crimped they couldn't be uncrimped, a minor inconvenience, unless you were stationed in the field or aboard ship where the supply of paper straws wasn't inexhaustible. He realized that straight straws could easily be transformed into bendy straws by adding a one-inch corrugation near the end of the straw that dispensed liquid, thereby no longer needing to dispose of straws which crimped simply because they no longer crimped. Bob sold the idea to the military which quickly benefited from their value. Bob then took a patent for bendy straws which set him up for a life of continued indulgence in his passions; expensive cars and motorcycles, which he never had lost a taste for, and beautiful, desirable women. He'd never lost a taste for them either.

Bob and Helen lived the good life after the war. Bob tinkered with his toys in the barn; Helen got involved in local charities and hosted lawn parties to raise money for worthy causes. They were seen frequently at the Suffield Country Club; Bob on the links; Helen in the card room. Some thought of Bob as feckless. Bob sometimes thought this of himself as well. Bob junior, aka Robbie, went to Suffield Academy, an all-boys prep school and temple of testosterone, where he excelled athletically if not academically. Diane, aka Dee Dee, went to Our Lady of the Angels Academy in Enfield, an all-girls estrogen preserve which acted as a feeder system for Suffield Academy. Both married well and moved out to start families of their own. Helen succumbed to breast cancer not long after, leaving Bob to rattle around alone in a house that began to take on the air of a museum. These were the circumstances when Bob and Angelo first met.

Bob's estate was just across the Enfield-Suffield Bridge on the Suffield side of the river. Angelo estimated it to be a 15- to 20-minute bike ride, so when Bob suggested that Angelo might be interested in working on some of Bob's classic cycles when he wasn't needed by the Porcellos, Angelo jumped at it. Bob wanted Angelo's help to get his "cycles" in running condition, because he'd decided that his riding days were over, and so he might as well divest himself of that part of his collection. Besides, he knew that Robbie and Dee Dee could both make good use of the money now, rather than waiting for years (hopefully many).

Angelo figured he'd died and gone to heaven when he saw Bob's "cycles." There were Indians and Harleys, BSAs and BMWs, Nortons and Triumphs and Vincents, (Oh My!) and a score of other lesser known makes, some of which were new to Angelo. It was truly "kid in a candy store" time, and Angelo dug right in, normally working on three bikes at a time, because he was always waiting for parts on one bike or another. As he had when he first wandered into Angelo's workspace at Porcello's, Bob often found his way into the bike barn (as he liked to call it) with a couple of cold Buds, where he kept a folding chair set up so that he could "protect his investment" which was code for shoot the shit with Angelo for a couple of hours.

Although they had come from two very different worlds, they shared a common passion for anything powered by an internal combustion engine.

They say that opposites attract, and never was this more accurate than when describing the relationship which gradually evolved between Angelo and Bob. Although they had come from two very different worlds, they shared a common passion for anything powered by an internal combustion engine. They also shared a common passion for wine, women, and song; that is, booze, sex, and sports, and they spent many hours together recycling these topics. They mutually agreed to avoid the subjects of politics and religion which was probably wise. On cold winter days Angelo enclosed his work place with heavy plastic, always allowing space for Bob who, because he felt the cold more as he aged, bought a space heater which benefited both. Sometimes Angelo stayed after work hours and cooked dinner for them. On those occasions, Bob would raid the wine cellar for something vintage and expensive, while Angelo was satisfied with anything that had a screw top in Bob's fridge. Roughly once a month, Angelo would invite Bob for an evening of entertainment at The Ringside, where a game was watched, pool was shot, and much beer was drunk, but always with Bob remaining anonymous so that the patrons would treat him like only "one of the guys."

This arrangement continued for roughly two years, with Angelo working his way through Bob's two-wheel collection to the point where he had reached about the halfway point, when Bob had the first of several heart attacks. It seemed that the ice cream was finally catching up with him.

Angelo continued working when Bob was hospitalized and kept him up to date on his progress with daily phone calls. During those times, Angelo was given the run of Bob's house. He didn't abuse the privilege, going inside only to use a bathroom, make a call, or grab a cold one which he kept stocked in Bob's fridge. Naturally he explored the rooms of the house which Bob had never shown him. He didn't find anything extraordinary about them, other than that some of the rooms looked like they hadn't been actively used for years. He was more interested in the other two barns on the property; the keys for both were kept in Bob's kitchen.

One day, with Bob still in hospital recuperating, Angelo's curiosity bested him, and he unlocked the second barn. He found it to be a warehouse of disused furniture and of old ice cream making equipment, and a depository for the archived records of Bob's Dutchland Farms business. When Bob approached the third barn, he found that, although he held the keys in his hand, he couldn't use them without deactivating what appeared to be a robust security system. Signs posted prominently warned anyone trying to break in that a security company and local police would be notified immediately. Angelo knew that the code for deactivating the system had to be somewhere in Bob's house, probably in his office desk, but Angelo had too much personal integrity and too much affection for Bob to take advantage in that way. "You don't bite the hand that feeds you" was a Frenchtown commandment. Angelo took only one small liberty in this regard. There was one board on the north side of the barn where a small knot in the wood had so completely dried out that it had simply disintegrated. Angelo peered inside. His view was very limited. The interior was illuminated only by a few very narrow shafts of sunlight. He saw cars, lots of them. Bob had alluded to his four-wheel collection a few times, but never in detail. If Angelo brought up the subject, Bob always found a way to change it. The cars which Angelo could see most clearly were mostly "squares," a term Angelo used to refer to older vehicles where right angles ruled (Model T's, Model A's, early boxy Cadillacs and Packards, etc.) as opposed to streamlined models which came along mostly in the 30's. He did get the impression of other, more modern shapes in the deep gloom, but that was about as far as his straining eyes could take him. His curiosity sated, Angelo returned the keys and went back to work.

Angelo peered inside. His view was very limited. The interior was illuminated only by a few very narrow shafts of sunlight. He saw cars, lots of them.

Two years later, Angelo knew the issue of Bob's four-wheel collection would need to be addressed, like it or not, because the end was in sight for the two-wheelers. Once finished, Angelo knew that Bob's last few bikes would go to auction, as had the previous ones. However, Bob died peacefully in his sleep before the fate of his four-wheel collection could be discussed and determined. And with that, Angelo suddenly, but not unexpectedly, found himself equally mourning both the loss of a friend and the loss of his part-time income. He attended the services where a lawyer representing Bob's daughter told Angelo that she wanted him to finish up Bob's bikes, but that when he finished, his services would no longer be required. Angelo spent a few months wrapping things up. He took down the plastic sheeting and stored the space heater in the second barn. His saddest task was to fold up Bob's chair, which he brought home to remember Bob by, and he sent his final invoice to the family's lawyer for payment. The check arrived in the mail the following week accompanied by a second letter from the same source which instructed Angelo to appear at the law offices of so and so on the morning of such and such at 10:00 sharp for the reading of Bob's will. Angelo reported as instructed, eager and expectant. Bob had left everything: the house, all of its contents, the land, all of his stock portfolio, bank and checking accounts, contents of various safety deposit boxes, etc. to his son and daughter. But he had willed the contents of the third barn to Angelo.

Bob had alluded to his four-wheel collection a few times, but never in detail. If Angelo brought up the subject, Bob always found a way to change it.

It is said that when Howard Carter first broke a hole in the wall which had sealed King Tut's tomb for over a thousand years, he squeezed his head inside, along with his arm, which held a lantern. When the others present begged him to tell them what he could see, he could only say, "Things, wonderful things." So, it was with Angelo when the security system for the third barn was deactivated, and the door was finally unlocked. When light flooded the barn's interior, Angelo saw Auburn Boattail Speedsters, Cord 812 Supercharged Phaetons, Duesenberg SJ's (a Roadster and a Convertible), Mercedes 500k, 540's, two 300 SL Gullwings, and a pair of matching Delahayes 135's, one in red and one in blue. Angelo's newly acquired "wonderful things" immediately proclaimed one loud and undeniable truth: Angelo Russo, husband to Carmella and father to Patsy, was now a millionaire.

On Stealing

Have you ever stopped to consider that three of the ten commandments are about stealing? I mean, obviously, there is one that's pretty direct: Thou shalt not… aka Don't Steal. But what about coveting? If you act on coveting your neighbor's wife or your neighbor's goods, that's stealing, isn't it? And if you just covet but don't act on it, is that a sin? Jimmy Carter said it was when he "lusted in his heart" and, in other words, committed telepathic infidelity. So is coveting worth two whole commandments? Or is God finding three different ways to say the same thing, or is it that each member of the trinity is speaking independently? Was God saying that it's a sin if I covet my neighbor's F150? Should I look at it and pretend it's a Ford Pinto? Is it bad if I think "Hey, I'd look good in that?" Was God saying that it's a sin if I think my friend's wife is hot? What am I supposed to do when I see her in short shorts, pretend that she got hit with an ugly stick? Is it bad if I think, "Hey, I'd look good in that."

The fact that just under a third of the commandments are about stealing is significant. It says something about the human condition. We may not be programmed to steal (most of us anyway), but maybe we're programmed to at least consider stealing. After all, we're animals, and animals steal from each other all the time. Take three dogs. Give each dog his own bowl of food, turn the dogs loose, and watch what happens when the first dog to empty his bowl sees that his fellow dogs still have some food left. Dogs are not likely to demonstrate canine political correctness.

So here are some questions:

Have you ever shoplifted anything? If yes, how many times? Once? Twice? More than twice?

How did it make you feel at the time? Did you feel differently later?

Did you need to steal it?

Did you keep it? Did you give it away? Did you throw it away?

I'll ask the question again.

Have you ever shoplifted anything?If no, did you want to?

So why didn't you? Were you afraid of being caught?

Did your conscience kick in? Was it a combination of both?

Do you now wish you had?

JOHN: Part 1
Five Finger Discounts

John had shoplifted many times, usually small stuff which could be easily hidden at home, or stuff of little value which he'd just throw away. His favorite stores were the Western Auto, Henry's Toys, and Chick's, a variety store in a small stand-alone building, just across the street from The Mill. Chick's was the easiest "mark," because the owner, store manager, stock boy, and counter clerk were all Chick himself. Of course, the same could be said of Henry's Toys, but many of the toys Henry sold were simply too large to conceal easily inside a shirt, under a jacket, or down the front of your pants. Chick, on the other hand, sold a lot of what thieves call "smalls" which made Chick's an easier mark than Henry's. The fact that Chick himself was almost universally liked (in the Frenchtown universe anyway) presented a bit of a conscience complication that John had to overcome—which he did regularly.

> John didn't know why he stole things, but it seemed as though he'd always done it. We knew about it, of course. And we asked him about it too, but he couldn't provide an answer, because he just didn't have one.

Chick's was always busy just before shift changes, when workers stopped in for a coffee and Danish in the morning and a coke and a Ring Ding in the afternoon, or just after shift changes, when Chick sold beer by the bottle along with pretzels and chips; dinner for some, breakfast for others. John avoided those busy times. For many of us, while in elementary school, Chick's was a mandatory stop on the way home. Chick always had hot cocoa on cold days (I think he just heated up some chocolate milk but we didn't care, because he had those little marshmallows in a bowl) and lemon ice on hot days (and I swear to you he had the best lemon ice I ever tasted. I'd kill for a Chick's lemon ice even now). We went there mostly to buy trading cards and candy, and baseball cards and airplane cards, which were my favorite. Each package contained ten cards and a thin slab of very dry bubble gum. We almost always threw the bubble gum away immediately. Someday, an urban archaeologist prospecting in the area where Chick's once stood is going to wonder at the two foot thick concrete hard layer of petrified bubble gum he'll find just outside of what was the store's entrance.

John didn't know why he stole things, but it seemed as though he'd always done it. We knew about it, of course. And we asked him about it too, but he couldn't provide an answer, because he just didn't have one. Joanne called it "compulsive behavior," and that didn't sound as bad. We told John that we wouldn't help him, and we didn't—at least I didn't. I don't know for sure about the others. The trouble was that sometimes you'd help him, but you didn't even know it. Like, for instance, John would pick something up to examine it, and he'd remove the price tag. Then he'd say to one of us who was approaching the counter to pay for something, *"Ask Chick how much for this; there's no price."* And we would ask while paying. Once Chick had rung us up, he'd come over with his little price gizmo to retag the item. By the time he returned to the counter, the stack of baseball card packs had gotten just a little shorter or a few fireballs had disappeared from their glass bowl. Chick never noticed because the thefts were small, but it wasn't the size of the theft that made a difference to John; it was the theft itself. Most of the time, we didn't realize we'd been accomplices until later, and sometimes not at all. We'd get angry when he told us, so I think he stopped telling us. We'd even talk about returning the things he'd taken, but how would we explain it without getting ourselves in trouble? "Gee, Chick, we found it on the sidewalk outside." How many times would that work?

Joanne even asked Ruth about it during one of their lessons. Ruth said that she knew and had known for several years. So had their mom. John's birth mom had pretty much abdicated the role of mother in Ruth's favor, choosing instead to live with her then-husband wherever he was deployed. That left Ruth to pay the rent, keep house, and be, if not a mom, at the least a mom figure for her younger brother. Ruth said that she'd even asked their family doctor, who had said something about John trying to steal attention or affection maybe. I didn't understand that stuff, but Joanne said that Ruth thought there was a hole in John's life, and he was trying to fill it up with the things he stole. She thought that John especially missed having a dad, because his dad never even sent John a birthday card, much less a Christmas present. Ruth used to buy him a present and put "from Dad" on the card. That was something I could sort of understand, because sometimes I used to pretend that I didn't have a dad either. That was easy for me, because he wasn't around much. That made me sad too.

I didn't understand that stuff, but Joanne said that Ruth thought there was a hole in John's life, and he was trying to fill it up with the things he stole.

On Feeling Sad

Do you ever think sad things just to make yourself sad on purpose? I do. Sometimes I'll imagine that somebody I really like died suddenly, like Tommy, for instance. Does that make me weird? I mean, we watch a funny TV show to make us feel happy. And we go to see a horror movie to make us feel afraid. So why would it be wrong to want to feel sad—just to know what it feels like I mean?

St Patrick's is the perfect place for me to make myself feel sad. It's something about the hard wooden benches and the marble columns, and the life size statues, and the cold stone floor, and the little lighted thing that hangs on the wall to remind you that God is home, and the huge Jesus on a cross, hanging right there in front, looking down at all of you with painted blood on his forehead and hands and feet and coming out of his side. Boy, that'll certainly lighten your mood. Jesus must have worked out, by the way, because, cross or no cross, he was ripped. Picture a fat Jesus. Not easy is it? Fat Elvis? Yes. Fat Jesus? No.

Anyhow, St. Patrick's was the perfect place for me to make myself feel sad, especially if I was bored, which I was most of the time at St. Patrick's.

JOHN: Part 2
Dadless

Imagining how I would feel if I suddenly didn't have a dad anymore made me think about John. Did he miss having a dad? Maybe he didn't, because his dad had never really been a part of his life. Then again, the rest of us all had dads, so maybe he did. How would we even know? Did he feel jealous when we did something with our dads? Tommy's dad took him fishing all the time. Tommy told us he didn't really like fishing, especially the parts where you had to put the worm on the hook, or where you had to take the hook out of the fish's mouth, but he said he still liked that he was with his dad. And Patsy's dad would show him things about car engines when he had a backyard repair project. My dad never had much time for me, because he was working such long hours, but at least I had my grandfather; John didn't have a grandfather either.

I always felt sorry for John on Father's Day and at Christmas. None of us ever said something like, "I have to buy something for my dad," or "This is a present from my dad," even if it was. We never talked about that around John. We all liked him. We wanted him to stay in our group, the Fab Four + One, but he knew that when he went "shopping," he was on his own. I guess being a friend means that you ignore things like that, things like John's "shopping," even if he dragged us into it sometimes. Still, we wished he would stop.

John knew that Joanne was helping Ruth. He also knew that Demetrius would pound him if he said anything about it, so he kept his mouth shut. Demetrius didn't know that Ruth was helping Joanne, however. He did once notice that Ruth headed off to Joanne's with her books and her makeup case, but then Annette came on The Mickey Mouse Club, and he forgot all about it.

On Discovering Sex

I don't remember who first explained sex to me. My mom tried, but she didn't get very far. I already told you about the picture she drew. It looked more like an onion than a womb. Anyway, she seemed embarrassed by the whole thing. If I had to guess who really explained it to me, I would probably pick some of the kids at school, likely the same ones who told me that Santa Claus was really my parents and that the Easter Bunny was made up too. I remember that when the mechanics of sex were described, I simply couldn't believe it. I thought it was the dumbest thing I'd ever heard. I mean, when you stop and think about it objectively, it really is pretty absurd, isn't it? "He does what with what? Where?! You've got to be kidding me!" What finally clinched it was when somebody asked, "Haven't you ever seen dogs doing it?" and, of course, I had. When I asked my parents about it, I was told that the dogs "were just playing," but I sensed that something else was going on. Now I knew about the "something else." We (the Fab Four) talked about it quite a bit when Joanne wasn't around, each of us adding a little something that we'd heard or seen until a composite picture took shape. And when it finally did, other things that we'd heard and seen and felt, especially felt, came into focus. No wonder we kept watching The Mickey Mouse Show to see Annette.

That epiphany turned us all into sex bloodhounds. Suddenly, almost overnight, we saw sex everywhere: in movies, sex; on TV, sex; on billboards, sex; in magazine ads, sex. We were surrounded by it.

We were drowning in sex. And those Sears-Roebuck catalogs with their drawings of girdles and bras? Serious sex. It had been there right in front of us all this time. How could we have missed it for so long? But we saw it now. Boy, did we see it now. We even secreted away some of our favorite images, hid them in private places where moms would never stumble over them even when spring cleaning. Or so we thought.

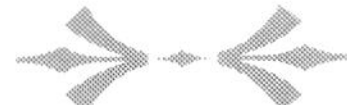

JOHN: Part 3
Blackmail

Ruth just flat out told John that he should go to the eighth-grade semi-formal dance. She used the argument that all his friends were going and that he'd look weird if he stayed home. His counter argument was that he'd say he was sick. Her counter argument was that being sick might work with some kids, but the rest of them would know he was chicken. He then said that it wouldn't be cool to go. She said it would be more uncool if his friends knew he was staying home alone to watch TV. And she would be sure they knew. He told Ruth that I had a date (Priscilla), that Tommy had a date (Carlene), that Patsy would probably take his cousin Maria (Patsy wouldn't take Maria and her mustache to a dogfight), and that he couldn't go without a date.

Ruth pounced, *"What about Joanne?"*

John was so surprised by this that he couldn't speak. He just stared at Ruth with his mouth open. Finally, he gathered himself.

"I'm not going to that dance with her or with anybody." He crossed his arms. As far as he was concerned, the matter was settled.

"How about if I give you two good reasons why you should go?" Ruth asked, *"Here's the first,"* she said striding determinedly to the telephone and dialing a number.

When it was answered on the other end, she said, *"Demetri, what we talked about. Tell him,"* and she handed the receiver to John who put it to his ear.

Demetrius spoke, *"Johnny, you owe your sister. She does everything for you. Now she's asking you to do something for her, and if you don't invite that girl I'll kick your ass, and I'll tell her later that I found out a couple of guys did it because they caught you stealing something from somebody they like."*

And with that Demetrius hung up. John handed the receiver to Ruth who replaced it in the cradle, all the while staring at her brother who had defiantly recrossed his arms.

Then Ruth said, *"That's the first reason; here's the second."*

With that she picked up her makeup case, opened it, and withdrew a group of clippings; it was John's secret sex stash. Time stopped. Nothing else was said. Nobody moved. John's face grew hot, and then very hot. He looked down, and Ruth knew she'd won.

She handed him the clippings and said, *"Next time, hide them better."*

She picked up her books and her bag and said, *"I've got a lesson with Joanne. I'm going to tell her that you want to ask her something."* And she swept out the door.

John went through all five stages of Dr. Kubler-Ross. Denial: At first he pretended that what had just happened hadn't happened. One look at his sex stash told him it had. Anger: Then he got really angry with Ruth for trapping him by threatening him with Demetrius, and with himself for not being more careful with his stash. There wasn't much point in being angry, though, because Demetrius wasn't going to go away and neither was his stash. Bargaining: He started to think that maybe he could blackmail Ruth into backing off, but he couldn't come up with something to hold over her head. If she'd been cheating on Demetrius, that would definitely have been blackmailable, but she wasn't. Depression: He felt defeated and spent a couple of hours sulking, which got him nowhere but bored. He even considered doing a little "shopping" to cheer himself up, but the others had really been on his case about that lately, besides, it was getting almost too easy, and the thrill was now gone. Acceptance: So, finally, reluctantly, he accepted the inevitable. He was cornered and he knew it.

He needed to lash out. He decided that there was still a way to get revenge. He would take Joanne to the dance all right, but he would have a lousy time. He would hate every minute of it, and he'd make sure Joanne would too. He'd hate the decorations, the punch, the music, the cookies; he'd hate everything about it. He'd hate wearing a jacket and tie, and he'd hate that Joanne was wearing a dress—and he'd hate the dress too, just for good measure. He'd get even with Ruth for making him miserable by making himself even more miserable.

That thought gave him a moment of satisfaction, but only a moment, before he acknowledged that it was an incredibly childish way to think—even for him. It wouldn't be fair to Ruth, and it certainly wouldn't be fair to Joanne, whom he liked and wouldn't treat that way. He and the others had made her cry once; he couldn't bear the thought of making her cry again. And, with that, he resigned himself to thinking about how to ask her.

JOHN: Part 4
Just Friends

John caught up with Joanne a few days later on their way home from school. They made small talk until he plucked up the courage to broach the subject.

John: *So, listen. Are you thinking about going to the dance?*

Joanne: *The Snow Ball?*

John: *Yeah, are you going?*

Joanne: *I'd like to go. I got asked.*

John: *Who?*

Joanne: *Jimmy Vella.*

John: *From Windsor Street? He's a seventh grader!*

Joanne: *So? Tommy's taking Carlene, and she's in seventh grade.*

John: *Oh.*

Joanne: *I mean if an eighth-grade guy can invite a seventh grade girl, why can't a seventh-grade guy invite an eighth-grade girl? Besides, we'd just be going as friends.*

John: *So you're goin'?*

Joanne: *Yes and no.*

He looked at her, puzzled.

Joanne: *I told him that I'd have to let him know because someone else had already asked me.*

John: *Who?*

Joanne: *Nobody else. He asked me two weeks ago, and I just didn't want to say yes right away.*

John: *Oh.*

John: *Ruth was saying that maybe we could go together.*

Joanne: *Ruth said that?*

John: *Yeah. She likes you.*

Joanne: *Is that what Ruth wants?*

John: *Yeah.*

Joanne: *What do you want?*

John: *Dances aren't cool.*

Joanne: *Stealing other peoples' stuff isn't cool. Using your friends to help isn't cool.*

John: *I stopped.*

Joanne: *For real?*

John: *Yeah.*

Joanne: *Good.*

Joanne: *So why is the dance uncool?*

John: *I don't know. You have to get all dressed up, so you start off uncomfortable even before you get there. And then you have to pretend like you're having a good time, even when you're hating it. It's so phony. Everybody is acting phony.*

Joanne: *Most people have a good time. I don't like the dancing part.*

John: *I thought all girls liked to dance.*

Joanne: *I don't really know how. Tommy and Carlene do because they took that class.*

John: *Ask Ruth! She knows how to dance. She's a good dancer. She puts on Connecticut Bandstand sometimes in the afternoon and she dances in front of the TV.*

Joanne: *By herself?*

John: *Yeah, I mean she tries to get me to dance if I'm around, but I won't do it. But she's pretty good, even just by herself.*

Joanne: *We could ask her to show both of us.*

John: *If we learn together, then we could help each other not look stupid.*

Joanne: *True.*

John: *Then maybe we could go together.*

Joanne: *Is that what you want?*

John: *Yeah. But just as friends.*

Joanne: *Okay. Just friends.*

John: *Yeah … friends.*

CHANGES: Part 1

There were changes (economic, political, and demographic) afoot during my grade school and junior high school years, but my limited life perspective simply left me unawares. Hindsight, as they say, is 20/20, and I recognize now what I was oblivious to back then.

The stakes were high in Frenchtown back then, for jobs, for bonds of family and friendship, for cultural and ethnic traditions, and for Frenchtown itself.

Rumors circulated, for instance, that the owners of The Mill wanted to relocate to a southern state where labor would be less expensive. I remember seeing posters for textile workers' union meetings on telephone poles and in storefront windows. The union hall was directly across the street from Bigelow's main entrance. The storefront was usually dark and appeared deserted. If you walked by and peered in, you saw lots of wooden folding chairs facing a dais on which there were tables, more chairs, and both the American flag and the textile workers' flag which featured a design of two conjoined hands. On meeting nights, however, the hall was ablaze with lights, and crowds, almost all men, spilled out of the hall's entrance onto the sidewalk. You could also sometimes hear shouting coming from within. After meetings, members would disperse slowly, often making their way to The Ringside, Mattie's and Frank's, and the Thompsonville Tavern where you got the impression that the real night's business then took place. On summer nights when it was just too warm to stay indoors, those crowds met on street corners, and you'd hear the same raised voices which would abruptly go silent so that all could listen to an announcer on someone's portable radio describe another Yankee's feat of wonder. The stakes were high in Frenchtown back then, for jobs, for bonds of family and friendship, for cultural and ethnic traditions, and for Frenchtown itself. My sense, now, is that events like this were playing out simultaneously in many New England mill towns.

Demographic changes were also reshaping Enfield. Farmers on the eastern side of town were finding it difficult to turn a profit by growing anything other than tobacco, and as the tobacco grown was used almost exclusively for cigar outer leaf wrappers, that market, although viable, was, at the same time, finite. Those same farmers felt the squeeze of higher property taxes imposed to service an increasing population. As a result, they sold off their farmland to housing developers who built "starter home" high density neighborhoods which resulted in still more increased population, which, of course, required even more services, thereby raising property taxes even higher, thereby leaving those same former farmers to start a new round of complaints about the effects they themselves had caused. More exclusive starter homes (later nicknamed "McMansions") soon followed. As before, I'm sure this played out (and still does!) elsewhere.

As Enfield's population shifted to newer neighborhoods in the east of town and farther away from the river which constituted the more affluent side's western boundary, the commercial center that was Thompsonville began to shift east as well. Businesses began to relocate closer to the main road, Route 5, which joined Hartford in the south with Springfield, Mass. in the north. Business-wise, Enfield was robust, Thompsonville was weakening but still viable, but Frenchtown was approaching life support status as its few businesses served only increasingly local customers. That being said, The Ringside and Mattie's and Frank's were still the go-to for dedicated drinkers, and Chick's remained Chick's.

To that population, Angelo could never be more than a Frenchtown lowlife for whom fate had punched a golden ticket.

Changes were very much on the minds of Fab Four + One families. Angelo could easily have afforded one of those "East Enfield McMansions," but, to his mind, this would only lead to social isolation. To that population he could never be more than a Frenchtown lowlife for whom fate had punched a golden ticket. To him, that population could never be more than "stuck-ups who think their shit don't stink." And so Angelo stayed put, surrounded by his family, his friends, and a culture that shared his values and his philosophy. He did, however, sell off Bob's collection a little at a time, which allowed him to buy Frenchtown's largest house, tear it down, and replace it with an architect-designed villa which incorporated lots and lots of stucco, Mediterranean design elements inside and out, an inner courtyard with stone benches, an in-ground pool with a stone grotto at one end, fountains, a sculpture garden, etc.

Ruth and Demitrius hadn't set the date yet, so she and John stayed put. She could have afforded a larger rental, on the east side of Route 5, but her ever-practical side concluded that she should bank the money for her upcoming married life. Joanne's mom was strongly attracted to the idea of moving her office into one of the new professional buildings which were springing up in professional "parks" which were developed to service newly arrived professionals, but she knew that some of those new professionals would have law degrees. Rather than compete with them and risk losing her legal monopoly in Frenchtown, she decided on staying put—but only temporarily. She felt that punching her own golden ticket was, unlike Angelo's, not fate-based, but would instead be achieved by raising her profile in local politics. Attorney Joyce Schultz would never be called out for having too little ambition.

My mom and dad moved their music business from Thompsonville to Route 5, which was increasingly being called "the tracks," as in Frenchtown being on the wrong side of the tracks and east Enfield being on the right side of the tracks.

Tommy's mom and dad were content for the moment, he working for the state, and she holding down the home front. They did, however, buy a spacious cottage on Cape Cod which they visited on most weekends. My mom and dad moved their music business from Thompsonville to Route 5, which was increasingly being called "the tracks," as in Frenchtown being on the wrong side of the tracks and east Enfield being on the right side of the tracks. Living in a three-generation house had an upside for my parents. Probably the most beneficial to them was built-in daycare, Bossa and her sister. The downside was that as the first generation, Bossa, her sister, and my grandfather, aged, they became more dependent on the second generation, my parents, who then found the idea of moving all three generations initially problematical, then increasingly impractical, and, in the end, virtually impossible.

There were changes in the school system as well. New elementary schools were being built, a new junior high was in the planning stages, and a new high school was ready to open. This was Fullerton High School. It was located in Enfield's southeast quadrant, and it served a very different population which was younger, more diverse, and more prosperous; in short: "upscale" as compared to the ethnically narrower population served by the older Enfield High School, which had become so overcrowded that double sessions had become the norm.

It was further decided that, even with a new high school set to open, the strain on the older school would still be too great even if it returned to a normal single session schedule. As a result, a lottery was held to decide which neighborhoods in the old school's territory would send its students to the new school. Among the neighborhoods in the School Board's crosshairs was Frenchtown, whose residents at first protested vigorously but ultimately became resigned to the new order of things. Their strongest argument, that Frenchtownies would be riding school buses for hours, didn't go very far because the new school was only ten minutes farther away than the old. And so the Fab Four + One were "designated for assignment" to Fullerton High School, and a very different world.

Although the 13-14 age group will never win points for being insightful where self is concerned, we, all of us, understood that childhood would soon be in our collective rear view mirror. The changes in our minds, bodies, and souls were simply undeniable; they had been so ever since we passed through the Purgatron and exited the Tween Ark. I was expected to inherit my parent's television business, Tommy had shown interest in a public service job or perhaps teaching, John toyed with the idea of professional shoplifting, but not for long. Ruth and the rest of us took the bloom off that rose.

The changes in our minds, bodies, and souls were simply undeniable; they had been so ever since we passed through the Purgatron and exited the Tween Ark.

Patsy thought about a trade. His dad, a World War II vet, suggested that he should enlist after high school graduation. That way he could serve his country while learning a trade on the government's dime. Patsy didn't understand why his dad was thinking so frugally when he could easily afford not to. But remember that Angelo had chosen to remain in Frenchtown despite his windfall, and frugality was part of the Frenchtown weltanschauung—more about "weltanschauung" in a minute.

If there was one of us whose path and future success was assured, it was Joanne. Her intelligence was quick to be showcased. Although the word "genius" embarrassed her, especially when one of us used it, the term was heard more and more often when her name was mentioned.

I remember that we all sensed that our eighth-grade summer would be our last as children, and that our looming ninth-grade fall would be our first as young adults.

It was sad, but it was also exciting.

On Weltanschauung

Weltanschauung is a German word which means world view. I don't remember where I first heard or read this word, but I fell in love with it immediately. It's just so darned teutonic in sound and appearance. Much of German is. It could mean anything, really, and still sound authoritative.

Conrad Veidt as Major Strasser to Humphrey Bogart as Rick Blaine in "Casablanca":

"You seem to have led your life as a soldier of fortune, Mr. Blaine. How exactly would you describe your weltanschauung?"

Or

Conrad Veidt as Major Strasser to Madeleine Lebeau as Yvonne, the sexy bar girl/starlet.

"Come over here and sit on my lap, fraulein, so that I can feel your weltanschauung."

A child's weltanschauung is defined by how far he is allowed to walk unaccompanied. Mostly, this means his backyard, but add a few years and his weltanschauung encompasses his neighborhood and those surrounding it. Attending school soon brings him into contact with others who live within this larger radius.

Bicycles change everything. Now his radius expands exponentially, filling up with new places (some nice, some not) and new faces (some friendly, some not). He also now recognizes differences in where and how others live, work, and behave. His backyard may even lose some of its luster in the process. *"Hey, Mom, Jimmy has a swimming pool. It looks like fun! Can we get a pool too?"* Nice try. His friends increase in number and diversity.

Automobiles change everything again, and, unlike a bicycle, a car offers privacy which shifts his weltanschauung into overdrive on both a public level as well as a personal one, offering "kid in a candy store" potential. Educationally, he's evolved from a narrow, grainy super 8 perspective to the widescreen wonder of Vistavision.

And so it was for the Fab Four + One who dutifully climbed aboard Bus # 7 right in front of The Strand Theater on a sunny September morning—full of anticipation to experience an entirely new and exciting weltanschauung.

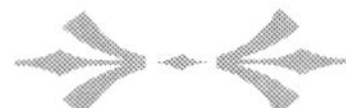

CHANGES: Part 2

Remember way back when I asked you whether or not you recalled your first day at school? I didn't. The first day I remembered was when Miss Sullivan retired permanently. What about your first day of high school? Do you remember that? If yes, what stands out? If no, what is your first memory of high school? And why does that day stand out?

Our first day started with our introduction to a new pecking order.

Our first day started with our introduction to a new pecking order. The bus was almost empty when we first boarded. Like most of the early pick-ups, this was our first school bus experience, meaning that the seating started out random and was defined by social clusters. As the bus progressed on its route through new neighborhoods, however, different seating criteria emerged. Rising seniors occupied the rearmost seats with rising juniors just in front of them, and rising sophomores just in front of the juniors. This new arrangement was dictated in some cases by threats of bodily harm, *"Move your ass or I'll pound it,"* or by supposed custom, *"Me and my friends always sit in this row,"* or, in a few cases even by rational explanation, *"Freshman have to sit near the front, or else."* The thought that three years would need to pass before those back rows could be occupied made them seem coveted forbidden fruit. Freshmen from neighborhoods closer to the school sat in their own cliques as they boarded, leaving us Frenchtown Freshman, as they soon came to be called, a small seated island in a larger seated sea.

When the bus pulled up in front of the school, passengers were shepherded immediately to the auditorium for an orientation assembly. Upperclassmen made a point of chatting familiarly with teachers and administrators on the way, in order to impress the underclassmen. Seating followed the same protocol; new meat down front, vets toward the back. Orientation was pretty much what you would expect with welcoming speeches from the Principal, the Vice Principal, the Dean of Students, and the Guidance Department Head. After ten minutes it all became a blur of platitudes. Juniors and seniors, who had already heard exactly the same speeches multiple times, soon tuned out. Their only interest was in faculty personnel changes, the school calendar, and a couple of new directives which they would ignore. They were dismissed to their classes first after being reminded to set a good example for the lower grades, their teachers, their parents, their school, and their town. Sophomores stayed about ten minutes longer, at which time the subject of "follying" was addressed. Apparently, there was a tradition at the school for sophomores to "folly" freshmen. The administration portrayed follying as good-natured and well-intentioned. It was described as harmless behavior, consisting mostly of silly pranks, meant to welcome freshmen to the "Friendly Fullerton" culture. Sophomores were, however, reminded that "follying" was never meant to degrade, intimidate or embarrass new students, aka subjects, aka victims. With those admonishments, sophomores were dismissed to classes. Freshmen soon followed under the supervision of Student Council members who directed them first to their lockers and then to their various classrooms.

FRIENDLY FULLERTON: Part 1

Outside of classrooms, high school life often centers on distinct interior locations: the halls, the library, boys' and girls' rooms, the gym, and the cafeteria. Outdoor locations like the parking lot, athletic fields, and informal smoking lounges, located just outside of less frequently used exits, might also sometimes be included, but the pecking order ruled mostly indoors. Follying was rampant, often pedestrian and always annoying. Being jostled in the halls between periods became commonplace. Boys' rooms provided opportunities for harassment. Imagine, for instance, trying to pee while someone stands right next to you commenting about the size of your package or asks you about how often you masturbate. And while Joanne had the benefit of a girls' room stall, lit, partially smoked cigarettes often rained down from above as break time drew to a close. If you went to the library to do some homework or research, it was best to go with a friend, because leaving a book unattended on a table while you perused the card file or the stacks was an invitation for both your book and your homework to relocate onto a faraway shelf. And Frenchtownies were as isolated in the cafeteria as they were on the bus. Tater tots smeared with ketchup became frequent missiles lobbed indiscriminately at our clutch of tables. The metal air vents in locker doors were also useful for the delivery of malicious mail or noxious liquids, which sometimes damaged books and destroyed clothing.

Add to all these follies, pervasive name-calling. John was spared because his last name was Damian, but Joanne was dubbed a Kraut or a Nazi. Tommy, Patsy, and I, however, were targeted more because we had committed the cardinal sin of being born with last names that ended in vowels. In Fullerton, Benners, Hathaways, and Andersons were welcomed; Russos and Ferraros were not. We were guineaus, wops, dagos, greasers, or, among the more creative, guineau wops, dirty dagos, and greasy guineaus. Was it possible to overcome "end" vowel stigmata? Yes, others had, mostly by distinguishing themselves with a unique talent for instance, or by demonstrating athletic prowess in competition which brought sports glory to the "Fullerton Falcons." Unfortunately, that left the original Fab Four out. Joanne was the only one of us who earned respect because of her superior intellect. She was taking sophomore honors classes by October of her freshman year and being afforded deference by 10th graders, even though much of their respect was tinged with jealousy.

I had the drums and Tommy had his fireworks, but Fullerton didn't offer opportunities for either. Patsy fumed helplessly. John just became sullen and withdrawn. Demetrius (Ruth's intended) offered him a part-time job as a stock boy in the family market and that helped a little. Harassment was an ever-present topic when the group gathered on the bus or after school.

The sheer disparity in numbers made resistance seem futile. The administration seemed to turn a blind eye as did most teachers, although a few feigned sympathy. Our moms, and to a lesser extent our dads, could see that we were troubled by something, but offers to mitigate were ignored. The Fab Four + One were unanimous in thinking that parental intervention would only make a difficult adjustment downright intolerable.

On Tribalism

My experiences during the first semester of my freshman year at Fullerton taught me a lot about discrimination. It came in many forms: racial, cultural, religious, age-based, gender-based, and just about any other "based" you can think of—Fullerton reaped a discrimination bonanza. I bundle all of the pathogens into what I call "tribalism."

We don't generally like to think of ourselves as being members of tribes. Then again, we don't normally think of ourselves as animals either, but every time we drink, pee, eat, poop, and have sex reminds us that we, indeed, are animals. And being animals we share in animal behaviors. Some of us, for instance, are alphas, while others are content to be members of the pack. What is your status? And what about fight or flight? We see this playing out on the news all the time. What's your preference?

My point is that just as we don't often consciously think of ourselves as animals, we also often don't acknowledge that we're part of a tribe, and yet, we are, and we demonstrate that we are every time we celebrate a cultural holiday (St Patrick's Day, Columbus Day), a religious holiday (Easter, Rosh Hashanah), a racial holiday (M.L. King Day), or simply when we walk into a Men's Room or a Ladies' Room. Are you a child, a pre-teen, a tween, a teen, a young adult, a mature adult, an older adult, a senior adult, a dead adult? Which is your tribe? And are your transitions measured chronologically or experientially?

Tribal thought and behavior seem to become more emphatic in times of stress. Some might immediately think, "there's safety in numbers." That would be true if the threat was physical. What if it's not? Then the adage would change to, "there's safety in similarity." Fortunately, we're more likely to indulge in tribal behavior for the second reason than for the first.

At Fullerton, we were "the other." Our names were different, frequently ending in vowels. Some of us were darker skinned. Back in the day, our annual school photos were always in black and white. One option available to your parents was to have your portrait "colorized' which basically meant tinted. If you lived east of Route 5, your colorization would start with a white/pink base. If you were from the west side of Route 5, aka Frenchtown, your base was olive.

Sometimes we dressed differently too—not intentionally, mind you. As freshmen, many of our clothes were still being bought for us by our mothers, so the clothes we wore were their interpretation of what fit in at Fullerton, and sometimes it just didn't. We spoke differently too, not language-wise of course, although communicating in Italian or Polish could sometimes be useful, if you wished to hide what you were saying about someone in his, her, or their presence. We were sort of ethnic Navajo Code Talkers in that regard. Those who were being talked about sometimes became really angry when we resorted to this tactic, because they assumed that we were saying things that were derogatory, which, of course, we were. But, how else could we counter tribal discrimination?

Force was an option, but not a realistic one, given how disproportionately we were outnumbered. Simply accepting without resistance was too much like surrender. Besides, if we were to acknowledge freely that they had the upper hand, wouldn't we then be acquiescing to victim status which might lead to more victimizing? Signing a proverbial peace treaty? Smoking the peace pipe? Finding common ground? Joining hands and singing kumbaya? There really was no easy answer. And, keep in mind that we were just as tribal as they were. We didn't want to relinquish any part of our collective identity to appease them. And there's another factor that I mentioned when I was writing about Bossa: Italians need enemies. They may have seen us as trespassers, but we saw them as interlopers; after all, we were here before they were. So what you had was a symbiotic relationship of dislike and distrust. Time would gradually reduce the level of animosity, but teenagers don't measure time by way of generational changes. The change wouldn't come from within in a timely manner; it had to come from without.

FRIENDLY FULLERTON: Part 2

The beginning of the end actually had more to do with the pen than with the sword. It began when Carmella went to Ruth to get her hair done. Carmella told Ruth about some of the things she'd heard Patsy saying in phone calls to friends when he thought she was out of earshot. Ruth then asked Dimitri if he'd heard John say anything on this subject. It turns out that John had confided in Dimitri, but he had also sworn Dimitri to silence. You know the old saying about catching more flies with honey than with vinegar? Well, Dimitri was the fly and Ruth had the honey. Before you can say "unzip it," Ruth pretty much had the whole story. She then told Joanne's mom who told Tommy's mom who told my mom. There was a lot of "Is this true?" going around all of a sudden. And, of course, it was too true, and this eventually caused Joyce, Joanne's mother, to place a phone call (ostensibly about buying advertising space) to Matt Molinski, who was the publisher, the editor, the reporter, the business manager, and the advertising director for *The Thompsonville Press*.

Shakespeare said, "Some men are born great, some achieve greatness, and some have greatness thrust upon them." Matt never aspired to greatness in any form on any level. He was perfectly content to live on a shoestring by publishing a shoestring hometown newspaper. Matt often "relied on the kindness of others" as Tennessee Williams would have said.

The Thompsonville Press was Matt Molinski and Matt Molinski was *The Thompsonville Press*. They defined each other, completed each other, and co-existed almost symbiotically. Nevertheless, his job gave Matt everything he needed in life to be content. And how many of us can say that and truly mean it? Matt could and did frequently. If there was one thing he could wish for, it was for both himself and *The Thompsonville Press* to be taken more seriously. Enter Joyce Schultz.

Outside of the occasional photo and story about the winner of the recent fishing derby, the newspaper featured death notices, which included days and hours when people could pay their respects to fresh stiffs at the Leete or Brown funeral homes.

Joyce read *The Thompsonville Press*, as did everyone else in Enfield, for a very simple reason: it was sent free to every address with additional copies distributed to diners, barber shops, hairdressing salons etc., etc., etc. The fact that it relied solely on advertising explained why it had always been, and would probably always be, a labor of love for Matt. Joyce saw that as her way in. Over the course of a long meeting held in a booth at The Donut Kettle, Joyce convinced Matt that *The Thompsonville Press* would enjoy a whole new "lease on life" if it became just a little bit edgy. When Matt asked her to explain, she stated that most people read the paper principally because they were interested in local public notices that made up the biggest part of the "copy," outside of the occasional photo and story about the winner of the recent fishing derby and the death notices which included days and hours when people could pay their respects to fresh stiffs at the Leete or Brown funeral homes. This Matt knew. Joyce suggested the addition of a gossip column written by an anonymous "Inquirer" (herself) in which she would answer fictional letters about local issues, personalities and events. After all, a good many tabloid newspapers and even some magazines proliferated in exactly the same commercial outlets where Matt delivered extra copies of *The T'ville Press* every week. Joyce also referenced the popularity of advice gurus like Ann Landers and Dear Abby. She strengthened her argument by asking Matt to take a slow, meandering walk to the men's room, while he cocked his ear to snatches of conversations taking place between patrons seated in other booths and at the counter. Given that The Donut Kettle kept afloat on a veritable sea of gossip, Mark returned from his little expedition almost won over. Joyce knew how close she was getting when Matt asked about liability. She explained that he would supposedly not know the identity of the anonymous columnist, whose columns arrived in the mail a few days before each issue went to press. She also said that saying the words "First Amendment" often had a powerful effect on the disgruntled. Mark gave her the benefit of the doubt in this regard; after all, she was "Attorney" Joyce Schultz. She also promised that, as editor, publisher, and chief cook and bottle washer for *The Thompsonville Press*, Mark would always have the final word when it came to editing Joyce's column. Mark was almost sold, but he felt that he still had one last card of his own to play. In addition to her burgeoning law practice, Joyce was a member of the Town Council, a first for a woman. Mark had fantasized about being elected to this august body of local governance and said so. If respectability for himself and for his raison d'etre was his goal, then a seat on the Town Council would go a long way toward reaching that personal destination. Joyce was impressed by this tack, sensed a quid pro quo in the offing, and promised to throw her future support behind Mark. That sealed the deal.

FRIENDLY FULLERTON: Part 3

Joyce's first few columns, entitled "About Town," were softballs. She made a conscious choice to start slowly and inauspiciously; she didn't want to ruffle feathers immediately. She answered "anonymous" letters from the local populace about the dates of upcoming church bazaars, the increase in cost of movie tickets and how the increase was being justified, the projected dates of high school graduations, birth announcements, which she called "new arrivals," death notifications which she referred to as "recent departures," etc. Each (fictional) letter was signed only with the sender's initials, and each column concluded with a request for more mailed-in inquiries and provided an address to which they could be sent. Potential senders were assured that their identities would never be revealed. In fact, they were requested not to sign their letters with anything more than initials, and never to write a return name and address on their envelopes. Joyce was particularly careful in her earliest columns to be personable and approachable, to be neutral, and to avoid controversy. However, she was equally careful always to include a little "juice." A good example was her third column, in which a letter from "S.P." hinted at the fact that Enfield police were sometimes intentionally parking their partly concealed cruisers at the bottoms of slopes, where passing cars naturally sped up, in order to issue more tickets and thereby fatten town coffers. Joyce assured the complainer that local police would never resort to such tactics (wink! wink!). Two weeks later "T.T." asked our anonymous host, "The Inquirer," if others had noticed that most town construction contracts always seemed to favor bids from one particular contractor. The Inquirer assured "T.T." that those bids were always given fair and equal representation, even if the usual successful bidder was the mayor's brother-in-law (nudge! nudge!). Before long, letters were arriving at *The T'ville Press* office in droves (a few were even read), and, next to the comics, "About Town" became the most popular feature, (the only one, actually), in the paper.

> **Joyce was particularly careful in her earliest columns to be personable and approachable, to be neutral, and to avoid controversy. However, she was equally careful always to include a little "juice."**

In her fifth column of "About Town," The Inquirer raised the issue of follying at Fullerton High School. She simply asked about examples of follying and wondered rhetorically if, in fact, its principal intention was always "just good-natured fun," which had always been the high school administration's "go-to."

That set the cat among the pigeons. For the first time in her brief journalistic career, Joyce could incorporate mailed-in quotes from actual readers about how follying frequently degenerated into harassment and intimidation. And about how Frenchtownies were frequently singled out simply because they came "from the wrong side of the tracks," the tracks in this particular case being Route 5. Significant also was the fact that follying was almost non-existent at Enfield High School where the population was more homogeneous. It wasn't long before Matt was fielding calls from the Office of the Superintendent along with a variety of school board members and of school board hopefuls—an election was pending. The more publicity "About Town" generated, the more The Inquirer "squeezed the lemon." And as Joyce squeezed, Matt seized—the opportunity, that is. He proposed a meeting of concerned parents and victimized students during which complaints would be fielded and addressed by school administration personnel, school board members, town council representatives, church officials, any and all public officials whose positions seemed relevant. He included a date, a time, and a place, The Textile Workers' Union Hall, directly opposite The Mill's main entrance. Matt designated himself moderator. On the appointed night, he arrived 15 minutes early to turn on the lights. He also recruited a few attendees, waiting at the door for him to unlock, to help set up a dozen folding chairs on the dais and two dozen on the floor. The meeting started almost half an hour late, the delay precipitated by the need to set up an additional 120 chairs. Standees were three rows deep in the back of the hall. The Fire Marshall would have disapproved.

I see no need to describe the proceedings. Those seated on the dais got an earful, (even town council member Joyce), for whom the irony was palpable. The most worrying comments, (for town employees), concerned contract renewals. The most worrying comments for elected officials concerned voting in the upcoming elections. They, in particular, were reminded that a vote from the west side of Route 5 carried the same weight as a vote from the east side of Route 5. The message was loud, clear, and delivered repeatedly: time to change the culture.

Change did happen, but not in dramatic fashion. Follying continued, but in a less malicious fashion, less destructive and less prone to physical intimidation. The name-calling continued, as did a host of other petty indignities. Like most issues where one tribe is forced to accept another tribe, the reaction to "the other" will always be, well, tribal. Acceptance is generational; it can only be imposed just so much. Teachers and coaches won't seriously advocate for acceptance unless they, themselves, have risen above a tribal response. Some did; some didn't. Life at "Friendly" Fullerton went on as usual. Joyce kept up with "About Town"; Matt dreamed about a seat on the Town Council. The election loomed large.

GENESIS

Patsy's birthday was in mid-December, a fact that always rankled him because of its proximity to Christmas. Every year, without fail, he'd complain to the others about his birthday cheating him out of a full-fledged gift blow-out on December 25. This was also his way of reminding the others about his upcoming birthday in case they felt obliged to throw a little party (with gifts!) for him—which they usually did. The other thing about Patsy's birthday that ruffled his feathers was that Carmella, his mom, saw his birthday as an opportunity to give him "educational" gifts, as opposed to the "fun" gifts he'd find under the tree on Christmas morning.

In the summer between eighth and ninth grade, Carmella, having chatted with Tommy's mom, who made a little side money giving piano lessons to locals, told Patsy that he should try playing an instrument. She referenced my playing drums and Tommy's reluctant piano playing as examples of what she hoped Patsy would aspire to. Her entreaties were greeted at first with casual derision and a "she'll eventually forget about it" attitude; that is; until she brought home a color catalog of musical instruments. They were laid out by family: stringed instruments, brass, reeds, percussion, etc. The pages which showcased gleaming horns were particularly appealing with trumpets, cornets, trombones, euphoniums, French horns, and tubas arranged on deep red and royal purple velvet, leaving them looking more like gold than brass. Patsy, reluctant to admit that he was dazzled, tossed the catalog carelessly onto the kitchen table, open to the trumpet page, and rushed out the door saying, *"Okay, I'll try one of those."*

In the process, the draft from the open door flipped to the next catalog page, which featured trombones. Subsequently, Patsy registered surprise while unwrapping one rather large birthday present and finding a trombone. At first, Patsy wasn't sure if he was disappointed or not. Angelo said, *"What's the difference? You blow in here and it comes out there."* Patsy had to admit that his dad had a point, and besides, he wasn't 100% sure he hadn't picked the trombone from the catalog in the first place. Angela wisely knew that he would never agree to lessons (she planned to work on that), so she included a couple of books on how to play and a bottle of slide oil.

> **Patsy registered surprise while unwrapping one rather large birthday present and finding a trombone. At first, he wasn't sure if he was disappointed or not. Angelo said, "What's the difference? You blow in here and it comes out there."**

The genesis of the band took place during the week between Christmas and New Year. Patsy had invited everybody over to check out his new "game room" in the villa's finished basement. It featured paneled walls, a carpeted floor, casual furniture, a TV set, and assorted board games. However, its crowning glories, Patsy's "fun" Christmas presents, were a jukebox stocked with current pop hits (and a few Dean Martin and Al Martino songs for Carmella) a ping pong table, and a pinball machine. Also, orphaned in a corner, were a folding chair, a music stand with "Learn Trombone Books I and II" on it, and Patsy's birthday present trombone on its stand. The Fab Four +One initially spent a couple of hours saturating themselves on pinball and ping pong. During a lull, I casually wandered over to the trombone, lifted it off its stand and started working the slide. I then asked Patsy if he'd learned any tunes. His response was, *"a few, but I can make great farts."* To which Joanne responded, *"We already knew that,"* which provoked snickers and guffaws. In response Patsy took his trombone out of my hands, put his lips to the mouthpiece and proceeded to let loose a cascade of fart noises from "left cheek sneaks" to "depth charges" to "earthquakers," Needless to say, we were soon rolling on the floor with laughter. We simply couldn't get over the sheer range of noises that he had explored. Every time the laughter would begin to subside, Patsy delved more deeply into his catalog, and we'd all convulse again. Once things finally began to calm down, Tommy asked Patsy to play something he'd actually learned. With that, Patsy walked over to the jukebox with a "watch this" facial expression. He punched a couple of buttons to select a record and the opening riff of a song we all recognized immediately started up: "Louie Louie." And Patsy played it! He actually played the opening notes! Da /Da-Da-Da /Da-Da /Da-Da-Da /Da-Da.

"Louie Louie" had been Number 1 on the Billboard charts for a month and didn't show any signs of relinquishing its position. People loved it for its musical simplicity, its infectious riff, and the fact that its lyrics were unintelligible. At some point, someone had interpreted the lyrics to contain all sorts of sexually suggestive references. The rumor then began to circulate that the lyrics were unintelligible for that very reason. Naturally, bootleg copies of the "real" lyrics began to circulate clandestinely, each set dirtier than ones that had already been handed round. The song got a second life from this "forbidden fruit" ethic. It soon became clear that the opening riff was the only part of the song Patsy had figured out. He said he was still working on the rest. Nevertheless, we were all impressed.

Just as Patsy started to replace his trombone on its stand, Tommy said, *"Hey, why don't we start a band."* Everybody paused for a moment and then started in to rank on him for saying something so ridiculous, but Tommy stood his ground.

"I'm serious," he said, *"We should start a band. We've got the core right here."* he said pointing to me, Patsy, and himself, *"We could have a lot of fun."*

John chimed in, *"What kind of music would we play?"*

"The kind we hear on the radio, like the stuff on Patsy's jukebox."

Patsy said, *"There's no trombone in those songs."*

Tommy insisted, *"Maybe not, but you can read music, and you just showed us that you've got a good ear, so play bass instead. Bass is easy because you never have to take a solo, so if you miss a few notes, who's going to know? And my mother can buy the sheet music from La Russa's; she's got an account there."*

Once they got past the *"Hey gang, let's put on the show in my father's barn"* stage, they started to address the idea's practicality. What other instruments would they need and who would do the singing? In order to answer the instruments question, they drew on what they'd been hearing in popular tunes and from a recent TV appearance that had generated a great deal of interest.

When the Beatles first appeared on the Ed Sullivan Show that was a watershed moment, not just for pop music, but for the music business itself. They looked good, they sounded great, and they wrote their own songs. What more could anybody want? The Fab Four + One drew on the British Fab Four for inspiration. The Beatles had lead guitar (George), rhythm guitar (John), and bass guitar (Paul) up front, with Ringo on drums in the back. Assuming that Patsy could learn how to play bass, that still left them at least a lead guitar short. They'd have to recruit. The other issue was how would John and Joanne fit in? Joanne, always the shy one, said that she didn't want to participate, but we all knew that Joanne could sing. She'd been in the Glee Club from fifth grade to present. In fact, she was the only "trained" singer of the bunch. We'd have to work on convincing her. Then there was John. He'd never taken music lessons, so he couldn't contribute instrumentally. He said that he could be the band's manager or agent or equipment tech. He clearly wanted to take part in some capacity.

Then Joanne asked a breakthrough question, *"Have you ever tried to sing?"* John, trying to hide his embarrassment by turning his answer into a joke said something about attracting dogs from miles around. But he was the only one laughing. Joanne then started over to the jukebox and punched in the code for Elvis' current hit, "Can't Help Falling In Love." She said, *"I know this won't be in all our keys, but let's start with it anyway. I'll go first."* And she did.

It wasn't bad given that Elvis was a baritone and Joanne was an alto. You could tell immediately that she could have sung it well if it had truly been in her range. She restarted the song and Tommy tried. He was a tenor, so this definitely wasn't his song. Joanne tried him on "Surfin' USA" by the Beach Boys, and he sounded really good covering Mike Love. Everybody was impressed. I was next, but I bailed out saying something about how drummers heard rhythm, not melody. Joanne made the point that Ringo sang but admitted that it was only rarely, so I got a temporary stay of execution. I told them I'd play "Wipe Out" as my feature; they liked that. By this point in the proceedings, Patsy had really gotten into the spirit of what was happening. In fact, enthusiasm for starting the band was now well into the "how" stage when Patsy chortled over to the jukebox and punched in "The Twist." Now Patsy was never going to be a crooner, and that's putting it mildly. He couldn't really "sing" a song, but he could damn well "sell" one, and sometimes that's all you need. With his stocky, slightly rotund build, his chubby, "cherub" face, and his medusa hair, he was a natural. Add to those qualities the fact that he almost sort of "danced" the twist as he sang it, and his vocal niche was filled. Which brings us back, once again, to John. Joanne went back to the jukebox and punched in "Can't Help Falling in Love" again. It took a lot of coaxing before John would even try it, but eventually, very tentatively, he did. The results were discouraging, but most of the notes were there.

Joanne said, *"Well at least we know you can carry a tune so that's good. We just have to find the right tune for you to carry."*

They tried him on "Return to Sender" (Elvis again, just okay), "Mean Woman Blues" (Roy Orbison, also just okay), "The Wanderer" (Dion and the Belmonts, not bad), "She Loves You" (The Beatles, forget it), "Love Me Do" (The Beatles again, not bad), and, finally, "Can't Help Falling In Love" (Elvis again, but much better). Everybody turned to Joanne for the final word on the subject.

She said, *"You can do this if you believe that you can do this."*

Silence. John looked unconvinced.

Joanne continued, *"Do me one favor. Pick a song you know, one that you used to sing, even from a long time ago, and try singing it."*

"Without music?" John sounded terrified.

No music," Joanne stated, *"just your voice."*

"And if it makes it easier," I said, *"we'll all face the other way."* And we did.

And after a short delay (and a lot of shuffling around and throat clearing), John launched into a spirited a cappella version of "Onward Christian Soldiers." We were all standing near each other facing the same far wall of the room. About halfway through the first verse, Joanne and I stole a sideways glance at each other, and she mouthed the words "Oh My God," and we both smiled at each other. We had our lead singer. When he finished singing, we turned back to face him and there were high fives all around—even a couple of manly half-hugs. John explained that his dad was a real "holy roller" who insisted on attending services and actively participating, hence the singing. In fact, John said that if your enthusiasm was lacking, you could probably expect to get a beating when you returned home, so you sang, and loudly. Tommy volunteered his mom to help John (and himself) learn the songs along with some rudimentary help with reading music for John. Assuming that progress could be made in that quarter, that left Patsy needing to get a bass (his mother, already convinced that he was a prodigy, bought one the next day) and learning how to play it, the Fab Four convincing the + One to participate, us needing to recruit a lead guitarist, and us again needing to come up with a name.

Everybody turned to Joanne for the final word on the subject. She said, "You can do this if you believe that you can do this."

THE SHADES

The musical challenges which confronted the Fab Four + One were daunting. Tommy's mother was a godsend. She worked mostly with Tommy and John, while Patsy worked mostly with Patsy. We suspected that he was getting help from someone, but he insisted that he was teaching himself, and we saw no purpose in calling him out. Joanne remained aloof and noncommittal, although she did attend most of the twice-a-week rehearsals in Tommy's rec room where his mom normally taught her piano lessons. Patsy and I brought the minimum of instrumental equipment necessary. However, in addition to buying Patsy a bass guitar, a small practice amp, and a larger amp for gigs, his folks had also gifted him with professional grade speakers, mixer-amp, microphones and stands. In short, we had everything a band would need to start performing in public except a song list, capable singers, polished players, a leader, and an all-important name.

Our Leader

Bruce Springsteen isn't called "The Boss" for nothing. He's called "The Boss" because he *is* the boss. A band can't function properly if it's a democracy. The E Street Band's smooth functioning is due in large part to Springsteen's authority. He calls the tunes, decides who will play what when within each tune, determines the length of solos, and keeps musical egos in check. The Fab Four + One needed a boss.

I bowed out immediately; drummers are never bosses because they're never out front. And for those who would cite Dave Clark of The Dave Clark Five, take it from a drummer, Dave Clark may have held sticks and sat behind a set, but Dave Clark was never a drummer. John would, as lead singer, be very much "out front," but he was first to admit that he was woefully unqualified to be the leader. This left Tommy and Patsy. Patsy was the stronger personality of the two, but his appearance was unconventional by the standards of the time, and his behavior (not just what he sometimes did, but what he sometimes said) was just unpredictable enough to make the rest of the group uncomfortable about letting him front the band in public.

That left Tommy. Not only had he proposed the band in the first place, but he also knew more about music than anyone else. And while it's true that I knew how to play the drums, there's some truth to the old saying, "There are musicians and there are drummers, and only sometimes do the two combine." So Tommy was it. His piano was the band's instrumental foundation, at least until we found a lead guitar, he sang lead tolerably well, he could show the rest how to sing back-up, he could deal well with "personalities," and his house provided rehearsal space. Most importantly, everybody liked and listened to Big Tommy Nitro. He demonstrated the wisdom of our choice right off the bat by announcing that Patsy would act as M.C. when it came to making announcements and introducing the tunes. We had chosen well.

Our Name

We all felt that choosing the right name was important. We looked to successful bands for guidance. Many bands way back when had names that didn't evoke a musical vibe. I'm thinking here of The Tornadoes, The Fabulous Twilights, The Drifters, The Exciters, The Enchanters, The Angels, The Cascades, The Kingsmen, and, of course, The Rolling Stones. Other bands were named for their leaders, Dion and the Belmonts (what's a Belmont?), Gerry and the Pacemakers (were the Pacemakers moonlighting cardiologists?), Shane Fenton and the Fentones (what's a Fentone?), B. Bumble and the Stingers (who wants to be a Stinger?), Joey Dee and the Starliters, Randy and the Rainbows (look, Ma, I'm a Rainbow), Ruby and the Romantics, and Martha and the Vandellas (what's a Vandella, and why do I envision Vikings?). We must have tried one hundred and more names like Jukebox Johnny and the Jokers, Tommy Nitro and the Nightlights/Spotlights/Headlights (take your pick), The Fabulous Fireworks (Tommy's idea), The Carpet Baggers (ostensibly for The Mill, but actually for the then popular Harold Robbin's novel which was wonderfully smutty), The Big Shots, The White Spots (there were Inkspots, so why not?), The Aces (too close to the Four Aces, but nobody would have mistaken us for them), Johnny and the Jesters (Patsy's idea, not John's, because Patsy could dress up like *"one of them guys with bells on his hat and tell jokes between songs,"* The Deltones, The Delphonics, The Mellowtones (sounded too much like The Monotones), Tommy and the Tattletales, and on and on. Patsy made it difficult to consider any name seriously, because he saw these "name-search" sessions as an opportunity to make us all crack up. Just as an example, one night he was into ass-related names like Patsy and the Poop Chutes, The Rectal Thermometers, and Little Anthony and the Enemas. Anyhow, we finally settled on The Frenchtownies

Patsy was into ass-related suggestions such as Patsy and the Poop Chutes, The Rectal Thermometers, and Little Anthony and the Enemas.

as a temporary title, but none of us really liked it. It reminded me of French toast every time I heard it. The thing about names is that they should do more than just document identity; they should be somehow aspirational, a vision of whom we wanted to become rather than of whom we already were. And combining identity with aspiration is difficult. Anyway, we decided to adopt it until something better came along. We couldn't choose our two actual favorites, Sister Kerosina and the Lapsed Katholics, and The Mighty Reltneys, for obvious reasons.

Our Guitar Player: Part 1

Residences which are pondside, lakeside and riverside are highly desirable now, but that wasn't always true. This was especially the case of rivers, and it was particularly true of the Connecticut River, which reaped a rich harvest of industrial pollutants and just plain, old household garbage from factories and households along its banks in Massachusetts' cities like Lowell, Lawrence, and Springfield. Connecticut contributed as well from factories like Bigelow-Sanford in Frenchtown, Dexter's and Montgomery's in Windsor Locks, Hartford, Middletown, New Haven, Bridgeport, etc. Where trash disposal was concerned, it was ecological "kick the can" all the way down to Long Island Sound. People who lived fronting the river almost always did so out of necessity rather than choice.

Just beyond The Mill was a railroad overpass and then the Enfield-Suffield Bridge. Sandwiched in between the overpass and the bridge entrance was South River Street, about one-half mile of narrow road squeezed between the river on one side and a high berm for train tracks on the other. If you lived on South River Street, you never bothered to look out of east-facing windows because all you saw was berm. The road didn't really end. It just sort of petered out as if embarrassed to go any farther. Between the sound of frequent train traffic, and the sometimes stench of polluted river water, South River Street would never be mistaken for prime real estate, even by Frenchtown standards. The few houses, like the people who inhabited them, could be described as "hardscrabble." Their paint peeled, their fences, where there were fences, were bent and broken from heavy, plowed snow, their shingles went missing here and there, leaving their roofs looking like so many gap-toothed smiles. The people were hard-working, honest, and God-fearing. They were also unskilled, poorly educated, and culturally deprived. But if you had occasion to be walking or driving slowly down South River Street, what you heard emanating from number 14 would surprise you. Muddy Waters, Blind Lemon Jefferson, Gatemouth Brown, Lightnin'

Hopkins, John Lee Hooker, T-Bone Walker, B.B.King, and more, all lived in 14 South River Street in the person of Suzie "Spike" Parker.

Spike Parker was a complete anomaly in Frenchtown. Many people could say they knew of her, but no one actually knew her. The town records showed that the house was in her mother's name, but the bank records showed the mortgage In Spike's name. No one could remember seeing her mother at or around the house, or anyone other than Spike for that matter. She apparently lived alone, the second to last house on a street which terminated with Freddy "Flash" Gordon's Used Auto Parts. Fred's house was backed by a barbed wire barrier which encircled a huge collection of junk vehicles cascading down the river slope into the river itself. If you wanted a 53 Chevy grill, you'd probably find it at "Freddy G's," but you might have to don scuba gear to retrieve it. Freddy was a fixture in *The T'ville Press* a few years back when he and the Town of Enfield locked horns over his business, which was technically on land zoned residential rather than commercial. Freddy G's contention was that his father had started the business before zoning was a factor, so the business should be grandfathered. As Spike was his only abutting neighbor, she was asked to attend. When questioned about how she felt living next to a junkyard, she said that she would tolerate his cars as long as he would tolerate her music. Spike and Freddy had gotten along ever since. In fact, he even offered for her to cherry-pick "his collection" free of charge, but he said he would have to charge her for the rental of his diving equipment.

Spike Parker was a complete anomaly in Frenchtown. Many people could say they knew of her, but no one actually knew her.

On the Other

When people use "the Other," it's usually in the context of referring to an individual or a group that identifies differently in some way—racially, culturally, religiously, etc. It's a reference that has always struck me as insensitive, inherently divisive, and vaguely sinister. However, I think that we're all wired to compartmentalize in this way; it's part of our involuntary brain circuitry to do so. We learn how to disguise it as we age and mature. We veneer it, but it's there, and if something happens to scratch the surface, then, as Tag Team said in song back in 1993, "Whoomp! (There It Is). Kids are much more honest in this regard, either because they're too young to conceal it, or because they simply don't think they need to. When I was quite young, "the other" was a witch. In fact, this particular witch was "the Other" to my friends as well. To us, a witch was an old woman who lived alone by choice or necessity. And, to our way of thinking at the time, witches could accumulate bonus points for being especially witchy. For example, if her house was old and decrepit, bonus points; relatively isolated, bonus points; spider webby, bonus points. If she dressed in black, bonus points; had cats, bonus points; had a black cat, mega bonus points. Her real name was Mrs. Pickens, by the way. To us, she was a witch; hence, she was "the other."

Now Spike wasn't a witch, but where she lived, how she lived, and how she dressed (pre-Goth), and the fact that no one could remember seeing her without sunglasses, even indoors, qualified her as "the other" to some, even though she had a classic "white bread" job. Spike was a mailman—in those days you were a mailman even if you were a mail lady. People on her route saw her all the time, some elders every day even. And she always seemed to enjoy conversing on common denomination subjects like the weather, sports, or the rising cost of first-class mail. A few even put Christmas cards for her in their boxes on the last day mail was delivered before the holiday. All this, the fact that she lived alone, kept to herself, didn't attend social functions, dressed in dark clothing even on summer days, always wore sunglasses (even indoors and during the winter), rarely engaged casually out of uniform, and searched through antique shops for old 78 records, made Spike "the Other" to more than a few. For some, even her age made her "the other." She looked like she could easily be of high school age, but she hadn't gone to school in Enfield. Some said they thought she might be originally from Rhode Island. Had she gone to school there? Had she graduated? Some thought she must have a high school sheepskin to hold down a government job. No one knew for sure, and The Fed wasn't about to give out her personal information. That just added to her mystique.

It was hard to tell whether or not that perception bothered her; it certainly didn't change her. Still, she must have suspected what others thought and how others felt. She had never been seen with a man, or with a woman either, for that matter. And what about her mother? Where had she gone? What had happened to her? Was she gradually decomposing in the cellar like Norman Bates' mother in

Psycho? (A huge hit at The Strand, by the way. The tagline about no one being admitted into the theater after the first ten minutes of the film had people lining up at the box office to buy tickets from Mrs. Driscoll—speaking of which Janet Leigh looked superhot in that bra—sorry for the detour). Spike seemed unfazed by what others saw, thought, assumed, and speculated over. But you really never know. The old saying, "still waters run deep" comes to mind.

Will we always have "the Other?" I think so. Will "the Other" always know that they're "the Other?" Probably. If you're reading this, are you "the Other" in someone else's eyes, or is someone else "the Other" in your eyes? Just asking.

Our Guitar Player: Part 2

We live in a disposable world. If something breaks or stops working properly, throw it away and buy a new one. That wasn't true back in the day, however, when my parents sold TVs as part of their music store business. Back then, a TV was basically a heavy, glass cathode ray tube, surrounded by a variety of other attendant electronic components, encased in a heavy wood cabinet. It was regarded as a genuine piece of furniture. If your living room furniture showcased maple, for instance, then you wanted a TV with a maple cabinet to match. Likewise, stereo phonographs, which consisted of a turntable, an AM/FM radio and speakers, in heavy wood cabinets, also had to match the room's decor. These electronics weren't disposable at all; they were investments. When your TV or stereo stopped working properly, you'd call Gatto's Music to schedule a service appointment, when a technician would usually put things right by coming to your home and replacing a few of the TV's myriad vacuum tubes—the predecessors to transistors and solid-state circuitry. If the TV couldn't be repaired "in situ," the technician would then transport it to my parents' store where it entered the kingdom of Harry Martin, my parents' repairman.

I don't use the word "kingdom" without intent. The back room, aka "the service center," was Harry Martin's fiefdom, and he was its chief fief. It was a small, dark room. The only natural light came from a frosted window in the back of the room, away from Harry's workbench. The window looked out on an alley, however, so Harry worked in permanent twilight. This didn't seem to bother him much. Harry was content as long as he had a soldering iron and his unfiltered Lucky Strikes. Harry had chain smoked all his life. His addiction even woke him out of a sound sleep a couple of times a night so that he could take a few drags. Everything in his universe, his house, his car, his clothes, his hair, even his skin, seemed impregnated with that stale cigarette smell. His small mustache and his fingers were nicotine brown. Even in an age where most everybody smoked, Harry stood out as a dedicated smoker.

Harry Martin was a living, smoking encyclopedia with an extensive collection when it came to vintage blues guitarists/singers, so he and Spike hit it off immediately.

My parents' store was on Spike's mail route, so she came in everyday, but she would make a special stop every Friday after work to check out the latest releases, because she knew that the singles and albums were replenished every Thursday by the rack jobber from the nearest record distributor. Sometimes she would buy guitar picks and guitar strings as well. My parents didn't sell musical instruments, but they did sell instrument accessories like drumsticks, saxophone reeds, and such. Spike didn't often buy records, however, because most pop music wasn't to her taste. She preferred vintage blues over rock. She asked my mother, one day, if my mother thought the record distributor might stock "her kind of music" for different markets within his territory. My mother said that she didn't think so, but she would ask Roger, her rack jobber. Meanwhile, my mom suggested that Spike should ask Harry in the backroom, because she knew that Harry listened to old 78s.

It turns out that Harry Martin was a living, smoking encyclopedia with an extensive collection when it came to vintage blues guitarists/singers, so he and Spike hit it off immediately. Every time Spike came into the shop to deliver mail, she'd have a brief word with Harry. He even eventually invited her over to his house to peruse his old shellac 78s, which he was methodically transferring to recording tape because of their value and fragility. Spike would bring her guitar, Harry would drag his out, and they'd spend a few hours together playing and singing along. After a session, Harry, normally a pretty reticent guy, would talk at length to my parents about Spike's knowledge and her talent.

And that's how I came to know that Spike might be exactly what The Frenchtownies needed, if she could be enticed to join that is, and if she could be enticed into playing rock.

Our Guitar Player: Part 3

We shelved the idea of approaching Spike for two reasons. First, there was no reason for her to say "yes." Second, she had every reason to say "no." Until we had a repertoire, there just wasn't much point.

So, we went to work on a song list. We rehearsed twice a week, trying to acquire one new song at each rehearsal. At particularly good rehearsals, we'd pick up a couple and maybe start on a couple more. At other rehearsals we'd come up empty. At the end of a month, we had eight: "Twist and Shout," "Louie Louie," "The Twist," "Wipe Out," (boy, did we miss having a guitar on this one), "Can't Help falling In Love," "Surfer Girl," "I Saw Her Standing There," and "Let's Dance," (on which Patsy would replace the line, "Hey, Baby, won't you take a chance, Say that you'll let me have this dance" with, "Hey, Baby, won't you take a chance, Come outside and pull down your pants"). He promised he wouldn't do that in public, but we had doubts.

Anyway, at that point we figured we had enough for one short set—maybe. We lengthened some pieces mostly by asking Tommy to play piano solos or by playing through a song two or three times—*"Don't worry, they won't notice if they're dancing."* Another tactic was to stretch a tune by slowing the tempo. "Can't Help Falling in Love" sounded positively dirge-like. At that point, we felt ready to try for Spike. If she wasn't interested, fair enough; we'd just continue to build our song list and look elsewhere.

My first thought was to enlist Harry Martin in an ambush. We'd find some excuse to rehearse at his house on a night she was coming over to listen to some of his "old wax." He wouldn't go for it. He said that it was dishonest, that he wouldn't lie to her for us, and that she'd see through it in a minute anyway. But he didn't turn us down either. He said that he'd tell her that he knew of the band through me (true), and that he'd ask her to listen to us just to provide us with some advice on starting out (sort of true). He was okay with that. In fact, he agreed to record the rehearsal on his fancy reel-to-reel Akai tape recorder, saying, *"It'll give me something to do."*

We shelved the idea of approaching Spike for two reasons. First, there was no reason for her to say "yes." Second, she had every reason to say "no."

On the appointed night, we dragged all of our equipment and our sound system over to Harry's house with the help of Tommy's dad's station wagon. John had "light fingered" the Fullerton Jazz Band's electric guitar and amp just for the occasion, with the understanding that he would return them the next day (and he did). We set up in Harry's smoky front room, the Fullerton guitar and amp conspicuously just off to Tommy's side. Joanne sat with Harry as an observer.

Spike arrived in her trademark black and her sunglasses. Harry introduced me and invited me to introduce the rest. She asked a few questions about how we got the idea to start a band, if any of us had any music background, when and how often we rehearsed, who and what our musical influences were, and what our intentions were for the band. That last one really threw us at first, but Tommy stammered out the right answer: *"To entertain people by playing good music well."* She liked that response. You could tell. She actually looked impressed by what Tommy had said. So she took a seat and said, *"Show me what you got."*

Spike called out a key change, repeated the guitar lead-in, moved to John's mic and started singing "Johnny B. Goode." Sister Kerosina would have orgasmed on the spot.

We started with "Twist and Shout" (Tommy lead), followed it with "Can't Help Falling in Love" (John lead), then "The Twist" (Patsy lead), and finally "Wipe Out" (my lead). We played "Wipe Out" through once, and then Spike stood up and waved us to a stop. Up to this point she had said nothing. We figured she may have heard enough.

She walked over to the Gibson next to Tommy and looked at it. Then she said, *"I presume this is for me?"* We just grinned sheepishly. She turned on the amp and tuned the guitar for a minute. Then she turned to Tommy and said, *"You can't play 'Wipe Out' on a piano. Just play chords."* Then she turned to the rest of us and said, *"From the top,"* and counted us in.

It sounded amazing. When it ended, she just nodded. Then Tommy asked her if she knew "Fun, Fun, Fun" by The Beach Boys, a tune we had started to work on with Tommy singing lead. She said that she'd heard it, but that she knew "Johnny B. Goode" better, and that it and "Fun, Fun, Fun" were basically the same tune with the same exact guitar opening and a few simple Beach Boy chord changes. She told Tommy that she'd play the opening guitar riff, and then he should come in with "Fun, Fun, Fun" lyrics.

She kicked it off, Tommy sang the lyrics, Patsy faked his way through it, and John sang with Tommy on the choruses. Just as we were coming to the end of the song, Spike called out a key change, repeated the guitar lead-in, moved to John's mic and started singing "Johnny B. Goode." Sister Kerosina would have orgasmed on the spot.

Our Guitar Player: Part 4

We played through the rest of our song list with Spike singing lead on "Twist and Shout," harmony and/or unison on "I Saw Her Standing There," "Let's Dance," and "Surfer Girl," and a blazing guitar solo on "Louie Louie" that went on for a good five minutes. That was the clincher. When it ended, everybody just stared. Silence. I think Patsy was drooling. More silence.

Spike finally broke the spell by saying, *"Thanks, guys, that was fun,"* as she replaced the guitar on its stand and turned off the amp. Tommy asked her if she could give us some suggestions. Her response was: *"Add to your song list, find a guitar player, and start booking some gigs."*

I jumped in at that point and asked her if she'd be willing to rehearse with again, *"just until we find somebody."* She said she would if she didn't have anything else going on. So that's how it was left. While we were packing up, Harry put on his latest blues compilation tape, and both he and Spike took out their acoustic guitars and started to sing and play along with some Howlin' Wolf. Tommy called his dad who ran us and our equipment back to his house where we brought everything downstairs to his rec room.

We were all still pretty wired by how good we had sounded with Spike, so we took some time to calm down and decompress. Patsy, always free with his parents' money, wondered if she'd take money to rehearse with us regularly so that maybe we could gradually rope her in. That led to a contentious discussion which paired those who were in favor, because we could increase our song list more quickly, build up our confidence for performing live, and possibly convince her to buy in, against those who felt that she might object to being treated as a "hired gun," and that we'd probably become too reliant on her with no guarantee that we could depend on her. Their thinking was that we'd be better off to find someone else now, thereby not having to reinvent the wheel later. Patsy and I were in favor of the "pay her to rehearse" position, while Tommy stood on principle.

> Spike played a blazing guitar solo to "Louie, Louie" which went on for a good five minutes. That was the clincher. Everybody just stared, speechless. I think Patsy was drooling.

When all eyes turned to John, he said, *"Ask Joey first."* So we did. She sided with Tommy and principle so it was a Mexican stand-off.

All eyes shifted back to John. Finally, he spoke.

"I've got an idea," he said, *"but I need some time to think it through. If we can get her to one or two rehearsals, I think it might seal the deal. That's all I'm gonna' say. You'll have to trust me on this."*

Patsy asked, *"When you say 'seal the deal,' do you mean that she'd join the band?"*

John nodded, *"Maybe."*

We all nodded in agreement, because we all really wanted her in the band, and because it seemed some alien had taken control of the shy "wouldn't say 'shit' if he had a mouthful" guy who used to be John.

Our Guitar Player: Part 5

We picked up a few new songs during the next few rehearsals, notably "Shout!" (Patsy lead), "Return to Sender" (John lead), "I Get Around" (Tommy lead), and "The Wanderer" (John lead). We even persuaded Joanne to try "Johnny Angel," which sounded really good, but, despite our compliments and protestations, she wouldn't sing anything else. We rehearsed with Spike at Harry's house a month after the first rehearsal with him again recording. And once again, the band took on a whole new dimension with Spike's guitar and voice. She liked our new songs and made some very helpful suggestions, especially regarding the harmonies on "I Get Around" and the background vocals on "The Wanderer," which consisted mostly of "shoop shoop's" and "wah wah's." John had cautioned us about not saying anything that could be interpreted as pleading, persuading, bribing, or begging. We didn't. We were all impressed by the changes in him. As he grew in confidence with his voice as a performer, he also grew in confidence with his voice as a contributor—and we were mightily impressed.

Six weeks to the day after our first rehearsal with Spike, we met with her for the third time, but this "decisive" rehearsal was at Tommy's house. Harry was invited but said he'd pass because Tommy had said his mom wouldn't allow smoking in the house, and Harry would never be able to go for long without his Lucky Strikes. Spike was surprised to find all of us dressed in black from head to toe when she arrived. We were following John's instructions to do so. When she commented about it, John covered by saying that it was "Dress-Up Week" at Fullerton, and our class had chosen "Back in Black" as its theme. Before she could ask a follow-up question, Tommy sidelined her with a question about the chord progression for one of the new tunes we had just started working up. We then warmed up on some of the songs we'd already rehearsed before moving on to the newer stuff. The last song in our warm-up set was "Twist and Shout," on which Spike sang lead.

Just as she was about to count it off, John interrupted. *"I've got an idea about making this our opening number. We all like it, and we all think we sound really good on it. But it needs something, something flashy. So, let's try this. Patsy and me stand in a line with Spike in the middle."* We did.

"Now me and Patsy face toward the back." They did.

"Okay, piano and drums, you guys can't face the back so just lower your heads and try to hide your faces." Tommy and I did.

"Now we play the intro just like this, but when each of us starts singing our individual 'ah's', me and Patsy face front, and then you guys (meaning me and Tommy*) raise your heads and look front. That way when we get to the fifth 'ah' we're all facing front and singing. Get it? Okay, I'm going to introduce the band with my back turned before the singing starts."*

There was a millisecond of silence before we started tripping all over each other to agree.

Now, I'm going to assume that you know the opening of "Twist and Shout," and for those of you culturally deprived cretins who don't, go to YouTube and worship at the altar of the Isley Brothers. It starts with a four measure instrumental introduction. Those four measures are then repeated with an ascending note sung and sustained on the first beat of each measure until all voices are in when the introduction ends. Then the first verse begins in a call and response pattern.

Spike counted it in, and we all started playing the four measure instrumental intro. It was a little difficult for me and Tommy to play and hide our faces but we managed. Because Spike was the only one facing forward, she didn't see the rest of us behind her back putting on dark glasses identical to hers which John had supplied to us before her arrival. He said something about them falling off the back of a truck. The final touch took place during the instrumental opening when John's voice came over the sound system saying, *"Ladies and Gentlemen, you got it made, with Spike and the Shades."* And the singing started right then.

When the tune ended, Spike took a moment to think. *"All right,"* she said, *"but there are three conditions. The first is that the name has to change. I don't want my name used because I might change my mind about participating at some point. The second is that I won't rehearse more than once a week, maybe not even that often. You guys work up some new stuff on your own, and then call me, but I'll help you pick out new stuff. And, speaking of new stuff, that's the third condition, some of it has to be blues. I'm not going to play back-to-back "bubble gum."*

Then she looked at us. There was a millisecond of silence before we started tripping all over each other to agree. Once things quieted down a little, she said, *"Get some gigs. We'll get better faster if we're not just playing for each other."*

At that point, Joanne, who had been a silent, almost forgotten observer spoke up. *"We've got one for the Student Government 'Snow Ball' in February,"* she said, *"and one for the St. Patrick's 'Spring Fling' in April."*

At a rehearsal where jaws had repeatedly been on the floor, they were again on the floor after Joanne's announcement. I managed to stammer out a few fragmentary words like "when" and "how."

Tommy finally came up with a whole sentence, *"How could they hire us if they never even heard us?"*

Joanne picked up a paper bag that was resting near her feet and withdrew our two rehearsal tapes. *"They have,"* she said.

Spike said, *"Nice going"* to Joanne. Then, while still addressing her, Spike said, *"The band needs a 'sweet, girly' voice for some of the top 40 stuff, and that's not me. The guys say you can sing, so it'll have to be you. Agreed?"*

We all nodded, including Joanne. At that moment The Fab Four + One became "The Shades."

PART 2

THE BALLAD OF JOHNNY AND JOEY: Part 1

Two Years Later

Johnny always needed help getting off the stage, because his concerts' encores climaxed with intensely bright lights and indoor pyro, leaving him "light blind" when it came to negotiating a path into the wings. He depended on Leo, his personal assistant, in times of vulnerability like these. The once hundreds, now thousands in the house would be roaring for still more, but Johnny's manager, Ben, was a stern practitioner of the "always leave them wanting more" school where his biggest clients were concerned, and Johnny Domino was about as big as they came. He fumbled a bit on the short set of offstage stairs, but Leo steadied him, got him onto firm ground, and led him over to the oxygen tank where he alternated between deep drags of 0^2 and deep gulps of orange juice ("with pulp" as stipulated in his contract). During this pause, Leo stripped off Johnny's heavy, sequined jacket and sweat-soaked shirt and passed them to Marcie, Johnny's wardrobe attendant. All the while, the rest of the band, along with some of the techies, were making their way to the green room to feast on the buffet, have a few (or more) beers, and generally decompress before boarding the band limos or techie bus for the short run back to the hotel. Groupies were everywhere; hook ups were expected.

Johnny's regimen was quite different. When he'd had enough gas and juice to recover at least temporarily, Leo and Johnny's two security men, Gus and Francis, helped him to run the groupie gauntlet in the backstage hallways to his private dressing room where Brad was waiting. Together, they reviewed the show and talked about possible changes to the set list and song order. Ben always kept one set of notes for Johnny, one for the band, and one for tech (stage crew, sound, lighting, and effects.) Johnny insisted they go over the notes that pertained to him right after a performance; the other notes could wait until tomorrow. Johnny sipped Drambuie on the rocks. They finished about a half hour later. Brad

Johnny insisted they go over the notes that pertained to him right after a performance; the other notes could wait until tomorrow.

called for Leo who threw a black sheet over Johnny's head and shoulders so that he wouldn't be recognizable to fans still desperately hanging around in the hope that the marquee, which now read "Johnny Domino has left the building. Please get home safely. Thank you and Goodnight," was all a lie, which, of course, it was. Leo, Gus, and Francis hustled Johnny out a side door and into a running limo with blacked out windows. In the short distance between arena door and car door, Johnny looked, to all the world, very much like Sister Kerosina.

On Talent

I've spent much of my life in and around the performing arts. Much of that time was spent teaching young people about the difference between acting and pretending. Some got it; some didn't. Inevitably, some of those who did get it would ask me if I thought that they had the talent to "make it in the biz." Because I didn't want my legacy to be a trail of broken dreams, my answer was that a person could succeed in the performing arts if three conditions were met. Those conditions were good training, perseverance, luck, and talent. I believed then, and I still believe now, that this is true. A successful career in performance requires three of these four criteria; however, I was always careful to make a distinction between success and stardom. Being successful in show business means making a living, not becoming a star.

So what is "talent" anyway?
Are you born with it?
Does it evolve?
Can it be taught? Can it be learned?
How do you recognize it?
Can it be lost? If yes, can it be regained?

The answer to all these questions is, "I don't know." And I really mean that. I don't know. It's one of those elusive, hard to define or describe, you either have it or you don't, kinds of things. Forty years ago, the husband of a woman who was then choreographing a show for me said, "Talent will out." Now that's true. In fact, it's about the only certainty I can commit to where talent is concerned.

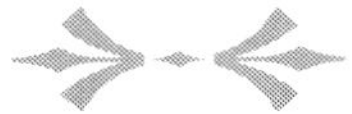

Talent will out. It always does. And it very much did when John found his persona with The Shades. He started off shakily, scared to death to be performing in public, but he got better by taking on a new identity, and, as his confidence grew, he got a lot better. The other Shades: me, Joanne, Tommy, Patsy, and Spike, used to kid him about it, but we couldn't deny or not be impressed by the change we saw taking place. John underwent a virtual metamorphosis, and the butterfly that emerged from the chrysalis had talent to spare. Gradually, the persona overtook the shy, virtually parentless, insecure kleptomaniac, and the persona became Johnny Domino. He had reinvented himself. Fortunately for the rest of us, the new John kept the size of his head in check. I credit his sister, Ruth, for that, and I also credit Joanne. She and John were close, but not in a romantic way. They were "best buds," and she could drag his tether back down to Earth and puncture his ballooning ego with one well-timed comment. She could deflate him better than anybody, and he both knew it and respected her for it.

John underwent a virtual metamorphosis, and the butterfly that emerged from the chrysalis had talent to spare.

John's Big Break: Two Years Earlier

The Shades made a name for themselves quite quickly. Spike was great when it came to marketing the band. She insisted that all proceeds from their first few gigs go directly to promotion. She had t-shirts printed with the slogan, "You Got It Made with The Shades." The band handed them out at dances, and they soon started showing up in Fullerton's hallways. Joyce, Joanne's mom, started hyping the band like crazy in her "anonymous" T'Ville Press column. Stories and photos appeared in the *Hartford Courant* and the *Springfield Republican*. Bumper stickers were next; a fan club soon followed.

Their "big break" came that fall at The Big E, The Eastern States Exposition in Agawam, Mass. The Big E was a New England tradition. Each state had its own building which showcased indigenous products and industries, such as maple syrup for Vermont, and blueberry everything for Maine. There was a huge carnival adjacent, every fast food vendor known to man, livestock displays and competitions such as biggest cow, prettiest llama, and best behaved pig, along with petting zoos, trolley rides, craft displays (who knew you could do that with clothespins and pipe cleaners!), craft shows and craft vendors, and a large arena for shows and concerts which were always country and western themed, such as Billy Bob's Rodeo and Bluegrass Blowout. And there was also a nightly "Battle of the Bands," which featured three local bands per night for three consecutive nights. Each night's winner became a finalist for the fourth night's finale. Spike convinced the others to send in a demo tape, and The Shades got the second slot on the first night. They won handily. They were well rehearsed musically and choreographically (Patsy's influence) and Fullerton provided a school bus, promptly dubbed the Shades Wagon, for their fans. They attended the next two nights to scope out the competition, which sounded formidable.

But The Shades were the total package. They may not have been the pick of the litter musically, but they had performance skills, they had presentation, they had charisma, they had a fan club (Fullerton provided three Shades Wagons for the finals), and, most importantly, they had Johnny Domino, the John persona. And that was all they needed to take the trophy. After the awards ceremony, and once the hugs and backslaps subsided, The Shades began the anti-climactic but still important task of breaking down, packing up, and loading out. It was during this process that a young man wearing a "WATC-TV Channel 3" blazer approached John and asked for a few minutes of his time.

Ben

Ben Thorpe, nee Ben Davidovich, started out as a DJ on WYOL, a small, low powered, privately owned radio station in Holyoke, Mass., called by residents in neighboring "metropolises" like Chicopee and Belchertown "the back of beyond." He was on the morning shift for three years, playing what was then called M.O.R. which stood for middle of the road, which, in other words, meant musical pap, too innocuous to be called rock, country and western, jazz, or anything else in the way of recognizable genre. Some radio stations attracted listeners by specializing in certain types of music. WYOL did the opposite; it offered the hall of fame of music mediocrity. But Ben was a natural salesman, and he paired that talent with a made-for-radio voice. He also sported good looks and a winning personality.

Ben could also be quite persuasive. For example, he convinced WYOL's owner to invest in remote broadcast equipment and to buy a used, oversize delivery van which he had emblazoned with the station's call letters, its frequency, and a larger-than-life portrait of Ben himself, under which was written "WYOL Radio Personality Ben Thorpe, The Voice of Western Mass."

Ben then took his show on the road whenever he could. The "WYOL VAN" became a common sight at store openings, county fairs, church carnivals, religious festivals, bar mitzvahs, brises, local sporting events, etc. WYOL got a lot of publicity, and, more importantly, so did Ben, who parlayed his growing popularity into a radio job on WATC in Hartford, Conn., a much larger market. Brad used the same strategy there to make the "A.T.C. Truck" a frequent visitor to Connecticut versions of Massachusetts events like those he visited while still employed by WYOL. An additional bonus came with his new position. WATC was a CBS television station as well as "Radio 103."

Ben saved his radio self for the biggest events. The Big E qualified. And that's how Ben got to hear The Shades for the first time.

Dick Clark's American Bandstand was the most popular teen television program nationwide back then. Girls loved it; boys called it "skanks on parade." Brad convinced the powers at WATC to launch Hartford Bandstand with himself as host. They did, he was, and the show aired twice a week at 4:00 p.m. Both it and Ben were instant hits. The station got Conn. Dairy Partners to sponsor it. Moms loved that milk was advertised instead of sugary snacks. Ben drank glass after glass on screen and would retreat behind the scenery during musical interludes to fart, while local teens strutted their stuff to popular 45's.

Once Ben became a TV personality, he began to lose interest in remote radio broadcasts. The A.T.C. Truck still made many appearances, as did Ben, in the form of his painted, oversized image, now drinking a glass of milk, which still adorned the truck, but the announcer was now often one of Radio 103's lesser lights. Ben saved his radio self for the biggest events. The Big E qualified. And that's how Ben got to hear The Shades for the first time. Ben had set his eyes on agentry, and he saw The Shades, and Johnny Domino in particular, as a potential client.

Ben introduced himself to John and wrote down John's telephone number saying that he'd give him a call about possibly appearing on Hartford Bandstand. John recognized him because Ruth sometimes watched the show. She even floated the idea of appearing on the show to Demetri who said he'd rather castrate a pig. When John explained to Ben that Tommy was The Shades' leader, Ben apologized about assuming that it was John, and made some excuse about having to hurry back to the studio. "

It's okay," Ben said, *"I'll call you and you can tell them."*

And with that, he left. Needless to say, everyone was very excited. Appearing live on TV would really be the cherry on that day's sundae. But it didn't quite work out that way.

Ben called a couple of days later. He started off by flattering John for his singing and his stage "presence." He also complimented The Shades, but it was pretty clear from the get-go that Ben mostly wanted to talk to John about Johnny, and, in particular, about one song that Johnny had sung at The Big E. It was called "It's Almost Tomorrow," and was an original that Tommy had penned. The Shades had started mixing in a few original pieces along with new pop covers and some rock classics. The Beatles, who wrote all but their earliest stuff, provided the inspiration for this "in house" composition, and many bands were experimenting. Most original stuff was drek, but "It's Almost Tomorrow" was good enough that fans had started requesting it. Brad said that he wanted the group to record it at The Galley Way, a professional recording studio in East Hartford. More importantly, Ben said that he'd foot the bill for one hour of recording time. Naturally, John agreed, and the following Sunday morning at 7:00 a.m. (recording at off hours was lot cheaper) a sleepy, hung over sound engineer immortalized "It's almost Tomorrow" on tape. The sound guy gave a copy to John and said that he'd get the other copy to Ben.

Most original stuff was drek, but "It's Almost Tomorrow" was good enough that fans had started requesting it.

The Shades went back to Patsy's house because he had the best stereo system, and because Angela made great waffles, and listened to the tape at least a dozen times. They were amazed at how professional they sounded, even though the sound engineer had dismissed it as "just a rough mix."

The next week and a half were endless. John fielded calls from everybody, except Spike, almost daily. They all wanted to know if he'd heard from Ben, even though he had promised to get the word out as soon as he did. Ben finally called two-and one-half weeks after the recording session. He apologized for not calling back sooner, but explained that he'd had one of the audio techs at Channel 3 remix and make additional copies of "It's Almost Tomorrow," and he'd sent them out to some record company executives he knew. He also said that he wanted to make a proposal to John, and only John, and he invited John and his family to meet him at Broadcast Center, Channel 3's Hartford Headquarters. John explained that he'd be accompanied by his older sister, Ruth, and her fiancée, Demetrius.

Ben made it clear at the meeting's outset that he would be negotiating only for John, not for The Shades.

Ruth: *"They're a good group."*

Ben: *"They're a good group, but just being 'good' isn't good enough. There are hundreds of good groups out there right now, trying to be the next Beach Boys or Beatles, and some of them are a lot more serious about the music business than The Shades.*

Ben noticed John shifting uncomfortably.

Ben: *Look, I'm not trying to bring them down, John, but you guys started as a kind of "hobby"; that's not the right word, but you know what I mean. What's going to happen when one of The Shades, or maybe more than one, goes off to college, or joins the Army, or gets married and starts a family, or starts working fulltime?*

John shrugged.

Ben: *Playing in a high school band is a lot of fun. You get to hang out with your friends. The attention you get is amazing. And, if you make good music, that's a real bonus. But every band has an arc, John.*

Ben made a rainbow shape in the air.

Ben: *You go up one side, you level off at the top for a while, and then you start the long slide back down to the bottom. The arc is inevitable.*

Ruth: *You think the Beatles are going to arc?*

Ben: *They will unless they can find a way to keep reinventing themselves, or if they have outstanding 'think outside the box' talent management. And that's why I invited you to come in. I want to be that management for you. I want to be your agent.*

Demetrius: *How exactly does that work? I mean what does an agent do for somebody just starting out?*

Ben: *My first job is to find more material for John to record. We want three or four tunes on a demo tape, and we pick those tunes to showcase John's range. "It's About Time" is a ballad; what we call a "crooner." We'll also need a couple of rockers, and something we call M.O.R.; it means, 'in the middle' not a rocker, but not a ballad either. Think Ricky Nelson's "Travelin' Man." Once we're satisfied that we've got a strong demo, we hawk it to record companies. I already set the stage for that step by sending out the demo you did at The Galley Way.*

Ruth: *So how do they see him? They're not going to come to a high school dance.*

Demetrius: *Hartford Bandstand!*

Ben: *Bingo! Right on the money.*

John: *What do I tell The Shades?*

Ben: *The truth. I'm giving you an opportunity that doesn't come along every day. For most people it never comes along. You'd be crazy not to take this chance. Besides, things don't usually happen all that quickly in this business. You'll continue with The Shades as normal. If lightning doesn't strike, then it'll be like none of this ever happened.*

Ruth: *But I think you should still tell them.*

John: *Yeah, me too.*

Ben: *That tune. 'It's Almost Tomorrow,' Tommy wrote that?*

John: *Yeah. He's written lots.*

Ben: *Maybe I could come to a rehearsal and hear you perform a few.*

John tuned out as the meeting progressed. He was more worried about how the rest would react to these developments than to the legalese about parental consent, commission percentages, copyright restrictions, union membership, venture capitalism, etc. Ruth, who had a sharp mind for business, handled most of these matters. When Demetrius excused himself to visit the men's room, John did the same. Once inside, John asked Demetrius if he thought that he was doing the right thing. Demetrius responded like this.

Demetrius: *You got to reach for the stars while you're young, Johnny. You got something the rest of us haven't got. You can sing. You got talent. You see people on TV all the time who don't sing any better than you. And they live in big, fancy houses, and they drive around in new, flashy cars. That could be you, Johnny. We don't know this Ben from nobody. He's just starting out too. That means he's hungry; he'll work hard, and he sounds like he knows what he's talkin' about. So why not give it a shot? What have you got to lose?*

John: *What if I have to drop out of school?*

Demetrius: *So what. Ruthie got her G.E.D; you could, too. Maybe you'll even show up on graduation day in a red Rolls Royce with a sexy blond in the passenger seat. How cool would that be, huh? Wouldn't you rather have the car and the blond instead of a Fullerton diploma? If you say 'no' to this, you're going to wonder for the rest of your life if you shoulda said 'yes'.*

When John and Demetrius rejoined the meeting, they observed that Ruth had taken copious notes on a legal pad. As John moved behind her to take his seat, he noticed that she had written "get lawyer/Joyce!!" on the top of the page. It was underlined and followed by two exclamation points. The meeting started to wrap up soon after. Demetrius, however, raised one additional, important question.

Demetrius: *Here's something I want to know. Why John? Okay, he can sing, but you must know a lot of people who can sing. It's part of your job. So, why John?*

Ben: *The music business, hell, all of show business, is about finding a hole that can be filled and then filling it. What does the public want? What are they not getting right now from existing talent? What's the hole right now, today, in the music business? We've got groups coming out of our ears. We've got the Brits, we've got the West Coast surf scene, we've got New York doo-wop like The Four Seasons, we've got the Detroit sound, Motown is going to be huge, trust me. But those are groups. What about male solo artists? Well, we've got those too: Frankie Avalon, Dion, Tommy Sands, Fabian, Del Shannon, Neil Sedaka, and on and on.*

Ruth: *You're forgetting Elvis.*

Ben: *No, I'm not. Elvis is the king, but the king has gone corporate. Colonel Tom Parker had him making bad movie after bad movie. They're drive-in theater shlock, and so are his soundtrack albums. Elvis doesn't make records anymore, Elvis makes deals. John's a good looking kid. He presents well. But John also has attitude. I saw that at The Big E. He can curl his upper lip just enough to turn a smile into a sneer and back again. There's a little bit of bad boy in John, and that's what I want to bring out. Attitude, it's all about attitude. Think of the lyrics to 'It's Almost Tomorrow.' What's he singing about? His girlfriend dumped him, right? He knew it was coming, but he didn't want to admit it to himself. She just told him it was over. How does he feel? He's angry, right? He wants to get even somehow, but mostly he's angry with himself. She made him her fool. So, outside of angry, what else does he feel? He feels hurt. She damaged his pride; she made him vulnerable. That's what I saw in you, John. I saw both anger and vulnerability. I saw the sensitive young guy who hides his soft side under a hard shell. Girls are suckers for guys like that. They're sexy. And sex sells. Sex always sells. That's the hole. That's what you're going to fill John. And from now on you're 'Johnny', not John. It gives you more of a little boy vibe. It contrasts more with your attitude. We want to emphasize the two sides of your personality. John keeps you simple; 'Johnny' makes you complex.*

John told The Shades about his meeting with Ben at the next rehearsal. Naturally, they had a hundred questions. The big question for the rest of The Shades, however, was "What about us?" and nobody wanted to be the first to ask that. Spike took charge of both the reaction and of the response. She said that they were all happy for him, that they hoped the career wheels would turn slowly so that he could play many more gigs with them, and that they'd be satisfied to split 50% of whatever he earned. That last remark broke the tension in the room. For his part, John said that it would probably all amount to nothing. But somehow nobody believed that—not even John.

The Star Factory

Hollywood used sometimes to be called a "star factory" for the way it assembly-lined young men and women into celebrities. That metamorphosis required press agents, hairdressers, fashion consultants, vocal coaches, make-up artists, even backstory writers who invented fictional biographies. Errol Flynn, for example, one of Warner Brothers' most popular leading men of the 1930-40's so-called "Hollywood Golden Age," was said to have been born and raised in England. There were even hints that he might have a distant connection to royalty. In actuality, Flynn was born on a coconut plantation in Tasmania. He'd already contracted and been treated for V.D. by the age of seventeen. The point is that Hollywood manufactured stars like Ford manufactured automobiles. The music industry took those lessons seriously and followed suit.

John was the perfect example. He went back to The Galley Way a few weeks later prepared to rerecord "It's About Time" along with one other song by Tommy and two additional songs that they had collaborated on. The Shades were not invited. That was Ben's doing. He wanted to start conditioning John to see himself as a solo artist. He justified replacing The Shades by saying that he had to utilize union musicians for an "official" demo. This was partly true. In any case, John never questioned it. The session itself went well, once John got over his nerves about playing with strangers. He was amazed at their sight-reading skills. The physical arrangement in the studio helped in that respect. All of the musicians and John were separated by distance and by sound "baffles" so that one musician's instrument or voice wouldn't "bleed" in another's mic. That way the recording engineer could control each individual microphone's volume and tone. Ben supervised and paid for the entire process, which took three hours in the studio for numerous "takes" to be recorded, plus additional hours of "mixdown" with Ben and the sound guy alone. John was impressed by how much of an investment Ben was making in him.

Several weeks went by before Ben called again. He wanted John to perform the same songs back in the studio with the same backup musicians for "some friends." When John arrived, Ben led him directly into the studio where the other musicians were setting up. He intentionally steered John away from the control room where several men in jackets and ties were already seated. They all seemed to be smoking cigars.

Soon, Liberty Records came through with what Ben called a "training wheels contract" which heavily favored the record company, and left John with little more than bragging rights.

The session went well; in fact, better than the last time because John wasn't as nervous. He felt more relaxed with the place, the other musicians, and the process. He sounded more confident and self-assured enough to give Ben a little more of the vocal "attitude" Ben had mentioned when they met back at Broadcast Center. When the session ended, Ben, smiling like the cat that ate the canary, guided John into the control room where he was introduced to "suits" from a start-up called Liberty Records. John had never heard of that label, but he tried to look impressed and answered all of their questions as best he could. He wanted to look and sound respectful, but he also wanted tto continue radiating that sense of confidence that he'd just found in the studio. The meeting ended amicably for John who was dismissed. However, it was also obvious that the meeting between Ben and the suits hadn't ended.

Soon, Liberty Records came through with what Ben called a "training wheels contract" which heavily favored the record company, and left John with little more than bragging rights. Ben then brought the deal to John who brought the deal to Ruth who brought the deal to Joyce, and the buck stopped there. Joyce said that John would accept the deal only if the fixed renewable contract was changed to a variable renegotiable contract. The telephone lines among Ben, Joyce, and the Liberty suits soon got a workout. The final compromise brought Johnny Domino, John's new "artist" name, a little more money but a lot more creative control, which, according to Ben, could sometimes be more valuable. And so, John signed on the dotted line. The most immediate results included a whole new Johnny Domino wardrobe and hairstyle. Both clothes and "do" were intended to project his new personality of a wholesome All-American boy in a black leather jacket with a couple of discreet studs. A "mild" D.A. haircut completed the look. Johnny Domino was approachable but he was also a bit "edgy." Ben gave him a list of expressions which he wanted John to work into his vocabulary, and Ruth was a great help when it came to showing John how to sit, stand, and walk "with attitude."

The most immediate results included a whole new Johnny Domino wardrobe and hairstyle. Both clothes and "do" were intended to project his new personality.

John did three appearances on Hartford Bandstand over the next two months. He mimed to songs on the demo tape. Ben paid close attention (when he wasn't farting behind the scenery) to how the crowd, which was largely made up of teenage girls, reacted. One particularly good sign was that they were equally enthusiastic whether John sang a ballad, M.O.R., or rock, with maybe a little more "swoon factor" for the ballad. The contract called for John to start touring with a Liberty Records "package" that consisted of other Liberty performers, a back-up band for the soloists, road managers, a wardrobe person, a hair and make-up person, and a couple of techies. The Liberty Record Hit Caravan would head west with one-night stands in every major city until they reached Chicago, where they'd have a short "residency," aka, a day off. Then they would head south to St. Louis and then east to Miami where another short "residency," was scheduled. They then would head up the east coast until they reached New York where the tour would end. Ben called the tour's itinerary the "eastern loop." The tour would kick off in Boston in two weeks and last for six. John told The Shades who immediately started auditioning replacements.

Ruth planned a "going away" party for the eve of John's departure. Everyone was there to wish him well. Joanne had everyone contribute to a "survival package" which they presented to him with ersatz fanfare. It consisted of a shoebox containing earplugs, eye shades, aspirin, throat spray, deodorant, toothbrush and toothpaste, cologne labeled "frew frew juice," pre-stamped postcards and a pen, a jar of what looked suspiciously like Noxzema labeled "ego cream" with directions to apply it liberally and often, a Johnny Domino Fan Club membership card with a 10% discount coupon on the back for Lenore's Fashions and Intimates, some candy bars, chewing gum, zit crème, etc. Joanne's survival kit was the hit of the party, along with a chocolate cake (Johnny Domino's favorite) and Italian pastries that Patsy's mom and dad had contributed. All in all, it was a bittersweet send off. When the last of the partygoers had started for home, everyone walking except Spike who had driven herself and had picked up Patsy on route, John stood alone in his front yard and watched Tommy and Joanne walking away.

Tommy got home first. John watched from across the street as Tommy let himself in his side door and turned off the porch light. Joanne reached her house a minute later. She turned at her door, looked in his direction, and waved. John waved back. Then she disappeared and her porch light went out. John stood alone for a moment, staring at a streetlight. Then he went around back of the house so that Ruth wouldn't come outside to see that he was crying.

The Virgin Tour

The Liberty Records Hit Caravan tour lasted six weeks, but to John, it felt like six months. They rehearsed the show for two full days in Alston, a seedy Boston suburb. During that time, they were quartered at The Hotel Belmont, mostly because they could make use of the hotel's ballroom which, although it had once hosted proms and cotillions, more recently had settled for barbers' conventions and trade shows. Still, the hotel rooms were clean and comfortable, and there was a "we're all in this together" enthusiasm from the first-time "tour virgins." The veterans of previous "Caravans" just looked resigned. In addition to Johnny, the backing band, and the crew, the remaining talent consisted of Teddy and the Tornados, a five-piece group with a second tier hit called "Your Satellite or Mine"; Tina Petit who sang "(I'm just)The Loneliest Girl in the World"; Davey Keith, who wondered "When Will She Notice Me?"; Alan and The Top Hats (yes, they actually wore them) who boogied suggestively to "You Need to Get It Now"; and at the top of the bill, The Girlfriends, who had a big hit with "My Prince Charming," and an album with the same title. It didn't take long for even a "virgin" like John to figure out whether each solo or group was traveling up Ben's "arc," had plateaued there, or had started down the steep slope to becoming old news. John decided, as Ruth had advised him, to learn what he could by listening and watching and to generally to mind his own business, at least at first.

Ben had given the tour's music director four new songs for John. Two were from Tommy; Ben had worked out a separate royalty-only contract with him. Ben paid the tour's music director separately to write arrangements for the new pieces and to rehearse them with John, with the band, and, finally, with John and the band. Of those four, a rocker called "Shout Now" really stood out. Ben had already pegged it as the "B' side of Johnny Domino's first single.

Tommy and the Tornados were up next. He heard them saying things to each other like, "How are we gonna top that?" as he was coming off stage. They didn't.

They left on a rainy Tuesday morning, headed for their first gig at a performance venue, The Majestic Hall of Music, in Buffalo. They went on at 8:00. The music director, who also acted as MC, introduced Johnny Domino singing his new Liberty hit single "It's Almost Tomorrow," which drew a lukewarm response from a still-arriving crowd, which, at its peak, still only filled about half of the hall. John, who had grown accustomed to singing his hit to rapturous local attention, was disappointed at the tepid reception. As a result, when the band broke into the second song of John's two-tune set, the rocker "Shout Now," John went into full high energy "sneer mode" prancing and posturing around the stage in order to demand the attention which he had missed with the ballad.

The audience couldn't ignore him this time; he wouldn't let them. He finished the tune by rushing directly toward them at full speed, then dropping to his knees and sliding the last few feet to the very edge of the stage. His momentum almost carried him into the first row of fans. In fact, the girls closest put up their hands to protect themselves. However, while he managed to stop in time, the sweat on his brow didn't. That same momentum carried it right onto the first row. Those same teeny boppers squealed with delight, especially when he gave them his full lip curl action from just a few feet away.

Tommy and the Tornados were up next. He heard them saying things to each other like, "How are we gonna top that?" as he was coming off stage. They didn't. In fact, at the closing number, when the whole troupe came out on stage to sing "Til Next Time," Johnny Domino's reception was second only to The Girlfriends.

The Grind

For most performers, the road to making a living is a tedious, laborious grind. Remember what I said earlier about success? I said it took a minimum of three of these four: good training, perseverance, talent, and luck. John couldn't complain too much about his training. Ben saw to that. It makes sense that he would, as John's success would fatten Ben's wallet. As for talent, John had it in spades. Perseverance was a harder nut to crack.

Touring tested John in many ways, some professional and some personal. Relationships were expected. John and his bus mates were young people in close quarters working in a high-stress environment. One thing led to another. The tour, in this respect, was a series of shake-ups, break-ups and make-ups. And then, of course, there were drugs, but the Liberty Suits had hired Billy Meyer as music director because they knew they could count on him to run a "clean" tour—and he did. Sure, there was drinking and "reefer," but only at motel room parties, never on the bus; well, almost never.

The most memorable thing that happened on what John looked back on as his "virgin tour" was a phone call from Ben which came while the tour paused for a rare day off in Miami. Ben told John that he'd gotten a call from Billy Meyers communicating concern from some of the other acts who were griping about the disproportionate (for them) amount of attention Johnny Domino was generating from the audience. Billy said that some of the others felt that John was "stealing the show." Billy told Ben that Ben had to rein John in. However, Ben told John that they were rearranging the performance order, and that John would now go on in the middle of the line-up, so Ben told John to "just keep stealing." And John knew all about stealing.

When John got off the train in Hartford, which he'd boarded in Grand Central, he was exhausted. He wanted Ruth's cooking, he wanted his friends, but he mostly wanted his bed. And he pretty much lived in it for the first two days of his return. When he finally "*rejoined the land of the living*" as Ruth put it, he called his friends. Tommy said that they wanted to get together as a group so he wouldn't have to answer the same questions repeatedly. They met in Patsy's family room three days later. There John described in sordid detail the "glamorous" world of a rising rock star, a world of fast food made the only option by a measly daily "allowance," of oft-interrupted sleep, run-down cheesy motels, furtive groping on a semi-dark bus, catering to pimply teenagers while feigning gratitude and dispensing illegible autographs, etc. Patsy asked John if he had at least enjoyed seeing parts of the country he would otherwise likely never have seen. John responded that, outside of their short stayovers in Chicago and Miami, most of the country passed by the bus windows at night in an endless stream of incandescent, florescent and neon light. *"The music was the only reward."* John said, *"We made good music. And much of the time we were making it for each other instead of the fans."*

John then told some stories about people and events on the tour. He had liked and gotten along with most of the others, but he had kept his distance from those he judged to have "issues," and especially from those *"who thought their shit didn't stink."* One thing that John was particularly proud of was his advancement on the bill, the order in which acts performed. John had started out on the bottom, meaning that he was a "warm-up," an act that would go on first while people were still coming in and jockeying for locations with the best sight lines to the stage. It was next to impossible to engage the audience if you were a warm-up. The only way you could do it was to be over the top, which meant intentionally exaggerating everything about yourself and your performance. Bigger-than-life facial expressions, gestures, and postures were the order of the day. And, in a way, this was good for John, because, when he was moved up during their short stay in Miami, he found that it was easier to turn down the performance "voltage" a little bit. Johnny Domino was still a character, but less a caricature. Also, with growth in respect from the fans had come growth in respect from his stablemates.

"The music was the only reward." John said, "We made good music. And much of the time we were making it for each other instead of the fans."

The Shades brought John up to speed on what had happened at school and in Frenchtown during his six-week absence. It all amounted to *"nothing much."* They had played a couple of dances with a substitute lead singer, Rich Rossi, whom John knew, but not well. The gigs had gone well; their fans were still enthusiastic, but there was a sense that some of their own past enthusiasm had waned. Something had changed. The Fab Four + One had changed, were changing.

Ben called often; John met twice with him in Hartford. He claimed to be very pleased with John's progress. He claimed that the Liberty suits were also very pleased with how well he had adapted to the lifestyle of a dues-paying musician. Ben told him that they were "seasoning" him for bigger things. In fact, the western loop tour would be with mostly "higher tier" acts in larger, fancier performance venues in bigger towns and cities.

The really big news, however, was that Liberty Records was going to "press" promotional copies of Johnny Domino's first single, with "It's Almost Tomorrow" as the "A" side and "Shout Now" as the "B" side. These would be sent to radio stations all over the country for DJs to play and gauge the reaction to. If listeners reacted positively, they would release the single for general distribution. If that went well, the single could lead to an album. John would need more material. Ben suggested that John try to spend as much time as possible with Tommy to hammer out some new songs. Ben said he thought Tommy would agree to that, as Ben had already sent Tommy a couple of token amount royalty checks to grease the skids.

Two weeks at home flew by for John. He spent as much time as he could with the others, singly and as a group, as their schedules allowed. He attended their rehearsals, and he even sat in for a couple of songs with the group at the one gig they played while he was home. He felt jealous of the rapport that had developed between Rich, their new lead, and the others, but he tried not to let it show. He didn't have to; they sensed it. Ruth threw a party, a barbecue, for John and The Shades on the night before he needed to get on a train that would ultimately take him to Dallas where he would join the next tour for another six weeks of the western loop. The barbecue was great fun. Spike had brought along her acoustic guitar to provide some entertainment, and that led to a singalong where they all had to improvise verses to a made-up song. There was a lot more laughing than singing. The evening ended with hugs and handshakes. John felt really sad when the last of his friends drove away; Rich was driving with Joanne in the passenger seat. John was doubly saddened to see Rich reach for Joanne's hand a couple of times during the barbecue and singalong. Joanne discreetly moved out of range, but the implication was pretty clear to John.

On Luck

I mentioned the keys to performance success a while back: good training, talent, perseverance and luck. John had the first three in varying amounts with talent leading the parade. So what about luck? John was a great believer in something Ruth used to say. *"You have to make your own luck. Nothing ventured, nothing gained."*

To describe the tedium of Johnny Domino's slow climb to success would only share that tedium. Instead, jump into Mr. Peabody's "Wayback Machine" with me again, put it in forward, and flash ahead two years. Now, exit the machine. Here's where we are.

John is a tour veteran, and a minor star. His first single debuted on the Billboard charts "with a bullet" and went to number three in a week, where it stalled. His first album, also named "It's Almost Tomorrow' was recorded and rushed into release where it sold only moderately well. Ben, John, and the Liberty suits all felt that John was on the cusp of something big. The fear was that he would remain there, on the cusp. John knew that his future hung in the balance. He knew that another hit single would help, but he wasn't sure if it would be enough. He decided, then, to "make his own luck." And this is how Johnny Domino went from recording artist to superstar.

The Grammys

The 7th Annual Grammy Awards Ceremony was held at The Beverly Hilton Hotel, in Beverly Hills California, on April 13th, 1965. As awards shows go, this one was notable for demonstrating the tug of war still going strong between rock and more traditional pop music. The Beatles, for example, were introduced by Arthur Fiedler of the Boston Pops. Louis Armstrong won for "Hello, Dolly," Petula Clark for "Downtown," and Stan Getz and Astrud Gilberto took the Record of the Year award for their collaboration on "The Girl from Ipanema." Sammy Davis Jr. also presented a moving medley of Nat "King" Cole hits as a tribute to the great singer who had recently died of lung cancer.

I think it's important to understand that the Grammy Awards back then were a rather simple and straightforward awards ceremony. The MC was always a familiar face to the attendees and to the middle-American TV audience. On that night, Steve Allen, known to most through his popular variety show and his occasional forays into jazz piano, hosted. He started the evening's festivities with a stand-up routine that poked fun at the artists up for awards and at the recording industry in general. The rest of the evening then became a routine of celebrity awards presenters who told a few, pre-scripted, lame jokes; read the list of nominees, and then announced the winners. The recipients then gushed their thanks to parents, friends, record companies, agents, and God, usually in that order. To provide variety to what always dissolved into a snore-fest for both the live and TV audience, record companies were permitted to provide artists who were promoting their latest offerings. For Liberty Records, that was Johnny Domino's "the wax is still hot" hit, "My Way or the Highway," which was considered mildly edgy in the sense that the singer is telling his girlfriend that she'll have to acquiesce to his demands or he'll be gone, in other words, "put out or get out." I know this now sounds incredibly misogynistic, but it didn't back then. Liberty Records was hoping that this presumptive hit would set the stage for John's second album. The genesis for what changed that night's ceremony from ho-hum to boffo started that morning when John paid a trip to the Beverly Hills Hospital.

The genesis for what changed that night's ceremony from ho-hum to boffo started that morning when John paid a trip to the Beverly Hills Hospital.

John went to the hospital on the morning of the awards ceremony to visit Billy Meyers who'd had a mild (if there is such a thing) heart attack the previous day. Billy's doctors had decided to keep him under observation for a couple of days while they considered all of the available options, such as additional observation, treatment with heart medication, open heart surgery, or death. John brought a bouquet of flowers which hid an assortment of condoms and a half pint of Cutty Sark Scotch, Billy's favorite. John spent a half-hour with Billy generally catching up and talking about the Grammy's, at which time, a nurse came in to wheel Billy away for "tests." The nurse tipped the scales around 230 and to call her "plain" would have been generous. Billy looked back at John as she wheeled him away and noted that he'd save both of John's "flowers" for another time. Then, as he was pushed through a set of singing doors, Billy wished John luck and said he'd be watching tonight.

John intended to make his way to a set of elevators, but got lost almost immediately. Somehow he ended up in the wrong wing of the building. He saw a sign that indicated a set of stairs, so he walked down one flight and emerged in the Children's Cancer Treatment Center where he first encountered a very pretty five year old. She spoke first, ***"Are you lost?"***

John was both amused and taken aback by this little girl's sagacity. He pretended to be offended by her question, *"Me? Lost? What makes you think that?"*

She crossed her arms and nodded knowingly, *"Okay, follow me. We'll show you how to get out."*

"We?" John asked.

"Yeah, me and Martha. I'm Emily and this is Martha." Martha stood about two feet taller than Emily. Her head was about twice the size of a grapefruit.

Someone creative had stuffed her pillowcase head with rags or cotton to give it shape. Eyes, eyebrows, a nose, and mouth were painted on. Martha had bright red lips framing a wide, beautiful smile, pretty blue eyes, and rosy cheeks. Emily, in contrast, was a beautiful little girl, but quite pale with faint circles under her eyes. Martha's hair was all brown curls topped by a facsimile of a nurse's cap. Emily wore a pale pink frilled cap which matched her nightdress. Starting at Martha's neck, buttons and a seam were also painted vertically down the front of a white sheet which completed her uniform. The sheet stopped just short of the floor, and John could see wheels peeking out from underneath. Someone had even painted a name tag on Martha's uniform. When Emily turned to lead the way, John could see that Emily was tethered to Martha by several semi-transparent, flexible tubes that may have contained liquid. The back of Martha's uniform was open to reveal several devices which sported lights, control knobs, and dials. They produced a faint humming noise that John hadn't noticed before. Wherever Emily went, Martha followed along obediently, as did John.

As the little parade passed a nurse's station, one of the nurses looked up and asked, *"Hey, Emily, who's your new friend?"*

Emily replied, *"I don't know. He got lost. What's your name anyhow, mister?"* Before he could answer, the nurse jumped in with, *"Wait a minute! I know you. I bought your album! Emily, this is Johnny Domino!"*

To which Emily said, *"Who?"* "

Johnny Domino," the nurse exclaimed, *"the singer! He sings that song you like, the one about tomorrow is another day or something. You know the one I mean? You're always singing it!"*

"It's Almost Tomorrow," John said.

"I like that song," said Emily.

"Then sing it for me," John said. Emily was clearly embarrassed, but John had the impression that she was also faking a little. With a little more coaxing from him and the nurse, she gave it a try. She started to mix up the lyrics after the first chorus, so John joined in, and they finished the song as a duet, by which time some patients and staff were standing in the hall. When they applauded politely, Emily hugged John's leg.

"Do you know what the Grammy's are, Emily?" John asked.

Emily shook her head.

"They're special music awards, and they're tonight. I'll be singing that song; you can watch on TV. You'll see me and the Supremes. Why, you'll even see The Beatles."

Emily's eyes grew wide at the mention of her favorite group. *"I love Paul,"* she said, *"He's so cute. Can you get him to write me something?"*

"An autograph?" John said, *"I'll sure try."*

I wish I could go," Emily said.

John looked at the nurse. She met his gaze and shrugged, as if to say *"I could ask."*

John nodded and she picked up the phone and started speaking to someone. John made small talk with Emily about where she lived, how long she had been in the hospital, what she was being treated for, and when she hoped to leave. He found out that she lived in Burbank, that her parents were both teachers, that she was being treated for leukemia, and that there was no set time for her discharge as she was being treated with experimental drugs. When the nurse got off the phone, she said that it might be possible for Emily to visit for an hour or so, but only if her mom signed off on it to absolve the hospital of liability. John said that he'd pay for a private ambulance and for any hospital personnel deemed necessary. He also told the nurse that Ben would greet Emily's party on arrival and usher them to their seats. When John left, Emily was very excited about attending so that she could see her music idol—Paul.

When John left, Emily was very excited about attending so that she could see her music idol—Paul.

The TV coverage of the Grammy's began at 8:00. Unlike present-day awards ceremonies, these Grammys were not preceded by three hours of Red Carpet "can you top this" fashions, which go from outfits which feature enough material to clothe the populations of small villages in Uzbekistan, to scraps of cloth that wouldn't conceal a squirrel's private parts. Press photographers made celebrities run the "Kodak Gauntlet," and a few TV cameras were discreetly placed near the hall's entrance to record some videotape that might be shown on tomorrow's network news. That was about it. No "layer cake" hair-dos, no lingerie being passed off as evening wear, no plastic faces, no silicone boobs and butts, no Botox brows, no "flavor of the month" stars and starlets with the half-lives of toilet paper, in short, no pretenders who were famous only for being famous. Yes, there was plenty of "lift and separate" on display, but the tuxedos were black, the dresses mostly pastel, (although a good portion of the TV audience would still be watching in black and white), and practically all else was left to the imagination. Johnny Domino got a respectable reception from fans in the galleries. It was relatively tame when compared to some of his casino shows in Vegas where women who were old enough to know better would throw their room keys on the stage for Johnny to ignore. He was amused by remembering his reaction to this phenomenon on early tours when he thought they had done this unintentionally. Back then, he collected the keys left onstage after the show and handed them over to management in case their owners returned to reclaim their "accidentally" misplaced property. His bus mates laughed themselves silly over his naivete.

Steve Allen kicked off the proceedings with a rather pedestrian and condescending monolog in which he stated that this was a time in music when, *"It doesn't hurt if you're a Beatle or a chipmunk or something like that. For people it's a little tougher."* Yuk! Yuk! The Beatles got their revenge for Allen's snark by winning Grammys for Best New Artist and Best Performance by a Vocal Group for "A Hard Day's Night." Another Brit, Petula Clark, won the Best Rock and Roll Recording for "Downtown."

Performances during the show's first act included Stan Getz and Astrud Gilberto performing "The Girl from Ipanema," which won Record of the Year, and a moving tribute to Nat "King" Cole in which Sammy Davis Jr. performed some of his most famous songs. Woody Allen's award for Best Comedy Album led off after a break for commercials. Jimmy Durante performed "Hello, Dolly" as a substitute for Louis Armstrong who was indisposed. Jerry Herman, "Dolly's" composer, accepted the Song of the Year award.

In keeping with the show's "traditional music/new music" format, John was scheduled to perform next. The ceremony was beginning to wind down at this point, but some of the biggest awards remained so people hung around. However, anticipating a traffic jam when the show let out, a number of attendees headed for the rest rooms and a few to the lobby bars when John was introduced.

The plan was for John to start off with his signature hit, "It's Almost Tomorrow," and then to segue into his latest offering, "My Way or the Highway." Steve Allen returned to the stage for a little patter and a remark about how he *"liked to put on a Rolling Stones' record so that he could take it off"* which generated polite laughter at best. He then introduced John as a *"Liberty Records' rising young star,"* at which point the orchestra started the opening vamp and Johnny Domino strutted out on stage and took the mic off its stand. This movement drew the immediate attention of Dwayne Herman, the show's director, who was watching in the control room up in back of the auditorium.

"What's he doing?" Herman asked.

In rehearsal, John had performed with the mic on its stand, and the TV cameras were set up accordingly. Now it looked like Johnny was going to walk around, which would disrupt camera placement and require some improvised re-locating. Herman didn't welcome Johnny's surprise this late in the broadcast which had run smoothly so far. A minute ago, he could almost hear the champagne corks popping, but Johnny Domino had changed that.

Johnny took the mic in hand, moved a few steps downstage, looked directly at Wayne LaChance, the orchestra's conductor, and made a slashing motion across his throat for LaChance to cut the music, which he did. Johnny then spoke directly to the attendees and to the TV cameras. He said, *"Good evening. I apologize for interrupting the show. I know that this is a very important night for you (gesturing to the audience) and for the music industry."*

The production crew was in chaos. Cameramen were panicking into their headphones. *"Should I stay on him? Should I pan to the audience? Should I go black or fuzz the image?"*

A few faint boos began, but they turned into gasps when John re-emerged leading Emily by the hand, in her pale pink nightdress and matching frilly cap, with Martha trailing behind.

In the control room, assistants to the director were asking, *"Should we cut away? Should we go to commercial? Should we cut off his mic?"*

Herman tried to remain cool. He said, *"Wait. Let's see where this goes, but cue Steve Allen to stand just out of sight in the wings and give him another mic. He may have to step in."*

John continued, *"But some things are more important in life, and I got a reminder of that today."*

He paused to collect himself. You could hear some members of the audience shifting uncomfortably in their seats. John continued, *"I want you to meet somebody who's going to sing the song with me."*

He strode to the side of the stage and disappeared from view for a second. A few faint boos began, but they turned into gasps when John re-emerged leading Emily by the hand, in her pale pink nightdress and matching frilly cap, with Martha trailing behind. Emily looked terrified; her eyes were wide open and her expression at seeing music royalty spread out before her was a mixture of shock and wonder. Martha's expression didn't change.

John: *This is Emily. Say hello to all these famous people, Emily.*

The best Emily could manage was a little, frightened wave. Tony Bennett, in the front row, next to Connie Francis, waved back, and Diana Ross, seated just a little farther along, said *"Hi Emily."* Emily's mouth fell open at the response, and she started to shelter behind Johnny's leg. John gently drew her out to stand alongside him and knelt down so they could share the microphone.

John: *Tell them where we met this afternoon, Emily.*

Emily: *At the hospital.*

Emily started at hearing her amplified voice for the first time; and looked up at the speakers that were mounted high above her.

John: *Where exactly at the hospital?*

Emily: *In the cancer center.*

Emily's reply stilled the audience.

John: *Are you a patient there, Emily?*

Emily: *Yeah,* she said, *I have leukemia.*

The audience was dead silent.

John: *And who's this next to you?*

Emily: *This is my friend, Martha. She has to come with me wherever I go.*

John: *Oh, why is that Emily?*

Emily looked fondly at Martha,

Emily: *Because she gives me medicine.*

John: *Is that what those tubes are for?*

Emily nodded.

John: *And you need that medicine to get well, isn't that right?*

Emily: *Yeah, cuz it keeps me alive.*

John: *Well, then Martha's the best kind of friend to have isn't she, Emily?*

Emily: *Yeah, I have lots of friends at the hospital now.*

John: *Maybe some of them are watching you right now. Why don't you look right into that camera over there and wave to them.*

Emily did.

The control room had quieted somewhat, but the tension was palpable. An assistant director kept asking, *"Should we cut away? Should we go to commercial?"* to which Herman responded incredulously, *"Cut Away? Are you crazy? This is fucking gold."*

"But General Motors…" the assistant persisted. *"Fuck General Motors,"* this from Herman and two other crew members.

John: *I'll bet some of the doctors and nurses are your friends too.*

Emily: *Yeah, I know lots of them. They're nice.*

Emily abruptly whispered something into his ear. John held the microphone close so the audience could listen in.

Emily: *Are those really The Beatles?* (whispering)

John: *They sure are. That's John, Paul, George, and Ringo right there.*

All four waved and said, *"Hi Emily."*

John: *And that's Paul"*

John whispered as he pointed.

Emily: *He's my favorite.*

John: *Better than me?*

Emily: *Kinda.*

An assistant director kept asking, "Should we cut away? Should we go to commercial?" to which Herman responded incredulously, "Cut Away? Are you crazy? This is fucking gold."

This drew sympathetic laughter. Emily was charming a nation.

John: *By the way, I like your outfit.*

Emily: *My mom made it. She's right back there.*

Emily pointed offstage.

John: *Well, I think it's very nice. I notice that Martha has brown, curly hair sticking out from under her cap, but I don't see your hair sticking out. Why is that, Emily?*

Emily: *Because I don't have any. The medicine took it.*

The audience reaction was audible. Some women began to fumble in their purses for Kleenex.

John: *But it'll come back.*

Emily: *"I hope so, They need to find the right medicine first. Then my hair will grow again, and I can go home.*

John: *What do you miss most about not being at home, Emily?*

Emily: *Riding my bike, and running around and playing with my friends. And my dog, I miss playing with Skipper.*

John: *When you go home, will Martha have to go home with you?*

Emily: *I think so, probably.*

John: *Well, I hope you get well and go home real soon, Emily, and I'll bet that everybody here hopes so too.*

The applause was long and genuine. Emily beamed. John stood and addressed the audience.

> *"The Children's Cancer Treatment Center at Beverly Hills Hospital is doing great work with children like Emily. There are many others like her—too many. If you have the means, it would be nice if you could make a small contribution. Cancer treatment is very expensive. I saw some kids in the ward today who were unable to move around as freely as Emily because they're tethered to IV stands. 'Marthas' are expensive, and there just aren't enough to go around. But you can change that."*

John knelt back down and spoke to Emily. *"Are you ready to sing our song now?* Emily nodded eagerly. The conductor cued the orchestra and Emily and John began to sing "It's Almost Tomorrow."

Yesterday's over
Today's nearly done
It's almost tomorrow
The dawn's nearly come
We'll face it together
We'll smile at the sun
Now and forever
We've only begun
Live each day just as though it's your last
When it ends it becomes part of the past
I'll be there with you
To share in the fun
Day after day together
We'll live them as one
And if you get weary
Too tired to stand
I'll put my arm around you
Or give you my hand
Live each day just as though it's your last
When it ends it becomes part of the past
And if there is sadness
And some days are long

At least we'll know now and always
There's truth in this song
That yesterday's over
Today's nearly done
It's almost tomorrow.
The dawn's nearly come
We'll face it together
We'll smile at the sun
Now and forever
We've only begun

The ovation was overwhelming—a mixture of cheers and tears. And, as for Johnny Domino, well, I don't think I need to tell you how everything changed for him in those few minutes.

THE BALLAD OF JOHNNY AND JOEY: Part 2
A New Fab Four + One

Joey's phone rang at 3:45 a.m. It was Dr. Ming, aka. Ming the Merciless, aka. Uncle Tochiro, calling to tell her that Uncle Maurice thought he had it figured out, and the coffee was on in the lab. Joey dragged herself out of bed, threw some water on her face, shrugged on her bathrobe, slid on her "fuzzy bunny" slippers and headed downstairs to the bike rack. It was a bit chilly, but the lab was only about a five- to six-minute ride. She was just glad she'd taken on the routine of staying "on campus" during the work week instead of being chauffeured back and forth twice a day in a car with blacked-out windows so you couldn't tell where you were even being taken—somewhere in Connecticut's northeast "quiet corner" she'd concluded. Even at this hour, it was difficult to make out the brightest stars because The Campus was always ablaze with light. It always struck her as ironic that a top secret military installation was so blatantly illuminated, and that it was only ever referred to as a campus; "base" would have been more appropriate, "concentration camp" better still, except for the obvious negative connotations. But "concentrate" they did; Task Force Five, that is. In fact, concentration as applied by a quintet of genius-level researchers was their raison d'etre, as Uncle Maurice, a Francophile to the end, would say.

Joey was waved through a checkpoint without even having to slow down. A security team passed her in a jeep doing routine rounds. The driver, Sergeant Morin she thought, gifted her with a wolf whistle. "You'll be lucky," she thought. All of the MPs on the graveyard shift were accustomed to seeing Joey and her fellow "boffins" (their name for her group) coming and going at weird hours and in weird dress. She couldn't remember the last time she wore anything other than slippers on campus—probably last year during her first winter there—outside of her running shoes of course. Running every day had become precious to her. She needed the alone time to decompress and to get her head outside of whatever project was current.

While some teams were assigned research projects by higher-ups, Task Force Five decided on its own projects, because, well, because there were no higher-ups.

Uncle Ming was lead on the team's latest. He had the most knowledge when it came to anything medical, so when the team voted to take on the obstacles preventing a vaccine for malaria, it was only logical that he should step to the fore. Joey had never led the pack; she was still too much a newbie, but she was developing a proposal for the rest. While some teams were assigned research projects by higher-ups, Task Force Five decided on its own projects, because, well, because there were no higher-ups. TFF was completely autonomous.

Joey used her daily running time to plan her first offering. She wanted the team to compute the probability of an asteroid colliding with the moon, to predict the consequences for the human race, and to propose a defensive strategy. The odds for such collisions with earth were well known. There were only two variables: the position and velocity of the Earth in its orbit around the sun, and the velocity and trajectory of the rogue asteroid. However, a collision with the moon added a third, and much more complex variable, the position and velocity of the moon as it rotated around the Earth. The moon's distance to earth varied as well, which made the calculations even more formidable. Would a collision with the moon at apogee cause greater damage to the Earth than if the moon was at perigee, or was the magnitude of catastrophe more determined by the size or speed of the asteroid? And what exactly would the damage be? Was being showered with moon debris the bigger concern or was it the sudden cessation of tides worldwide? This type of mathematical calculation was right in Joey's wheelhouse. In fact, she first came to TFF's attention by solving an incredibly complex mathematical problem, called Plumar's Puzzle, as her high school science fair project.

Robert Plumar, Earl of Shaftesbury, was an eccentric. If you watch British TV, you sometimes get the impression that the UK is overrun with eccentrics, and in some parts of "Old Blighty" you mightn't be that wrong. He was born into great wealth in 1784. He inherited the title and an estate of several hundred acres from his father, William Plumar, who died when Robert was 14 years old. Although there was talk of a regent to help Robert manage the estate, (in particular its finances), the appointment of a regent proved unnecessary as Robert proved himself to be remarkably adept at all things numerical from quite an early age. In fact, a veritable parade of private tutors dubbed Robert a mathematical genius. As he never had to work a day in his life, Robert could, therefore, dedicate himself to his great love: the investigation of mathematical calculation at a level only a very few had achieved before him. He spent hours alone in his study, sometimes not sleeping for days at a time and only rarely eating, in his pursuit from the practical, to the theoretical, to the visionary. No one then living could completely comprehend the breadth and scope of his work. The greatest minds of his generation stared at his writings in wonder, hoping to glean fragments of comprehension.

In order to amuse himself, Robert devised convoluted problems for others to solve. These problems were not complex to Robert in the slightest. But he took a perverse kind of pleasure in watching others struggle to solve puzzles, which he, himself, found ludicrously easy. His greatest achievement was a problem called Plumar's Puzzle which wasn't convincingly solved until 1954. The answer was 1 = 1, but arriving at that answer could take months for some. Others who attempted simply gave up. Only six had solved the problem between 1954 and 1965; seven counting Joey.

Only six had solved Plumar's Puzzle between 1954 and 1965; seven counting Joey.

Joey was invited (i.e. ordered) to interview for a position on TFF when an article from a proud mother (Joyce) about her wunderkind daughter appeared in her *T'ville Press* "About Town" column. *The Springfield Daily News* picked up and printed Joyce's article, and it briefly made Joey something of a local celebrity. Someone in a federal government "clipping service" office saw the Springfield article and passed it up the chain of command. And before you can say $E=mc^2$, Joey was picked up outside her home and transported, in the back of a black sedan with all its rear seat windows blacked out, to what she now called "The Campus."

She met there with the team which consisted of the four men she now referred to as her "uncles." They asked her many questions about how exactly she'd come to solve Plumar's Puzzle, and about what would motivate her to do so in the first place. The man she now knew as Uncle Ward, who spoke with an affected Southern drawl, made the mistake of saying that "it wasn't a typical female teenager pastime." Joey didn't even try to hide her anger at his use of "female" in his statement. Uncle Andrew, an African American gentleman, clearly older than the others, immediately jumped in to reduce the tension by observing that the team's sequestration meant that they had little opportunity to work with women and even less opportunity to get to know teenagers, which was exactly why Joey had been invited to interview to fill a vacancy created when a former member of TFF had passed away unexpectedly. Uncle Ward, ever the Southern gentleman, apologized as well, and then sought to change the subject by asking if they could examine the notebook Joey had been asked to bring, which contained her Plumar's Puzzle proof. The notebook was then passed from hand to hand as the interview continued. Uncle Tochiro was the last to peruse it. When he handed it back to her, he asked about a second notebook she had brought. Joey explained that when she finally arrived at the Plumar's Puzzle solution, 1 = 1, she had decided that it might be interesting to work from the puzzle's answer back to the question. That required an entirely new approach to Plumar's Puzzle. Nobody had ever done that; nobody except Joey, that is.

The man she now knew as Uncle Ward, who spoke with an affected Southern drawl, made the mistake of saying that "it wasn't a typical female teenager pastime." Joey didn't even try to hide her anger at his use of "female" in his statement.

Uncle Maurice and Uncle Tochiro were already in the conference room that morning when Joey arrived. Uncle Maurice's laptop was open, his experiment protocol projected onto a screen. Joey fixed herself a coffee and made small talk with France and Japan while waiting for Chattanooga and Senegal to arrive. Uncle Maurice was clearly excited by his revelation, while Uncle Tochiro scrutinized the equations on the screen skeptically. When the chit-chat trailed off, Joey's mind started to wander. It did that sometimes at 4:00 a.m. "What a strange lot we are," she thought, "an Asian, an African, a Frenchman, and Beauregard T. Cornpone, each with his own quirks and nuances."

Uncle Tochiro was Mr. Details, sometimes to the point of obsession. The comment most directed at him by the others was some variation of "Try to see the bigger picture, Tochiro," but Tochiro's OCD would never let him embrace "the bigger picture" until every nuance of the process that went into displaying the bigger picture was thoroughly explored and addressed. Joey was sure that if she could see into his campus apartment, everything from toiletries to scientific journals would be arranged parallel to the lines on the surfaces on which they rested. His shirts would be color coded and all hung facing in the same direction. He was the Felix Unger of scientific geniuses.

Uncle Maurice was flamboyant. He flaunted his gender preferences openly. He liked nothing better than drawing uncomfortable stares from what he called the "testosterone towers," aka MPs, who guarded the base. Sometimes, when he felt particularly frisky, he'd parade from his apartment to the lab, wearing an elaborate red and yellow boa. He'd sweep into the lab to stares from the others and immediately go into his "Who? Me?" posture. Then he'd look out the window and give little waves to "the boys" below with his boa's tail, all the while muttering self-deprecatingly, *"They want me. They all want me. I haunt their dreams."*

Uncle Andrew was the most contemplative and the most inscrutable. He didn't speak often which gave his sparse remarks gravity where the others were concerned. He was very proud of his children, all three scientists, and his grandchildren, who excelled both in the arts and in athletics. Joey thought of him as particularly private, but she felt a sense of the paternal in him that she didn't feel as strongly from the others. Sometimes, when she just needed a break, she'd go into his office and invite him to play a game of chess on the board he kept there. During those matches, which he usually won, she'd open up to him about her feelings towards the job, the place, the others, and her parents and friends. She felt comfortable discussing such things in his presence, and she liked to think that the insights he shared with her were as close to being mutual as he could get.

Uncle Ward was a large presence in size, speech, and attitude. He was the proverbial "life of the party," but he was also like a party guest who had overstayed his welcome and had also perhaps consumed one too many. He was prone to bluster, which Joey hated, but the others, particularly Uncle Maurice, didn't hesitate to rein him in, insisting that he apologize when he spoke out of turn. Ward did so, but almost always by adopting the pose of a recalcitrant child. Joey sometimes felt that his apology was more about getting caught than about his inappropriate words or behavior. Andrew would usually bring the issue to closure with a remark about "maintaining decorum" and setting a mature example for the youngest member of the team. Ward would then try to smooth things over by saying something about how Joey knew him well enough to know when he was just "spouting off" about this or that. And she did, but that didn't mean she'd ever like it—or him. Still, he was brilliant when it came to "thinking outside the (scientific) box," and the team needed him for just that talent.

The others arrived in due course looking rumpled and disheveled. Uncle Tochiro was the only one of the group who was fastidiously dressed and groomed. During a lull in the conversation, during which Maurice was reassuring Tochiro for the fifth or sixth time that Tochiro's postulates were valid, Joey's mind again gave in to its cerebral wanderlust. How strange for an ersatz high school senior to be deemed so valuable that she should be under 24-hour surveillance on and off campus. How wondrous that she'd soon be talking with her four "Uncles" about altering the DNA sequence of a malarial "host" in order to generate antibodies, which might be the first step in a process to rid the world of a disease that brought misery to millions. Meanwhile, her classmates back in Fullerton were probably changing into gym shorts, or listening to Mr. Philips, the Earth Science teacher, extol the virtues of certain beneficial fungi.

She missed her friends, though; Tommy, Patsy, and John. She missed John most. "I wonder where he is now," she thought. He was probably banging the lights out of some compliant Hollywood starlet with pneumatic breasts. The vision disturbed her, so she erased it, but it was hard to avoid those fan mags and tabloid newspapers that littered beauty salons and dentists' waiting rooms, which often featured him with his babe du jour on their covers. She tried to steer her mind back to the present, but it resisted. At least he still had his twin stick necklaces intact. She'd read somewhere that he'd had them fabricated; two platinum drumsticks, each about two inches long, with a hole drilled through the butt end so that they each could be threaded on its own neck chain. It was the only jewelry he wore, and, according to the source, he'd someday gift one half of the pair to "the one."

The drum sticks were the only jewelry he wore, and, according to the source, he'd someday gift one half of the pair to "the one."

Some time ago, she had an epiphany when she realized that TFF was a more adult version of The Fab Four + One. Still, many would envy her. "It would be nice to feel that, to be envied a little, especially by my snotty peers at Fullerton," she thought, "but how could that happen given the secrecy that now surrounds me, physically and metaphorically?"

Uncle Ward's foghorn leghorn voice wakened her from her reverie. He pronounced Uncle Tochiro's proposal valid but suggested that they "sleep on it" for a month or so to dispel any lingering, or as yet unforeseen, doubts. The others agreed. Malaria had existed without a cure for millennia. It wasn't going anywhere. A one-hour recess was called so that everyone could wake up properly and find something for breakfast besides yesterday's Danish. The sun was just beginning to rise when Joey headed back outside to pedal back to her apartment where she could dress in "daytime clothes." But she decided to retain her fuzzy bunny slippers for the rest of the day. They brought her luck, and she decided that she might need it, because she'd also resolved to put forward her own proposal when they reconvened.

THE BALLAD OF JOHNNY AND JOEY: Part 3
New Digs

Johnny and Joey never attempted to keep in touch when he was away from home. Home for Johnny, by the way, was now on Mockingbird Lane in Somers, a three house cul de sac which the locals dubbed "The Music Mansions." Granted, they were large, expensive homes, but they weren't mansions. As for the "Music" part of the name, however, they were that. Johnny owned one, Neil Sedaka owned another, and Gene Pitney, aka "The Rockville Rocket," owned the third. The three didn't often see each other. In fact, it was rare that all three were in residence at the same time, and, even if they were, they didn't socialize much more than casual greetings or a quick over the fence chat. The three had virtually nothing in common socially or musically.

The size of Johnny's house, although impressive, was a reminder that living alone wasn't all that great. Sure, he had privacy—too much of it, in fact, but there were rooms in his house that were devoid of furniture and wall hangings. He avoided even going into them because they just made him depressed. When Ruth moved out of the rented house in Frenchtown to live with Demetri in Suffield, John had collected all of his worldly goods and transported them to his new home. His entire (material) life, outside of clothes, occupied one small corner of his basement. He found the sight of that little pile depressing, so he didn't go down there unless necessity dictated. The funny/weird thing was that Johnny sometimes actually liked being depressed. Joey had once suggested that, but he had vehemently denied it. But John had to admit that she had a point.

On Fear and Melancholy

Fear is fun; at least it can be when it's intended to entertain. Who doesn't like a good horror movie scare? Those 1950's nuclear-mutated insects, *Them, The Black Scorpion, Tarantula, The Fly,* etc. scared the crap out of us every Saturday afternoon at The Strand. They had to or else we'd feel cheated out of our 30-cent admission. And why else would you tolerate those concession stand ice cream cones that had the texture of wet cardboard and tasted about the same? Then there were the William Castle horror-fests, *The House on Haunted Hill, Macabre* (we didn't know how to pronounce it), *The Old, Dark House, 13 Ghosts,* and who can forget Vincent Price's panicked voice interrupting *The Tingler* to warn us that the malevolent caterpillar was suddenly loose in the theater? *Godzilla, Rodan, Mothra*, and other Asian menaces, were a whole separate category but equally worthy of our frightened attention. Those movies were great fun.

It's interesting that all of those 1950's monsters were non-humanoid. I don't remember exactly when that changed, but it did. Today's monsters are variations of us; Freddy Kreuger and Jason Vorhees, for example. If you watch any of the classic 1930's Universal horror movies, you feel a mixture of repulsion yet sympathy. *Frankenstein, The Wolfman,* and *King Kong* are good examples of creatures that generate that curiously mixed response, *Dracula* less so. But Freddy, Jason, and their clones just don't. We revile them, but they still entertain, sometimes even amuse us. Part of the fun is the predictability. You know immediately that those randy, young teenagers who are sneaking off to a carnal carnival in a storage shed will be the first to be splattered, just as surely as you know that the minute the "heroes" think they've killed Jason good and dead, he'll sit up and resume the carnage.

Fear is fun, whether it's in the form of films like these, the occasional television series, or thrill rides at an amusement park, because we know the threat isn't real, and because we know that it's transitory. What happens immediately after we get a good jump-scare? We laugh. Why? Because we're relieved, but mostly because it was fun.

Genuine fear, on the other hand, doesn't release in laughter. However, it's equally interesting to "fun fear" but in a different way. Bill Cosby, before he started wearing a prison jump suit, once remarked that being truly afraid unmasks us. The facade of control and dignity crumbles, and we show the world who and what we really are: animals caught up in a fight or flight dilemma. Genuine fear is primal. It is positively debilitating. If we escape it, the release is in relief, but certainly not in laughter. It does have one positive effect, however. Genuine fear teaches us about ourselves in a way that fun fear does not.

Melancholy is also fun; at least it is to some people on certain occasions. England's nineteenth-century Romantic poets reveled in it, sometimes feeling most productive when in its throes. I think that we all sometimes induce melancholy in ourselves, because it, like fear, can entertain. Who hasn't imagined the death of a loved one in order to be voluntarily saddened? Or try to deny that you haven't mused on your own unexpected death and how it would affect your families and friends. Sure you have; we all have. The mixture of sadness with pleasure seems oppositional, but it isn't always. Choosing depression as a form of self-expression, self-entertainment even, is just part of the human condition, especially when you know, in the back of your mind, that it's self-imposed, and can, therefore, be dismissed. Genuine depression, like genuine fear, is much more problematical and debilitating. However, genuine depression, like genuine fear, also teaches us about ourselves in a way that "fun" depression, aka melancholy, does not. Church was the perfect setting for me to be melancholic, especially St. Patrick's Church with its funereal atmosphere. I gave into those feelings easily there, especially around the holidays which we usually associate with emotional responses, like Christmas, for instance.

John hated Christmas. I've already explained that, as a child, it was difficult for him to reconcile himself to not having active parents in his life. Yes, they mailed gifts, but only as a formality. And the gifts they sent were almost never age-appropriate, usually being too young for him. It was as though he was frozen in time to them; they sent gifts to whom he was when they last saw him. Even at a young age he could distinguish their gifts from the ones Ruth bought and passed off as having come from them. He couldn't help but be jealous of the Christmases celebrated by his friends' families. He tried to shrug it off, but every place he went, everything he heard, and everything he saw reminded him of what he couldn't have. And there was no escape from that feeling. All the stores were decorated to the hilt and played Christmas carols inside, and a few even set up outdoor speakers. TV was all Christmas themed shows and holiday specials. Christmas greetings hung from lampposts. Banners were strung across streets.

Christmas in Frenchtown

Frenchtown's mostly Italian population saw Christmas as an opportunity to see who could outdo whom else with outdoor decorations that went beyond extravagant to the truly bizarre. The Rinaldi's, for example, mounted a full-size spotlighted replica of Santa's sleigh and its reindeer (including Rudolph) on the roof of their two-story house. Giovanni Rinaldi, the family patriarch, donned a Santa Claus outfit each night starting mid-December and mounted an extension ladder, concealed out of street view, to the roof, where he climbed into the sleigh and sat "ho-ho-ho'ing" to each passerby between the hours of five and eight and usually half freezing to death (the half-pint he brought along helped). Even so, I didn't envy him the hypothermic descent of the extension ladder, but you couldn't fault his religious devotion or his self-aggrandizement, depending on how you saw it. And St. Patrick's? SRO for Christmas Eve and Christmas morning masses.

The Morellos, who lived directly across the street from the Rinaldis, countered with a "living" crèche. Tony Morello constructed a foldable wooden manger with yellow excelsior left over from Easter on the roof and spread around on the ground to represent straw. He wrapped himself in a bed sheet dyed brown to portray Joseph, while Maria, his wife, wore pale blue sheets. Maria, by the way, was pushing about 225, so Frenchtownies referred to her as "Chunky Mary," but never to her face, because that would have been disrespectful to her—and to Mary. Baby Jesus was daughter Antonia's Betsy Wetsy doll wrapped in "swaddling clothes," a.k.a. a white dishcloth, and the Three Wisemen consisted of the twins, Tony Jr. and Vincenzo (Vinny). The third Wiseman was made of sculpted, painted Styrofoam as were two sheep and a donkey, and a monkey—which Patsy's sister contributed. Antonia had painted the names of each character on white cardboard. She set the cardboard labels on the ground and propped them up so that passers-by would have no doubt about whom each family member represented. She also drew arrows pointing upward to each character. She even made signs pointing upward for the sheep and the donkey (and the monkey). The stereo in the living room blasted Christmas carols, and the windows that looked out on the crèche were left open so that music could compliment the devotional atmosphere. The spell broke frequently, however, when passing relatives and friends greeted Tony and Maria by name, and when Tony Jr.'s and Vinny's friends strolled by making snide remarks about the fact that the twins looked like they were wearing dresses.

Tony was a pretty dedicated smoker, two packs of Viceroys a day, so whenever there was a break in the action, he'd duck behind the manger for a cigarette. That led to catastrophe one year when a hastily discarded butt set the excelsior on fire and the manger quickly became an inferno. No one was hurt, but by the time the fire department hosed everything down, the manger was so much charred plywood, the Styrofoam sheep, donkey, third Wiseman (and monkey) were unrecognizable, and Baby Jesus had melted in a black blob. Ironically, more people went out of their way to see what was left after the holy conflagration than had visited before. *The T'ville Press* did a two-page spread which included a photo of the family, in costume, standing in front of the still smoldering ruins: Tony Senior as Joseph, Tony Jr. and Vinny as two of the Wisemen (the third Wiseman was toast), and Chunky Mary cuddling what was left of a charred Betsy "Baby Jesus" Wetsy. That edition of *The Press* was a big seller.

While Frenchtown went all out for Christmas, John, home alone, went all in; no decorations, no Christmas carols, no tree, and obligatory presents only. His neighbors, the Sedakas and the Pitneys, concluded that he was Jewish.

While Frenchtown went all out for Christmas, John, home alone, went all in; no decorations, no Christmas carols, no tree, and obligatory presents only. His neighbors, the Sedakas and the Pitneys, concluded that he was Jewish. All of the others invited him to their homes. Spike invited him to her sister's house where she celebrated with nieces and nephews, but John said no to everyone. To him, Christmas was just another day in the year. He did the same for Thanksgiving, mainly so that he wouldn't offend several by accepting an invitation from one. Thanksgiving, too, was just another day in the year where John was concerned. He even considered checking into a hotel wherever he had performed last on the days leading up to holidays, but he was drawn to home, friends, and general familiarity, although he couldn't explain why—even to himself.

THE BALLAD OF JOHNNY AND JOEY: Part 4

Markers

Sometimes relationships leave markers. Call them metaphorical milestones if you like. What happened between Johnny and Joey left four milestones. This is about the first.

It came about when Joey invited John to join her and her family on Thanksgiving. She fully expected him to say "no" as he had for several consecutive years. Patsy was in basic training at Camp Lejeune, Spike and Tommy had given up trying; I had, too. John didn't disappoint her when he turned down her offer, but he surprised her by accepting her offer to bring over some leftovers on the day after Thanksgiving. She arrived late in the afternoon and popped everything into his oven, which looked like it had never been used. When she went to throw something away, she couldn't help but notice that much of his kitchen trash consisted of TV dinner boxes and crumpled aluminum trays.

Their conversation began with talk about the other Shades. Tommy was in school studying to become a pharmacist. He and Carlene were still a couple. He spent Thanksgiving with her family in Rhode Island, and she spent Christmas with his. Wedding bells were a virtual certainty. Joey had written to Patsy ever since he left for what he called "Marine School." She wrote every week; he replied sporadically. He seemed content with his decision to enlist. Angelo, a Marine veteran himself who had served during the Korean War, had encouraged Patsy's choice, saying that it would "make a man out of him." Spike was Spike. She delivered the mail every day with a smile and a happy thought, and spent most nights in concert with Muddy Waters, Howlin' Wolf, or B.B. King. The Shades were a thing of the past, long ago supplanted by newer groups of teenage musicians searching for their own collective and individual identities.

John was curious about Joey's job, but there really wasn't much that she could share. He knew that she worked as part of a team made up of older men, and that she worked in a high security facility. He also knew that the two men parked in a black sedan across the street were there because Joey was here. When he asked what she did all day, she answered like this:

Joey: *Well, first of all, our workdays are pretty erratic. We make our own schedule depending on the project at the time. Some days are nine-to-fivers, but other times we virtually live in the lab for days at a time, just heading back to our apartments to shower, change, and sleep for a* *couple of hours. It really depends on where we are in the project's progress. What about you? I'm sure your days are much more interesting than mine.*

John: *You might think so. Most people do; the "wild and crazy rock n' roll lifestyle" and all that. Sure, there's some of that, but it's not usually my scene. My publicist or one of the "Liberty suits" usually has something scheduled for me in the late morning or early afternoon, like a TV show or radio interview or press. Radio and press interviews are better because then I avoid dress-up and make-up. I try to visit children's cancer wards in local hospitals once a week, depending on where I am and for how long, but I have to space those visits out because too many can be depressing.*

Joey: *How's Emily, by the way?*

John*:* *I call her when I can. She's home now so I'll try to swing by to see her next month when I'm in L.A.*

Joey: *Well, it's good that she's home.*

John: *Yeah. Maybe. I don't know. Sometimes you get sent home when they know they can't do anything more for you. I'll know more next month.*

Joey: *Couldn't you call the hospital to find out?*

John*:* *Nope, family only.*

Joey nodded, and asked: *What are your afternoons like?*

John: *Rehearsal. We go over rough spots in the show, and we try out new material. If we're doing one-nighters, it's just me, the back-up singers, and the piano player. Sometimes we add bass, drums, and lead guitar. If we're doing 2 or 3 nights in the same place, then we can use the full set-up with lights, sound, and the running crew. Then off to dinner, a quick nap, and 'it's showtime, folks'. After a show, we debrief and then it's back to the hotel for a few hours of sleep, and then we start all over again tomorrow. Pretty glamorous, huh?*

Joey: *When do you have time to date?*

John: *Date?* (laughing)

Joey: *Well, you're on the cover of all these magazines with all of these hot babes.*

John: *My publicist sets up those photo shoots. I usually just show up and go through the motions.*

Joey: *And ...?*

John shifted uncomfortably.

John: *Everybody in "the biz" wants something from somebody, Joey. And the higher up you get, the more they want it from you.*

Joey: *You mean like fame? money?*

John: *Yeah, both of those, but sometimes they just want to be valued.... I don't know how to say it.*

Joey: *You mean validation? They want to be validated.*

John: *Validated, yeah, that's the word. They want to be validated. They want me to validate them, like my opinion is special. They want to make sure that they're really as good as the people around them tell them they are, because they're, like, living in an echo chamber, you know? Sure, your people are going to tell you that you're killing it every night. They have to make you believe that because their jobs depend on you believing that. So, then, who can you trust to tell you the truth? And what if you trust the wrong people, and then it's too late?*

Joey: *Are you talking about them or yourself?*

John: *Both. I need to be validated as much as they do. Who do I turn to?*

Joey: *You trust your friends who aren't in the biz: me, Tommy, Patsy, Ruth, Spike. You trust us.*

John: *But you're not around, Joey, and, besides, what do I do when I'm on the West Coast and you're locked up in some high security lab saving the world from itself? It's not like I can just pick up a phone and say, "Joey, I'm feeling insecure. Validate me."*

They both laughed.

John: *I wouldn't even know how to contact you.*

Joey: *I'll give you the number. Will you actually call it if you're feeling like that?*

John: *Yeah. I would. I will.*

Joey: *Okay. Just don't mix my number up with your bimbos.*

John: *Joey, the women are beautiful, and sexy, and available. The men are handsome, and sexy, and available too, depending on your personal preferences. Listen, you know Freshwater Pond in Thompsonville, how shallow it gets during the summer when it's a heatwave and we haven't had rain for a while?*

Joey nodded.

John: *Remember how you could take your shoes off and walk from one side to* *the other and how the mud would suck you right down if you didn't keep walking?*

Joey: *Yeah, I remember.*

John: *Well, that's what those beautiful women and handsome men are like, Joey. They're shallow, as shallow as that pond in summer, and if you pause with them for too long, then they'll suck you right under.*

John: *Okay, your turn. Are you still seeing Richie?*

Joey: *When I can.*

John: *Don't you guys date?*

Joey: *We try, but my job makes it difficult. My team keeps crazy hours, so it's difficult. Most of our dates are last minute, because I really can't plan ahead.*

John: *That's a royal pain.*

Joey: *Yeah, it is, but Richie's good about it. He understands. The team is trying to find a solution, because we're all starting to feel like we're married to our jobs.*

John: *Can't you just take weekends off?*

Joey: *We'd love to, but sometimes one or more of us will have a breakthrough, and then we have to go in. Our brains don't work regular hours.*

John: *Doesn't help a relationship, though, does it?*

Joey: *Definitely not.*

John: *Aren't you afraid that Richie will start looking around for somebody else? I mean, after all, he's a good- looking guy.*

Joey: *I wouldn't blame him if he did. To tell you the truth, I'm surprised he's put up with it this long.*

John: *We both have crazy jobs, and we both keep crazy hours.*

Joey: *It's ironic when you think about it. You're the rock star, and I'm just a researcher, but my schedule is as bad as yours.*

John: *Take the "just" out of "just a researcher" and substitute "genius" because that's who you are, Joanne Shultz. You wouldn't even have that job if you were anything less.*

Joey: *Stop.*

John: *It's true. I admire the hell out of you.*

Joey: *But you're famous, not just for music, but for your charity work, too.*

John: *For five minutes, Joey. I'm an island in a shallow ocean for five minutes. The stuff you're doing will last a lifetime, maybe several lifetimes. You're the star, Joey, not me.*

Joey stared at her plate for a long time. Her bottom lip quivered a little.

John: *You okay?*

Joey: *That's the nicest thing anyone has said to me for a long time.*

John: *And it's true. Believe it. Now, what's for dessert?*

THE BALLAD OF JOHNNY AND JOEY: Part 5
The Hot Tub Summit

The second milestone in the Johnny-Joey journey began a few weeks later, on December 14th, in a most unusual location: in an outdoor hot tub, on a very cold winter night.

John was reclining naked in his hot tub on the back patio, wreathed in steam, when Joey walked around the side of the house. It was bitter cold, and the ground was rock solid but snow free, so the only issue she had negotiating her way was her own slight inebriation. The hot water pump had just kicked on so the steam from the water made only John's head visible, along with his hand holding a glass filled with a gold-colored liquid and some ice. The bucket and a half-filled bottle of Drambuie sat within arm's reach.

John: *Well, this is a surprise.*

Joey: *Yeah. For me too. I rang the bell, but nobody came. Then I saw the lights on back here. Aren't you freezing? It must be in the teens out here.*

John: *Probably, but I like it like that. I get the tub cranked up, and then I turn it off. As the water cools, the steam settles, and then I can take in those fantastic winter constellations, just like the ceiling at The Strand. Remember?*

Joey: *Yeah, I heard it closed again.*

John: *That's a shame. I'll miss that place.*

Joey: *Buy it. You can afford it.*

John: *Just what I need. Coming home from a date?*

Joey: *Something like that. I need a drink.*

John: *You know where the glasses are. Help yourself.*

Joey: *Always the gentleman.*

John: *Hey, I'll be happy to serve you if you don't mind seeing me bare ass.*

Joey: *You're not wearing a bathing suit at least?*

John: *I wasn't expecting company.*

Joey: *Fair enough.* (Joey entered the house and reemerged with a glass.) *What are you drinking?*

John*: Drambuie.*

Joey*: Good enough. And, by the way, I've already seen your family jewels.*

John*: Where?*

Joey: *That ad for Piping Rock with you in the white briefs didn't hide much. (She mimics) "Piping Rock. After Shave, After Shower, After Anything." Not too suggestive. And don't tell me that photo wasn't touched up to showcase your "attributes."*

John: *Just the opposite, actually. It was toned down.*

Joey: *You're so full of shit.*

John: *My, my. Listen to the princess. Is that the way you talk in the lab to your "uncles?" Hey, have you been drinking?*

Joey: *A little. So what?*

John: *Nothing. You're a big kid. You going to tell me what's going on, or do I have to play "20 Questions?"*

Joey: *Suit yourself.*

John: *Prickly. Prickly. Okay, are you coming home from a date?*

Joey: *Yeah.*

John: *With Richie?*

Joey: *Yeah.*

John: *Did you go to a movie?*

Joey: *No.*

John: *Did you go get something to eat?*

Joey: *No.*

John: *Did you go to the submarine races?*

Joey: *To the what?*

John: *Parking. Did you go somewhere to make out?*

Joey: *Yeah.*

John: *And is that where Richie broke out the bottle?*

Joey: *Yeah.*

John: *Should I stop asking questions now?*

Joey: *Yeah.* She shivers.

John: *I want you to do something.*

Joey: *What?*

John*: Go in the house and get a robe out of the guest room closet, one of the big, white, fluffy ones. Then take off all your clothes, put the robe on, and get into this tub with me.*

Joey: *What?!*

John: *Or you can sit there and shiver until you get sick. Or have your buds out in the driveway take you home.*

Joey: *Is this one of your groupie fantasies you're acting out?*

John: *I'm trying to be nice, Joanne.*

Joey: *Sorry.*

John: *Besides, I've never invited a groupie to get naked.*

Joey: *Because you don't have to.*

John*: No comment. Get naked, get the robe, and get in the tub. I'll close my eyes when you say you're ready.*

He refilled both glasses. She reappeared in a robe.

Joey: *I'm ready.*

John: *My eyes are now closing.*

Joey: *You swear?*

John*: I swear.*

Joey: *And you swear you'll never tell anybody about this.*

John: *Joey, for Christ's sake....*

Joey: *Swear!*

John*: I swear! I swear.*

Joey: *Okay, I'm getting in.*

John: *Tell me if it's too hot or too cold.*

Joey: *Okay, I'm in. You can open your eyes now. And the temperature's just right, but make sure it keeps steaming.*

John: *I have just one thing to say.*

Joey: *What?*

John: *You have a magnificent ass.*

Joey: *You son of a bitch! You swore you wouldn't look! You bastard.*

John: *I'm kidding! I'm kidding.*

Joey: *You better be.*

John: *And great tits too.*

She splashed him. It turned into a brief water fight. When the splashing ended, they both laughed.

Joey: *We broke up.*

John: *You had a fight. It's not the same.*

Joey: *We broke up!*

John: *Okay, okay. Are you angry? Are you sad?*

Joey: *Relieved.*

John: *Really?*

Joey: *It's been coming for a long time. We both knew it. He was just trying to get what he could before time ran out.*

John: *Oh.*

Joey: *Yeah, "Oh." I mean, why does it always have to be about sex?*

John: *Ask Mother Nature. You'll get back together. He'll call.*

Joey: *I won't answer.*

John: *C'mon.*

Joey: *We're done. He was never right for me. I just kept denying it.*

John: *I'm going to turn off the heat for a minute, just so that we can look at the stars.*

Joey started to object.

John: *Just for a minute. There'll still be plenty of steam, but not clouds of it. The whole point of being out here is to see the winter stars.*

Joey: *Just for a minute.*

John: *A minute.*

John turned off the hot water pump, and the steam gradually started to disperse.

Joey: *Wow. It's so clear. They're like diamonds. Where's the moon?*

John: *It rises later. It's better without it because that way you can see more stars.*

Joey: *What's the one with three stars in a row?*

John: *That's Orion's belt, and those dimmer stars right under it are his dagger.*

Joey: *Neat. And what's that really bright star over there?*

John: *That's Jupiter. And that one just to its left is Saturn.*

Joey: *You should be an astronomer. We probably have a few where I work.*

John: *No matter where I am, I can look up at those stars, and they'll be the same.*

Joey: *And you like that?*

John*: Yeah. It makes me feel connected to you guys at home, because you could be looking up and seeing the same thing. So we're not as far apart.*

Joey: *Your world has changed.*

John: *I haven't.*

Joey: *There's nobody special you miss out there when you're here, at home?*

John: *Nobody.* (He jingled his drumstick necklace).

Joey: *I read about that.* (She refilled her glass).

John: *Maybe someday*. (He gestured to her glass). *Easy now.*

Joey: *Yes, Daddy. The water's starting to cool.*

John: *Yeah, it is*. (He turned the hot water pump back on, and the steam gradually returned.)

Joey*: I don't think you'll be alone for long. I'm surprised that you haven't found somebody.*

John: *Not yet.*

Joey: *Are you looking?*

John: *Sometimes I think that it would be nice to come home with somebody, or to somebody.*

Joey: *What would she be like? Beautiful?*

John: *No. Attractive. Maybe even pretty. But not beautiful. You?*

Joey: *The same. Good looking, but not handsome.*

Joey: *Sexy?*

John: *Definitely. But intelligent too.*

Joey: *Sounds about right. What else?*

John: (He thought for a minute.) *Style. She'd have to have her own style.*

Joey: *You must see plenty of that.*

John: *Actually, I don't. I see a lot of fashion, but that's different. All I see is a lot of people with style copying other people with style. You get glamor blind for a while, but then you realize that everybody looks the same, dresses the same, wears the same make-up and perfume. I want someone who makes her own style.*

Joey: *That's an interesting quality in a person.*

John: *Exactly. She has to be interesting.*

Joey: *Interesting.* (They both laughed when they realized what Joey had said.) *Okay, so far we've got good looking, sexy, intelligent, stylish, and interesting. How many is that?*

John: *Five. You're drunk.*

Joey: *So what? I'm sitting in a hot tub with a guy. It's probably 10 degrees out there. We're both naked. And I'm having fun. It doesn't get much more surreal than this. Let's see if we can get to 10.*

John: *That might be a stretch.*

Joey: *Let's try. I say kind, you know, compassionate.*

John: *Yeah. Kind is good. I got one. I can't think of the word. It's like "pathetic."*

Joey: *Sympathetic? Wait, I know what you mean, empathetic. Like you can sense what someone else is feeling.*

John: *Yeah, empathetic. I like that. Your turn.*

Joey: *I got one. A good one.*

John: *Yeah?*

Joey: *Creative.*

John: *Excellent.* (They high fived in the air.) *Okay. So where are we? What are we up to?*

Joey: *Eight? Let's see. Good looking, sexy, intelligent…*

John: *Stylish, interesting…*

Joey: *Kind.*

John: *Creative.*

Joey: *You missed one.*

John: *Yeah, I know. I'm pulling a blank.*

Joey: *Empathetic.*

John: *Right. Empathetic. Two to go.*

Joey: *What else are you looking for?*

John: *A good friend. A buddy. A best friend.*

Joey: *You mean somebody you can just hang out with, without any of those other things getting in the way?*

(They thought for a long time. John turned off the hot water and they both looked skyward as the steam subsided.)

Joey: *What about love? We haven't mentioned love.*

John: *You know, I thought of it, but I'd rather have a good friend.*

Joey: *Really?*

John: *There's something you get from a really good friend that you might not get from a lover.*

Joey: *What?*

John: *It's hard to explain. You can tell a good friend anything and not be embarrassed. I mean even the most personal thing. Like, you could tell your best friend if you were afraid, or lonely, or sad, or depressed and not feel self-conscious about revealing those things. A good friend doesn't judge.*

Joey: *You're talking about intimacy. Like exposing yourself, emotionally I mean, without shame.*

John: *That's it, I think. Intimacy. Personal intimacy. I'll settle for that over sex anytime.*

Joey: *Isn't that part of love?*

John: *I suppose it could be, but I don't think it has to be.*

Joey: *What if you could have both?*

John: *Then half this necklace comes off.*

John and Joey headed up to bed shortly thereafter. She made him promise to keep his eyes closed again as she stepped out of the tub and into her robe.

He reopened his eyes after he heard her go through the slider. He turned off the heat and waited a few minutes for the water to start cooling. He had a lot to think about. Something had happened, but he wasn't sure what. When he entered the house, he called Joyce to assure her that Joey was sound asleep in his guest room. She was grateful for the call, and she didn't sound surprised by the breakup.

As his last act before bed, John put on slippers and hurried down his front path to the idling black sedan at the base of his driveway. When the window rolled down, he explained that Joey had had a little too much to drink and was spending the night in his guest room. They mumbled a few words of thanks, said that they'd be staying where they were, and rolled the window back up. John went back inside, fished around in a kitchen drawer and pulled out a spare key to give Joey the next morning. His neighbors, the Sedakas and the Pitneys, both had private security services which sent cars by frequently, and he didn't want her to get arrested for breaking and entering if she was spotted sneaking around to the back of his house. He knew that was unlikely to happen, but so was her visit tonight. Anyway, he decided that somebody he could trust should have one. And that was Joey.

The last thought that went through his mind as he was drifting off to sleep was a question: "Why were those guys in the car wearing dark glasses?" He decided to ask Joey about it tomorrow morning, but he'd forgotten by then.

THE BALLAD OF JOHNNY AND JOEY: Part 6 Hooray for Hollywood

The third milestone started off somewhat contentious. It occurred one week after the hot tub summit when Joey called Ben, still Johnny's agent, and asked him to get a message to John that she'd used his loaned house key to let herself into his house in order to leave him a holiday surprise. John got the message along with a slew of others which demanded more immediate attention at the time. He registered it for a moment, but it was gone in the next.

It was Thursday, Dec 22, and John was just returning from a location photo shoot on and around the glorious beaches of Southern California. It might be all freeze and frost in the Northeast, but it was still fun in the sun in the Southwest, where Ben has secured John a strong supporting role in a "teen flick" tentatively titled *Beach Blanket Blowout*. It was slated for release the following summer. John was opposed to the idea for a number of reasons, but Ben eventually convinced him by arguing that it was great exposure, that his presence was only required for a couple of weeks, and that it was quick, easy money. More importantly, it would introduce Johnny Domino to the "Hollywood Movie Factory" community, which might lead to bigger, even more lucrative roles down the road. Elvis had crossed over, so why couldn't he?

Although the film starred Hollywood's perpetual teenagers, Frankie Avalon and Annette Funicello, Ben had made certain that Johnny would be featured singing, which meant lip-synching, two songs off his latest album, said album to be included prominently in the movie's promotional package. John hoped that the movie-making experience would be exciting, but it turned out to be mostly boring, as there were long breaks in between "set-ups," where cameras, microphones, and lights were repositioned or relocated. He played cards with the extras, read, answered some fan mail, and napped a lot. The cast and crew were pleasant enough, and clearly accustomed to the slow pace that was gradually driving John crazy. It was typical of the way things were done in La La Land.

Frankie was a nice guy, perhaps a bit taken with himself. Although he and John were only five or six years apart, he seemed older. That was partly due to his music, which was no longer "timely" in the always changing pop world. It was also due to his family, three kids with a fourth on the way, and his prematurely graying hair. He claimed that this was genetic, and he may have been telling the truth. In any case, his hair received a frequent color rinse, and his chest hairs were also touched up. The make-up crew wanted to pluck the offenders, but Frankie said it hurt too much. Now you know why he's the only guy in the movie who always wears a windbreaker for close-up shots on the beach.

Annette was very nice. John liked to ask her questions about her Mickey Mouse Club days. It turns out that the show's host was a letch and grandfather figure was a rummy. John found Annette attractive, except for her liberal use of depilatory cream which smelled pretty awful when she first applied it. She and Frankie were well matched in hairiness. She had a boyfriend who didn't seem to mind, but what really kept John at a distance was that she was so incredibly Catholic, "probably a true Sister Kerosina disciple where sex was concerned," John concluded.

John played Frankie's best friend, a surfer-type named Hot Dog. He was matched with a British import, named Beverly Andrews who played an English import nicknamed Wipe Out. The name was ironic because Bev couldn't swim much less surf, but she was wholesome-sexy and had a great accent. She also had "come to bed" eyes. She and John quickly became an item on the set and off. The fan mags picked up on this almost immediately and started paying big money for photos of the two which immediately became cover fodder. *Hollywood Today Magazine* became particularly aggressive. It claimed to have "love spies" amongst the cast and crew who reported on every nuance of the "Johnny-Bevy" intercontinental romance. A photo of the two heading into John's on-set trailer was gold. The truth was that the couple wasn't going inside to "burn rubber," as was implied. They just wanted to stop having to keep on the lookout for camera lenses. Johnny's fan club, by the way, started to receive hate mail about the fact that he wasn't dating an "all-American" girl.

John liked Bev a lot. Their backgrounds, even though they grew up three thousand miles apart, were remarkably similar; small town for him, small village for her; he raised by his sister, she raised by her aunt and uncle; discovered performing with local band for him, discovered after winning a local talent competition for her; etc. She had a ribald sense of humor, which he found both disarming and provocative. He promised a combination of naivte and smoldering sexuality which she found irresistible. They made a good pair, in bed anyhow, where they spent a lot of their time together. The Hollywood press heard distant wedding bells. One photo of the couple caused a sensation. In it, Johnny was shown wearing only one drumstick necklace. The second had been airbrushed out in a darkroom and had been crudely superimposed to appear as though hanging around Bevy's neck. The photo was an obvious fake, and was soon debunked, to the delight of legions of Johnny Domino fans, mostly but not exclusively female, who could still hold out hope for themselves. Still, expectations for the real thing ran high. There was something, though, something about Bev that kept John from going all in, "all in" for him being defined as committing on the level of personal intimacy that he and Joey had discussed in their hot tub summit. He couldn't put his finger on his reservation, but it was there.

One photo of the couple caused a sensation. In it, Johnny was shown wearing only one drumstick necklace.

The subject of Joanne's "holiday surprise" didn't even occur to John again until he pulled his Hertzmobile into his driveway. The Sedakas and the Pitneys had gone in heavily for outdoor Christmas décor, with the Sedakas mostly favoring traditional red and green, while the Pitney's went for the less conventional, but equally striking, white and blue. What really caught

John's eye, however, were the white electric candles in each of his own home's windows. He got out of the car, retrieved his suitcases from the trunk, and walked up the path to his front door, still somewhat bewildered. The lanterns on either side of his front door, although curtained, glowed with light from within. When he unlocked the door and stepped in, he saw why.

His foyer and living room were a festival of white mini-lights. They were everywhere, on the bookcases in his living room, on his dining room table and hutch, on his kitchen counter and cabinets, on his bar, and on the staircase leading upstairs to the bedrooms. They hadn't been applied randomly but had been artfully arranged. And he could see the all the lights were plugged into timers. A scattering of red and green Christmas tree ornaments added color to the festive atmosphere. John immediately called Joanne's work number. When the switchboard operator told him that Joey was temporarily unavailable, he chose to leave her a message stating that she could retrieve her lights at any time, and that, if he wasn't home, she could let herself in. They'd be waiting for her in a cardboard box on his living room floor.

His foyer and living room were a festival of white mini-lights. They were everywhere ...

On Communication

I've heard it said that good marriages require genuine communication between partners. I think that's true, but communication can be complicated. On the surface, it seems simple enough. One person sends; the other receives, but sometimes the message is distorted by intent. If the sender is in one place, emotionally or experientially, and the receiver is in another, then intent can be misperceived by the receiver, and then the message is misinterpreted.

A woman arrives home from a beauty salon. She asks her husband, "How do you like my new hairdo?" He says, "Yes, it suits you. It's a nice change. I'm surprised that you decided on a traditional style." She says nothing. What resonated was the last thing he said.

Was it his intent to suggest that her taste was out of fashion? Maybe.

Did he intend to needle her about her appearance, perhaps because she sometimes criticized his choice in clothes? Perhaps. In other words, was his intent to be critical or was his remark just an off the cuff half-distracted observation?

And what about her? What if she picked that particular style thinking that it would give her a more youthful, more contemporary appearance but then realized she'd erred when she looked in the mirror at the finished product?

In short, she had disappointed herself. Her new hairstyle was yesterday's news, but she now had to live with it for a while. So, his remark, unwittingly, confirmed her opinion. He unknowingly rubbed salt into her wound. So, who's at fault here? The sender or the receiver? Neither? Both?

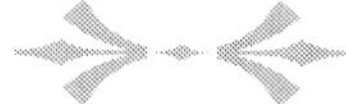

Did Joey overreach? Or did John overreact? Neither? Both? Bueller? Bueller?

Hooray for Hollywood (continued)

Joanne was angry when she first got John's message. It had taken no small effort on her part to find time away from the lab to decorate his house. Her first impulse was to drive over and reclaim the lights while saying nothing to him. She also considered calling and telling him to leave the box on his front porch where she could pick it up without even setting foot in his house again, and that she'd put his house key in an envelope and leave it in his mailbox.

She then transitioned from anger to sympathy. She knew that John was wounded where family was concerned, and that he'd always struggled around the holidays. Although her intent was to help him re-engage with the season, perhaps she'd done just the opposite. On the other hand, he was a completely changed personality now, so why should he resist a friend helping him to find a newer, happier direction? Or was it that, at bottom, he hadn't changed all that much, maybe not at all. Maybe he didn't want to be happy. Maybe he preferred "Woe is me."

Should she be angry at him? Or was she masking embarrassment with anger? Was she really angry because of his rejection to her overture, which was his right? So, should she be angry at herself? Should she feel sorry for him? Should she try to empathize more with his circumstances?

She called Ruth. Ruth summed him up succinctly.

Ruth: *He's being a shithead, Joey. He's always a shithead at Christmas. You know that.*

Joey: *I know it's a tough time of year for him. I guess I thought maybe he'd changed.*

Ruth: *He has changed, Joey, but not about this, not about Christmas. Not yet anyhow. He won't come here over on Christmas Eve, or on Christmas Day. He just says he'll drop some presents off before New Year's. And Patsy's having a big Russo Christmas Carnival at his place the day before Christmas Eve. Everybody's going to be there. You got an invitation, right?*

Joey: *Yeah, I go every year. It wouldn't miss those Christmas cannolis his mother makes for anything. But John's never there.*

Ruth: *And he won't be this year either. I already asked him.*

Joey: *Do you think I made it worse?*

Ruth: *You didn't. Don't beat yourself up. I've tried to talk to him. Demetri tried to talk to him. I even asked Tommy to call him. Nothing. He just mopes around feeling sorry for himself until the holidays are over, and then he comes out of it, like it's a spell or something, you know?*

Joey: *It's just such an awful time of year to spend alone and be depressed.*

Ruth: *For us, yeah; for him, I don't know. I used to think that maybe he liked it because it made everybody feel sorry for him.*

Joey: *He liked the attention you mean.*

Ruth: *Yeah, I think he used to, but it's different now. He's isolated himself. And that's his choice, so he can live with it. Some people like to feel bad sometimes. Maybe he needs to see a shrink. He can afford it. I'll bet you half the people he works with now probably have their own personal shrink couches, especially those movie people. Johnny and Bevy. That whole Hollywood thing makes me sick. Don't get me started. She's a no-talent Brit bitch who's only interested in making him make her look good.*

Joey: *Wow. I had no idea you didn't like her. Have you even met her?*

Ruth: *He offered to bring her home on one of his trips. I told him that I wouldn't even open the door for her. I hate her. And I hate him for not seeing her for what she really is.*

Joey: *So, listen, about this Christmas thing, you think it's best for me just to back off?*

Ruth: *I do, yep. Eventually John's going to realize who his real friends are. You can't force that. It has to come from him.*

Joey: *Do you think it will?*

Ruth: *I don't know, Joey. I hope so. Go get your lights. Call Brad and find out when he's not going to be home. I know he's visiting kids in local hospitals while he's here. Go over and get your lights and leave your key. Then it's his move. Let him spoil Christmas for himself if he wants, not for you.*

Joanne eventually decided that Ruth was right. It wasn't her place to fight John's battles. That was for him to do, if he even wanted to. She called Ben and told him only what he needed to know to find out about John's schedule; then she went over to retrieve the box of lights.

However, rather than put his key in an envelope and leave it in his mailbox, she decided to write him a note, and to leave it, along with the key, on his kitchen counter where John couldn't miss it. The note read:

> *As you can see, I picked up my lights. Here's your key. I see no reason to hold onto it. I left one electric window candle in the large window over your front door. It's on a timer. You used to say that you got homesick when you were away for too long. Do you still feel that way? Or is your home somewhere else now? If this is still home to you, then that light in the window will signify that a little of you is always here, even when you're there, wherever 'there' is. And here's something else about that light. It also signifies friendship. Are we still your friends? Or are your friends somewhere else now, too? Or do you just need the one friend now? If we are, then let the light stand for the friendship you still share with me, and Tommy, and Patsy, and Spike. We only want what's best for you, John, and we think you still want the same for us. I hope so anyway. If I'm wrong about any of this, then unplug that last light and throw it away.*
>
> *I'm not going to apologize for what I did. I know it was tough for you. We all do. We always did. But life is very different for you now. You've changed. We've all changed.*
>
> *We used to feel sorry for you that we could spend Christmas with our moms and dads and you couldn't, because your family was different; it was just you and Ruth. But we all have other families now. I have my uncles, Tommy has Carlene and her crew, Patsy has his soldier friends,*

(He's home now, on leave. Got back yesterday. Did you know?), so "family" means something else now, something different, something bigger than when we were growing up.

I read somewhere that the only constant in the world is change. It's true, John. Let the past go. Do it for Ruth. Do it for us. More importantly, do it for yourself. Change.

—Joey

THE BALLAD OF JOHNNY AND JOEY: Part 7 Patsy's Party

The Russo Christmas Party had become something of a holiday tradition in Frenchtown, especially since The Strand Christmas Party was now only a memory. The Chez Russo's bash had also become quite extravagant after Angelo punched the golden ticket where classic autos were concerned. The grounds and the house, inside and out, were a virtual explosion of Christmas décor courtesy of a professional party company, Edward's Events, out of Hartford.

Joanne arrived at 8:15, later than most, because she had been wrapping up loose ends at the lab. As a result, she had to park on the side of the street a good distance from party central. The night was calm and cold, but not frigidly so; in the mid 40s she guessed. The closer she came, the brighter the lights, the louder the Christmas music, and the more people she saw. The place was packed, inside and out. She had brought Christmas cookies—after all, you couldn't arrive empty handed—along with a bag of wrapped gifts for Tommy, Spike, and, of course, the man of the hour, Patsy, whom she caught sight of immediately. He was fresh from boot camp and resplendent in his dress uniform. He was encircled by well-wishers and didn't see her at first, so she decided on trying to catch "the belle of the ball" later, when things might quiet down a little. She greeted Angelo and Carmella, left her cookies on a table already piled high with enough of the same to last several Christmases into the future.

She then picked up a glass of Asti and headed out onto the patio with her bags of gifts, where she ran into Tommy and Carlene. Both were taking classes at the University of Connecticut. Tommy was enrolled in a program that would eventually lead to his becoming a pharmacist, (he was hoping for a job with one of the national chains, like Rexall, for instance), while Carlene was working toward elementary school teacher certification. The cost of Tommy's education was supplemented by royalties he'd earned from some of the songs he had written and was still writing (when time permitted) for John. As Joanne stood there talking to them about this and that, she was thinking, "My God, look at you two holding hands. You look like you just stepped off the top of a wedding cake. All that's needed is a bridal gown for her and a tuxedo for him. You are the perfect couple. You are living salt and pepper shakers, a perfectly matched, mutually complemented pair. How lucky you are to have found each other." Naturally, her thoughts also turned to her own single scientist status, where she was surrounded by old men and uniformed military testosterone. What were her chances of ever being as lucky as Tommy and Carlene? She had brought a gift for Tommy, but the envelope which held it was marked, "Merry Christmas to Tommy and Carlene," because they were one entity to the world now. Joanne was happy that Tommy was happy, but in him gaining Carlene, she couldn't help by feel that she'd lost half of Tommy, and that saddened her. The envelope, by the way, contained a gift certificate for a two-night stay at the Jug End Barn and Inn in South Egremont, Mass., the perfect romantic weekend. His gift to her was a watch with a stopwatch function that she could use to time her daily reservation runs.

Naturally, her thoughts also turned to her own single scientist status, where she was surrounded by old men and uniformed military testosterone. What were her chances of ever being as lucky as Tommy and Carlene?

They had just exchanged gifts when Spike strolled over to join them. She was accompanied by Ray, new to the postal service and assigned to the Enfield branch. Although Spike had long been welcomed in the Russo household, (she and Angelo had even drained a few together at The Ringside), Ray was a Frenchtown virgin, truly a stranger in a strange land on this notable night. Joanne, Tommy, Carlene, Joanne, (and Spike, of course), did their best to make him feel comfortable in surroundings where half the guests spoke in Italian, and old timers, who had once probably had mob connections, sat well apart, making the "evil eye" sign to each other by drawing crosses on table tops and dragging their thumbs across their throats to simulate slitting.

Meanwhile, Uncle Leo, who really wasn't anyone's uncle at all, tried to teach the tarantella to teenage girls so that he could watch their dresses fly up when they twirled. Joanne had brought Spike a bottle of Jack Daniels in a Christmas-themed ceramic container which featured graphics of "A Tennessee Christmas." Spike said she knew just the right records to sip it to. She presented Joanne with several eight tracks which featured some of Spike's favorites performing their most well-known hits. She told Joanne that the tapes were "music to experiment by." Spike told Ray that she'd explain to him what she meant later on, probably after the decanter had been uncorked. Joanne had the distinct impression that this wasn't their first date and probably wouldn't be their last.

She was happy for both couples: Tommy and Carlene, and Spike and Ray. Her own status left her feeling more bittersweet.

She was happy for both couples: Tommy and Carlene, and Spike and Ray. Her own status left her feeling more bittersweet.

She asked if anyone knew if Patsy had come up for air yet, and Ray said that he'd seen him talking to someone out on the patio. At that, Joanne excused herself, wished both couples a Merry Christmas (with hugs for Tommy and Spike), and went off in search of Patsy. She found him sitting on a lawn chair just out of range of the patio lights. He was sharing a beer with John.

Joanne tried to hide her surprise at seeing John but knew she hadn't succeeded when Patsy stood to greet her and said, *"Check this out! The Ghost of Christmas Past has decided to make an appearance."* She gave Patsy a big hug; she gave John a cursory one. Joanne couldn't get over the change in Patsy. It wasn't just the uniform or the missing Medusa hair either. He stood differently; his posture erect. He had presence. He radiated confidence. Everything about him was so much more mature, so much more authoritative. Joanne could hardly believe that this was the same person who once amused them (her, and John, and Tommy) with the fart noises he made on his trombone. John broke the spell by inviting her to sit with them and offered to get her something. She asked for another glass of white wine, and he went off to get one.

Joanne: *Well, look at you. I can hardly believe it. You look so different from the last time I saw you.*

Patsy: *Yeah, the Marines will do that.*

Joanne: *Are you okay? I mean I didn't know what to think when you stopped writing.*

Patsy: *Yeah, sorry about that. I'm good, Joey. And thanks for the letters.*

I might not be very good at writing them, but I always look forward to getting them. Please don't stop. They make me feel connected to this world. Sometimes I need that, you know?

Joanne: *I won't. And don't worry about writing back. I know they keep you busy. So, what's next for you?*

Patsy: *A few weeks of Advanced Infantry Training. Then I'll have to decide if I want to become a specialist in some field, which will mean a few more months, and then I'll probably be deployed.*

Joanne: *Vietnam?*

Patsy: *Possibly, but I might also be assigned to another base stateside. It depends on my specialty.*

Joanne: *I hope so. Pick a specialty that doesn't involve shooting at people.*

Patsy: *Maybe. So, how are you? Still seeing Richie?*

Joanne: *No, we broke up.*

Patsy: *I'm sorry.*

Joanne: *Don't be. He wasn't for me. I keep busy with my job. There isn't much time for dating anyway.*

Patsy: *John told me about the super-secret stuff you do. Not that he knows much. Not that anybody knows much. I told him that I think you guys probably caught a UFO, and that you're trying to figure out how to talk to aliens.*

They both laughed.

Joanne: *Nothing that interesting, I'm afraid.*

Patsy: *So, what do you think of our hometown superstar?*

Joanne: *I don't know, Patsy. Sometimes I think he's got everything he wants but not what he really needs.*

Patsy: *Which is?*

Joanne: *I don't know that either. But I think there's something missing for him. And I think he knows that, too.*

John: *He'll figure it out. He's just going through his usual holiday mood. He'll snap out of it.*

Joanne: *Yeah, you're probably right.*

Patsy: *He told me about the lights.*

Joanne: *He did?*

Patsy: *Yeah.*

Joanne: *It's my fault. I just overdid it.*

Patsy: *I told him he was an asshole.*

Joanne: *Really?*

Patsy: *No, not really. I told him he was a first class, "A" Number one, leader of the pack with oak leaf clusters asshole.*

They both laughed.

Joanne: *Did you really say that?*

Patsy: *I said it, and I meant it. You don't treat somebody like that who's just trying to help. That's complete bullshit.*

Joanne: *Thanks.*

Patsy: *Someday the penny's going to drop for him, Joey. I hope for his sake that you're still around when it does. You were always the best of us, Joey. Always. You still are.*

He took her hand then, and she was both surprised and very moved by his words and his gesture. She only had a moment to wonder where the old Patsy had gone, and who this was now sitting next to her, when John returned with her glass of wine and two more bottles of beer for himself and Patsy.

They made small talk for a while, mostly about how much change had taken place and how quickly it all seemed to have happened. Angelo came out a few minutes later to get Patsy. He said that some of the older people were getting ready to leave, and they wanted to say goodbye to Patsy before he had to report back. Patsy excused himself and headed inside where the old men who had been giving each other the evil eye just minutes ago were now locked in tearful embraces with each other, apologizing and swearing enduring friendship, while their wives, each one wearing black and sporting huge matching handbags, just rolled their eyes. And no-one's Uncle Leo, the tarantella lecher, dozed on the couch, visions of nubile sugarplums dancing in his head.

Meanwhile, the atmosphere back on the patio bench was frostier than the late December night.

John: *I don't know what to say.*

Joanne rose and started to leave.

Joanne: *I'll make it easier for you.*

John: *Can't we just talk? We used to just talk.*

Joanne sat down.

Joanne: *The floor is yours.*

John: *I won't apologize.*

Joanne: *I'm not asking you to.*

John: *I can't change this.*

Joanne**:** *Change what?*

John: *About Christmas. The way I feel.*

Joanne: *You can't or you won't?*

John: *Can't. I'm happy to be what I am?*

Joanne: *Then whence cometh Johnny Domino, your alter ego?*

John: *That was Ben's idea.*

Joanne: *And how much did you resist? And why perpetuate another personality? You're famous now. You don't have to.*

John: *I'm happy to be who I am, Joey.*

Joanne: *I envy you then. I truly do. I know some people are like that. Comfortable in their own skins. Content. I envy them, too. That's not me. And, if that's you, why did you ever leave Frenchtown in the first place? Why didn't you stay content here, like Tommy or Spike?*

John: *Sometimes I ask myself that.*

Joanne: *Then again, if you'd stayed in Frenchtown, you would never have met "Bevy."*

John: *Please.*

Joanne: *When you pay one of your hospital visits at Christmas, how does it make you feel when you see the wards all decorated with Christmas lights? And trees. Do they have trees?*

John: *Yeah, at the nurses' stations.*

Joanne: *And when you see those trees all lit up, and the kids—their faces, when you hand them a wrapped present. Don't you share in their joy? They don't even care what you give them, whether it's candy or your new album. They don't care what it is. What counts to them is that it's a present, and it came from you, a stranger. And it's Christmas. You must take joy in the giving.*

John: *I do.*

Joanne: *Then take joy in the receiving.*

John: *I can't change this, Joey. I can't change me.*

Joanne: *I don't believe you. You can't change because you don't want to change. Maybe you're afraid to change. Is that it? Are you afraid? Of what? Why choose melancholy? Here.*

She reached into her bag and extracted a wrapped present.

John: *I didn't get...*

Joanne: *Why break tradition?*

John: *What is it?*

Joanne: *Open it.*

He carefully unwrapped it. It was a photograph of The Shades; Tommy, Spike, Patsy, and Joanne. They were arranged, some seated, some standing, around a loveseat in Patsy's family room. The photo was obviously quite recent as Patsy was in uniform. Across the bottom of the card was printed "Merry Christmas."

Joanne: *Turn it over.*

He did, and on the reverse was a personal greeting from each. Each greeting reflected its writer's individual personality, some sentimental, some humorous, some profane (Patsy), but all combining to say ***"We love you. We miss you. Share yourself with us."***

John was stunned. He opened his mouth to speak several times, but no sound came out. He knew what he wanted to say, but he was embarrassed that his voice would crack in the saying of it. Finally, he spoke.

John: *But how did you? When did you?*

Joanne: *It wasn't easy, but everybody wanted to do it, all of your friends. And there's a photo lab at The Campus where I work. It cost me a few six packs. It wasn't hard, John. Bringing joy isn't hard, but you have to want to do it.*

John stared at the photo for a long time, flipping it from the front to the back and then to the front again. Finally, he leaned back and looked up at the sky.

John: *I kept the light you left in the window.*

Joanne: *You did? The vigil light?*

John: *The what?*

Joanne: *It's called a vigil light because it holds a vigil for you until you return.*

John: *Yeah, I liked what you said about me thinking about that light when I'm far away, that A little of me is still there, home. That something, isn't it? That has to count for something.*

Joanne*: It's a start.*

John: *Yeah. See.*

Joanne: *But that's not about Christmas.*

John: *Oh.*

Joanne: *It's not enough.*

John: *It's the best I can do.*

Joanne: *Nope.*

John: *It's the best I can do right now.*

Joanne: *I want something that says "Christmas."*

John: *Like what?*

Joanne: *A concession.*

John: *A what?*

Joanne: *A concession. I want a concession. A Christmas concession.*

She stared at him as he began to understand.

John: *Oh no. No, no, no, no, no.*

Joanne*: Oh yes. It can be artificial or real.*

John: *No.*

Joanne: *Small enough to sit on a table.*

John: *No.*

Joanne: *An end table.*

John: *No.*

Joanne: *One of those awful ceramic things that light up and bubble when you plug them in.*

John: *No.*

Joanne: *A bush.*

John: *No.*

Joanne: *A shrub.*

John: *No.*

Joanne: *A poinsettia.*

John: *You're not going to let this go, are you?*

Joanne: *Never. Because this matters to me. Because you matter to me. It's Christmas, John. The whole world is happy at Christmas. The whole world wants you be happy. Your whole world wants you to be happy: Ruth and Dimitri and Tommy and Carlene, and Spike and her mailman boyfriend, and Patsy and all those kids you love and who love you, and me, John, I want you to be happy. We all want you to be happy. Let us in, please?*

John: *I don't know, Joey.*

Joanne: *Try. Please.*

John stared up at the stars for a long time.

John: *Do you think that the fire department has any trees left?*

Joanne: *I'll bet they do.*

John: *Just a little one.*

Joanne: *Just a little one. I'll bring just one string of lights, just one. And a half dozen ornaments.*

He started to object.

Joanne: *Okay, four, one string of lights and four ornaments. That's it. That's all I'll bring.*

John: *I'll try it.*

Joanne: *That's all I ask.*

John: *Okay, I'll try it.*

They said their goodbyes shortly after. There were hugs and best wishes all around. The most heartfelt were the ones directed to Patsy who would be heading off to resume his military career early in January.

THE BALLAD OF JOHNNY AND JOEY: Part 8
The Morning After the Night Before

Joanne picked John up late the next morning. John started to freak out when he saw that she was driving her father's old station wagon, but Joanne reassured him that this wasn't about accommodating a large tree. Instead, it was the most practical vehicle at hand, and would prevent pine needles from collecting all over the back seat of her Volvo or his Hertzmobile. Joanne's posse followed close behind in their own blacked-out sedan.

Joanne then asked John if he had bought anything for Ruth and Dimitri. The look on his face when she asked the question provided the answer.

Pickings at the Enfield Fire Department were pretty lean, but they finally managed to find a small, nicely proportioned tree that had gone unnoticed because a much taller, rather misshapen tree had been leaned against a chain link fence in front of it. They had to stop at a hardware store to buy a tree stand. Joanne then asked John if he had bought anything for Ruth and Dimitri. The look on his face when she asked the question provided the answer.

So, they made another stop at the Enfield Mall. John had been in malls before, but never when they were all decked out for Christmas. It was a dull, gray day, so little natural light came through the mall's ceiling skylights. Instead, most illumination was from the Christmas decorations and the stores' display lighting. Costumed carolers sang seasonal songs in the central plaza, while a line of children, hand-in-hand with their moms, waited impatiently to make last minute Christmas present demands to a mall Santa; an elf collected two dollars admission for each audience with the old fraud. The youngest kids, wide-eyed devout believers, were always the cutest. (The same is true at Halloween.) Shoppers hurried about or milled around with arms full of presents, some wrapped at the mall's "wrapping station," and others carrying gifts which they'd wrap themselves at home. John noticed a cluster of embarrassed-looking men standing around an "Intimate Apparels" counter near the entrance to Filene's while shop girls behind the counters wrapped their purchases. John wondered if the wrappers were amused by their customers' obvious discomfort.

John and Joanne wandered in and out of a good many stores, before John, with Joanne's help, finally settled on a really nice, expensive new dinner set to replace the old, mismatched set that Ruth had brought from the rented house. They had lunch in the mall while the dinner set was wrapped by Santa's helpers, and then they drove over to leave the gift with Ruth and Dimitri. Ruth nearly fainted when she answered the doorbell to find John standing there with a large wrapped Christmas gift in his arms. She started to tear up almost immediately. Then she invited them in to see her and Dimitri's tree and to share a cup of Christmas punch-which delivered just that. She said that it was Dimitri's grandfather's recipe, and that the principal ingredient was ouzo, a potent Greek liqueur. Dimitri joined them shortly thereafter, his father's store closing early on Christmas Eve Day, and he proposed several traditional Christmas toasts.

Instead of earthquakes and tidal waves, they sat around, quietly killing a bottle of wine while watching Jimmy Stewart and Donna Reed wait for an angel to earn its wings in *It's a Wonderful Life.*

John and Joanne left an hour later by which time they were both feeling decidedly buzzed. They picked up some take-out Chinese on the way home for dinner, and ate it sitting on the floor at the base of the lit, sparsely decorated tree.

Now, you're probably expecting me to tell you that, after a dinner of pork low mien, shrimp tempura and vegetable spring rolls, the two retreated upstairs to the bedroom where our lovebirds declared their true feelings for each other, pledged their undying fidelity, and made passionate love which culminated in seemingly endless mutual earthquakes. Nope. No earthquakes, mutual or otherwise. Nope. Didn't happen. Sorry. Or, maybe you're thinking that they never made it upstairs to the bedroom at all, but instead ravished each other right there on the carpet, quickly and ferociously, their wild thrusting accompanied by groans of pleasure and screams of ecstasy until they were lifted and carried on tidal waves of pleasure. Right? Nope. No tidal waves. No lifting. That didn't happen either. Sorry, again.

Instead of earthquakes and tidal waves, they sat around, quietly killing a bottle of wine while watching Jimmy Stewart and Donna Reed wait for an angel to earn its wings in *It's a Wonderful Life.* Then they picked up and cleaned up, and Joanne put on her coat. John said thanks at the door, and they hugged. As Joanne started to leave, John said, *"I owe you."*

Joanne hesitated for a moment about halfway to her dad's wagon. Her "posse" was parked just behind it. She looked back over her shoulder at John, now framed in the doorway, with the lit Christmas tree behind him and the vigil light in the second-floor window directly above, and said, *"Yes. You do. And I won't forget."*

Then she smiled and walked to the car. Although it certainly didn't sound ominous, John knew for sure that Joanne would eventually call in that marker.

He watched as the station wagon and its omnipresent escort turned off Mockingbird Lane onto Battle Street and then disappeared. He felt lonely. He'd felt lonely before, but now he felt somehow lonelier than before. He stood there staring up at the winter stars for a long time.

Christmas Orphans

When John finally stepped back into the warmth and closed his front door, the tree was there waiting for him. It was too early to go upstairs to bed, and he didn't particularly feel like watching TV. Besides, Christmas Eve programming didn't offer much in the way of program variety unless the Mormon Tabernacle Choir was your thing. It wasn't John's thing. So, instead, he just sat and stared at the tree. He might have dozed off, he might have remained wide awake, or he might have entered that fugue-like state that awaits somewhere in between.

Were it not for him, that tree would still be crushed against a chain link fence by a much larger, rather misshapen brother, but it had a pleasing shape and decent proportions. Why had it been hidden from view? Was it a coincidence? Serendipity? Bad luck? A case of conscious or unconscious misjudgment on the part of some anonymous vendor? An act of intentional cruelty on the part of a tree truck unloader? Or had someone hidden it there purposely in order to return to purchase it later?

John liked that explanation best. He could envision someone walking by the Christmas tree display, thinking, "That's a nice tree, but I just spent my last twenty on a present for Susan. I know! I'll hurry home, drop off my packages, grab some more cash, and rush back to buy it." He then hid the tree out of sight so that no one else would come along and buy it out from under him. But he didn't come back. Something came up, or maybe another tree of equal attraction caught his eye first. So, there it sat, hidden from view, overlooked, until John and Joey rescued it. But what of the trees that weren't rescued? Were they still sitting, forlorn, in that lot? "They must be," John thought. "That's sad." Here these trees have given up their lives for a holiday meaningless to them, and they didn't even make it inside, out of the cold. Nobody will enhance them with decoration, no one will prolong their gradually diminishing life force with a plastic watering can, and no children will be delighted by the presents nestled beneath them.

"Did trees know? Were trees sentient?" John wondered about this. Other living things were sentient, so why couldn't plants be sentient, too? When you sawed a limb off a tree, it bled. Its blood was clear of course. "But isn't sap basically tree blood?" John wondered about this as well. Where did you draw the line between sentience and lack of sentience with living things? A whale was certainly sentient, but what about a clam or a scallop? Were scallops sentient? Does an oyster feel pain when it's shucked? And does a tree scream, in its own "tree way" when it's cut down by an axe, or a saw, or a chainsaw?

John didn't know the answer to any of these questions. The one thing he did know, however, was that he was glad that he had brought this one tree, the one now before him, in from the cold.

John didn't know the answer to any of these questions. The one thing he did know, however, was that he was glad that he had brought this one tree, the one now before him, in from the cold. And he felt badly about the others, so many others, that had been passed over, and who now had only each other for company, their future prospects reduced to a landfill, or a shredder, or both.

John's musings about whether or not orphan Christmas trees were sentient led him to speculation about dogs. He knew dogs were sentient. But how rudimentary were dogs' emotions? He knew they could express joy. He knew they could show fear. Could they mourn? There was plenty of anecdotal evidence to say that they did. But were they mourning the absence of someone in particular or of just a caretaker? And he'd read somewhere that dogs don't really possess long-term memory, and that's why they sometimes binge on food. They don't know if they'll be fed again, and that joy they demonstrate when you return from an errand is not a demonstration of affection for you on your return, but a show of relief that their source of food and water has returned. John had thought of owning a dog, but he dismissed the idea because it wouldn't be fair to the dog to spend most of its life in a doggie daycare kennel. Then again, do dogs sense fairness, or was he just projecting his guilt on the dog?

His thoughts then turned to dogs in pet stores. They were always fun to look at, and they always tugged at your heart strings, begging to be liberated from those tiered cages. And they were so incredibly cute! As a child, John had always thought that, if only he'd had enough money, he'd buy them all and bring them home. But the sobering reality was that those tiered cages would just be refilled in a day or two with more winsome Weimaraners et al. He'd seen some pet store dogs while with Joey at the Enfield Mall. Their cages were decorated on the outsides with Christmas wrap and ribbons. Each cage also had a little sign that said, "Take me home for Christmas," or "Give the gift of love this Christmas," or "I'm a Christmas gift the kids will never forget."

John's eyes had been drawn to one cage in the lower left-hand corner. A dog huddled there toward the back of its cage. It had drawn its blankie up around itself. John wondered if that blankie was for protection, comfort, or both. He thought that it was probably a mixed breed, what Ruth would call a "Heinz 57," and it looked older than most of the other dogs displayed, most of which were in varying stages of puppyhood. Unlike those other more exuberant, more enthusiastic candidates for adoption, which frolicked and yipped at every passerby, this one dog just stared out of the saddest brown eyes John could ever remember seeing. He wondered now about that brown-eyed dog. Did it know Christmas? How many of its brethren had it seen delivered into open, welcoming arms? More importantly, John wondered if it was awake right now, alone in a silent, deserted mall, with Christmas piped-in music playing to no one. Was it awake, and, if it was, was it lonely? And, if it was asleep, was it dreaming about being delivered into open, welcoming arms, too, someday? Or was its future a landfill too?

The grandfather clock in John's foyer chimed three o'clock. Surely he hadn't been awake all that time. He concluded that he must have fallen asleep upright in his living room chair. He got up, grabbed his jacket and keys and headed across his kitchen to the door that opened into his garage. He backed down the driveway into the street, and then he paused and got out of the car. The stars were incredibly bright and crystalline. Orion was low in the West, pursued there by Canis Major, The Great Dog. There was no Santa, no Rudolph, no moon. Just stars. He returned to the car and started driving to nowhere in particular. He let the car and his subconscious set the route. What he saw along the way was more important than a destination anyway, so he let the Hertzmobile decide. Traffic was almost nonexistent at this late hour. He wondered about the few cars which passed. A Christmas Eve party that ran late? Early morning Christmas present deliveries? Relatives travelling overnight to spend Christmas Day with family?

What interested him even more, however, was houses lit from within, especially ones where the curtains were drawn back to showcase living room trees. But why were those other lights on in the living room? The dining room? The kitchen? Was someone up late still wrapping presents? Were children trying to stay awake to greet Santa with milk and chocolate chip cookies? Maybe insomniacs lived there. And what was he, John, doing awake driving around aimlessly on Christmas morning? At times he felt like he was almost spying on people in those homes. At other times, he felt jealous of them.

And here he was on the real night before Christmas, parked on an empty road in an idling car, wanting to communicate somehow with someone else, a friend, someone he cared about, and someone who cared about him. But, of course, he didn't.

Eventually, he found himself in Frenchtown. He couldn't recall how he got there or why he came there, but there he was. There was the house where he grew up with Ruth. He pictured his old bedroom with its uneven floor and draughty window. There was Tommy's house. It was in darkness. And there was the Russo house, Patsy's house, or what used to be Patsy's house before Angelo punched the golden ticket. John wondered who lived there now, and who now rented or maybe owned his and Ruth's old house.

He stopped the car in front of Joey's house. He had the sudden urge to lean on the horn or maybe just gun the engine loudly enough to wake her so that he could see her bedroom curtain move a bit. Maybe even catch a glimpse of her face peeking out to see "what was the matter"—he suddenly remembered that line from "'Twas the Night Before Christmas." He used to like having Ruth read that story to him. He never got tired of listening to it. And here he was on the real night before Christmas, parked on an empty road in an idling car, wanting to communicate somehow with someone else, a friend, someone he cared about, and someone who cared about him. But, of course, he didn't. Joey had issued that invitation a few hours ago, a few days ago, weeks ago, months ago, even years ago. Now wasn't the time or the place. He drove on.

Eventually, he started to leave Frenchtown; the way out took him by The Mill. The long, "loom building" ran for block after block. It was dark now and silent; its silence, in fact, much more notable than its darkness, but just before he reached the end of the building, just before he emerged from Frenchtown, he spied a light. He slowed to investigate. It was a lone, bare bulb. Someone had left it on in a nondescript mill workshop, maybe accidentally, maybe on purpose. John would never know. And did it even matter? Probably not. What mattered is that it shone. It kept vigil in that empty space, and it illuminated a small, bare tree sitting on a workbench, a tree without lights or ornaments, probably artificial, but a Christmas tree nevertheless. The vigil light shone down on it, dispelling some of the shadows in that room, empty now of all except the ghosts who haunted there, empty for just this one, rare silent night. John pulled away then. He turned left out of Frenchtown onto North Main Street and started home. As he did so, he passed a dog, probably a stray, trotting down the center of the road, a dog that seemed bent on some destination, or maybe just hurrying to some warm place where it would find welcome, and love, and shelter from the pre-dawn cold and from the loneliness of self-imposed isolation. John didn't know which. And did it even matter? Probably not. Maybe to the dog.

THE BALLAD OF JOHNNY AND JOEY: Part 9 Susie's Dare

Joey called in her marker just short of a year later. During the interim, she had continued her work with her four uncles. Her proposal had been accepted but had to be put on the back burner. The government had dictated that a more urgent problem involving an infectious disease would take precedent. This caused Joey to consult with technicians whose job it was to test proposals under laboratory conditions that grew out of research done by Joey's team. In other words, Joey and her uncles generated ideas for treatment and cures, and the lab crew devised experiments to test their hypotheses. Joey acted as a liaison between the two teams. She enjoyed the opportunities to interact with people closer to her own age in different surroundings than her usual duties afforded. She and Susie, one of the lab techs, sometimes ran together on the base, and they even tried to meet once a week to "blow off steam" over beers in the local pub, often along with Paul and Lucie, the other two techs.

One night in particular, in mid-November, Susie, Joey's running partner, brought up the subject of the upcoming Christmas party, which was held in the base country club. Joey had attended the previous year. "Attended" isn't really the right word; "put in an appearance" would be more accurate. She went stag, as did Uncle Maurice, while her other uncles, Ming, Ward, and Andrew, escorted their wives. Paul and Lucie went as a couple. Susie's boyfriend was part of the base's security detail. He was one of only a few soldiers present at the party, as there existed a tacit understanding with the on-base military contingent that this occasion was mostly for non-military personnel who worked on the base. The uniformed population held its own, more raucous gathering at the Pub Hub, a popular base watering hole. The party, which Joey had attended stag, started out as a pleasant diversion. The buffet was excellent, the liquor flowed, a band played, and people danced (Joey danced with each uncle). Still, Joey's solo status had made her feel increasingly conspicuous as the evening wore on, so she left quite early and headed back to her apartment.

Joey told Susie that, in regard to the upcoming party, she wouldn't attend again without an escort. Susie immediately offered to have her MP boyfriend fix Joey up. Joey declined Susie's offer. What happened next grew out of the fact that Joey was one beer over her usual limit, and that Susie could sometimes be annoying about lording it over Joey when the opportunity arose. Joey had been on the receiving end of remarks from Susie that had convinced Joey, over time, that Susie was actually rather jealous of Joey's elevated status as compared to her own. Technically, Joey was Susie's superior, although Joey had always treated her like an equal. Nevertheless, on occasions when Susie had a question in the lab about some "request" from Joey that Susie was required to implement, that acted as a constant reminder to Susie that she was clearly the subordinate. And on occasions like that, Susie sometimes loosed the green-eyed dragon. This was one of those occasions.

Susie casually remarked that Joey should make a greater effort to attract male company, lest she turn into "an old maid lab rat" before her time. That hit a nerve with Joey; her hackles went up. She commented that the reason she was unescorted the last time was that her boyfriend was filming a movie on the West Coast. Joey could tell from the look on Susie's face that she'd counterpunched effectively. Naturally, Susie asked whom Joey was talking about. When Joey told her, Susie was left speechless. That was when the devil had his moment with Joey, who casually announced that Johnny Domino had promised to be her escort for this year's Christmas party. If you've ever instantly regretted something you've said, you'll know exactly how Joey felt at that moment. However, putting Susie on the defensive made Joey feel that her seemingly casual remark was worth it. Naturally, Susie fired a battery of questions, and, also naturally, Joey was more than happy to embellish. "In for a penny...," she thought. When Joey awoke the next morning, somewhat hung over, it was to acknowledge that she'd led Susie to believe that she and Johnny were much more than casual friends. She also had to acknowledge that Susie had dared her to prove it, and that she, Joey, had accepted the dare.

The Christmas Tour

Christmas parties were the last things on John's mind heading into this same holiday season. Ben had been pushing the Liberty suits to put together a European tour (three performances in each of two different locations in England, France, and Germany) along with print and radio interviews and guest shots on network television programs. The entourage was to leave two days after Thanksgiving, and was scheduled to return on Thursday, December 21st. Neither John nor the other solo artists and groups were enthusiastic about the timing; they'd all have to do Christmas shopping before Thanksgiving but the opportunity to see how Europeans celebrated Christmas appealed, along with the fact that few of them had ever been abroad. The Liberty suits bought into Ben's idea when it had first been floated back in July. Their strategy was to time the European release of the troupe's singles and albums for the tour, thereby guaranteeing brisk sales as Christmas gifts.

Their strategy was to time the European release of the troupe's singles and albums for the tour, thereby guaranteeing brisk sales as Christmas gifts.

On the personal front, Johnny and "Bevy the Brit" were ancient history. John had moved on, closely followed by his fans, and by the media which fed their appetite for more Johnny Do-Mania, which was fueled by an advertising campaign for a male fragrance company which Johnny was paid handsomely to endorse. The fragrance, sold as both after shave and cologne, was called Afterglow, a not-too-subtle reference to post-coital satisfaction. Its black and white print advertising featured models in diaphanous negligees reclining on beds which showed rumpled sheets and two pillows, one vacant but with the clear impression of the recent occupant's head. Johnny was featured in only one print ad, but it was a lulu. The black and white photo was taken by a fashion photographer stationed on a second floor balcony of a Las Vegas hotel where John was playing at the time. John was lying alone on a pool chaise, resting after rehearsal and before dinner. His eyes were closed. He wore only a brief white swimsuit. The suit was just tight enough to be slightly revealing. The slanted rays of the late afternoon sun, through a trick of light, created elongated shadows, and, as it happened, created the impression that one of John's "assets" was rather impressively elongated as well. It was hard to tell, however, where reality ended and the impression of reality began. In any case, the print ad was a sensation. Afterglow's manufacturer received so many requests for copies of the ad, that they rushed a poster size version of the ad into print and distribution. It quickly became the male equivalent of the *One Million B.C.* poster that started out as a promotional photo for a very forgettable movie. If Raquel Welch's poster was required wall décor in teenage boys' rooms, Johnny Domino's poster was de rigueur for teenage girls' rooms. There was a famous ad campaign at the time for Memorex audio tape which touted the fidelity of sound recordings by asking, "Is it Real, or is it Memorex?" It wasn't long before this question was frequently asked of John's image on the poster. Young women whom Johnny had dated were quick to enhance their own reputations by enhancing his. Meanwhile, Afterglow sold by the gallon.

There was a famous ad campaign at the time for Memorex audio tape which touted the fidelity of sound recordings by asking, "Is it Real, or is it Memorex?" It wasn't long before this question was frequently asked of John's image on the poster.

The truth is that, while he kept company with a string of attractive singers and movie stars, he never stuck with any one for long. Most recently, he'd been keeping company with a red-headed beauty named Scarlett Rhymes, or, to his fans, Scarlett the Starlett. She was one of a growing number of beautiful young women in the entertainment industry whose greatest talent seemed to be in the field of self-promotion. She couldn't sing, and her roles in movies were decidedly as "B" characters, but she knew how to make herself look beautiful and desirable, and, for fan mags, that was often enough. Those less kind described her as "vapid."

John had released two singles in the past year, both off his latest album, "Second to None." The first single was the album's title song, which Tommy had written, and the second single, "All Over Again," opened the album's B side. Both singles placed in Billboard's top five for several weeks, but the fact that they were both taken from the same album made the album Billboard's Number One for six weeks, a first for Johnny Domino.

As proud as he was of that musical accomplishment, however, it paled in his mind when compared to the visibility he'd brought to Children's Cancer Centers in hospitals across the country. When he appeared at this year's

Grammys, back in February, he was surprised to be greeted onstage by Emily, this time without Martha, and the ovation was thunderous. She presented him with the American Society of Composers, Authors, and Publishers (ASCAP) annual Humanitarian Award, which touched him deeply.

John and Joanne saw each other every time he came home; in other words, about every six weeks. Their meetings were never treated as dates by either. Instead, they were opportunities for two friends to have dinner, sometimes see a movie, hang out together for a few hours, and generally catch up. No earthquakes. No tidal waves. Just two old friends, who had seen each other's warts, enjoying their time with each other. Nothing else. Nothing more. That is, until John's last visit home before his holiday European tour.

Just two old friends, who had seen each other's warts, enjoying their time with each other. Nothing else. Nothing more. That is, until John's last visit home before his holiday European tour.

It was Thanksgiving night. Joanne had spent it with her parents; John had gone to Ruth's. John had invited Joanne over to his place for leftovers, but neither was hungry, so they snacked on popcorn and pizza rolls and talked. Much of the discussion centered on John's upcoming holiday tour. Joanne was curious about whether John would celebrate Christmas this year or just use his late return as an excuse to return to his previous Scrooge mode. He surprised her by saying that he would like to participate, as long as it stayed "low key." She asked him if he wanted her to buy a tree for him before his return. He said that he would very much appreciate it if she did, and that he also hoped that she would help him set it up and decorate it as she had last year. She agreed as long as he would concede to two light strings and a few—just a few—additional ornaments. He conceded. She then saw her opportunity and took it.

Joanne: *I have a favor I'd like to ask.*

John: *What kind of favor?*

Joanne: *It's about the annual Christmas party at the base. I was wondering if you would be my date.*

John: *Your date?*

Joanne: *Yeah, my date, my escort, just for this one night. I went stag last year, and I stood out like a sore thumb. I want to go, but I don't want to* *go alone. I thought I could ask you. It's just for the research and lab personnel, so there won't be many people.*

John: *Isn't there anybody else you could ask? When is it?*

Joanne: *The day after you get back from the tour, Friday.*

John: *Joey, I hate those things.*

Joanne: *I knew you'd say that, but you owe me Domain or Domino or Mr. Scarlett Rhymes in the parlor with a meat cleaver, or whatever you're calling yourself these days.*

John: *You said that you didn't like standing out like a sore thumb last time. So now you want me to stand out instead?*

Joanne: *You wouldn't. There'll only be a few young people. Most of the people there are older, like my uncles. They won't know the difference between Johnny Domino and Vic Damone. It's just for a couple of hours. I'll help you do Christmas shopping?*

John: *I'm planning to pick up a few things while I'm travelling and bring them home with me.*

Joanne: *Oh.*

John: *Yeah, okay. But just this once. All bets are paid, right?*

Joanne: *Well....*

John: *What do you mean "well?" Well, what?*

Joanne: *There's just one more, little thing. You see there's this girl, a lab tech I work with. Her name is Susie, and....*

Joanne then told John the whole story, about Susie's jealousy, about how angry Susie's "old maid" remark had made her, about the night in the pub when she, Joey, had had one too many, and about how the words had just come tumbling out of her mouth before she could stop herself saying them. John listened in silence.

John: *That might complicate things for me. See, I've been thinking of asking someone to partner-up with me, and I was planning to do it when the tour ended, like for Christmas.*

Joanne: *Oh, wow. You mean you're getting engaged?*

John: *Hardly. I was thinking more like going steady, but that's not right either. Besides that sounds so corny, so 50's. You know?*

Joanne: *So more like engaged to become engaged?*

John: *No, that's too strong.*

Joanne: *So, maybe you mean more like exclusive. Exclusive to each other.*

John: *Yeah. That's better. Exclusive. Yeah, I like that. If she'll even go for it.*

Joanne: *Are you kidding? Every teenager in America will hate her.*

They both laughed.

Joanne: *I don't suppose you're willing to divulge....*

John: *What?*

Joanne: *Her identity, stupid. Who is it? And you'd better not say Bevy if you ever want me to speak to you again.*

John: *I don't want to say anything else until I know she'll accept. Otherwise, I'll just end up feeling embarrassed.*

Joanne: *And looking embarrassed. I mean, it's bound to get out.*

John: *That too.*

Joanne: *Meanwhile, your fans will celebrate a second Christmas if she says "no."*

John: *Maybe.*

Joanne: *Is it Scarlett the Starlett?*

He just looked at her.

Joanne: *Okay, okay. I get it. I'll stop.*

John: *Please.*

Joanne: *Done. So, how's this? The morning after the party I call everybody there and explain that I was just pranking Susie; that it was all a joke. I was planning to call her anyway. So, I'll make a few more calls. Not a big deal.*

John: *Yeah, but if someone takes a picture....*

Joanne: *Private cameras aren't allowed on base. They're too great a security risk.*

John: *But what if somebody sneaks one in?*

Joanne: *Can't happen. You're practically stripped naked before you're even allowed to enter.*

John: *Really?*

Joanne: *There are signs posted all around the perimeter of the base that say "No Trespassing! Lethal Force Authorized." Believe it.*

John: *But even without photos, somebody could still talk to the press.*

Joanne: *So, where's the proof? I'll deny it. You'll deny it. Where's the evidence? It was just a joke, a prank. Besides, what happens on the base stays on the base, John. Trust me on this one.*

John: *So, I have to pretend like we're a couple.*

Joanne: *Hold my hand, and tell me that I look nice. That's it. You can manage that for a couple of hours. I'm not asking that much. Then you can go back to treating me like a tomboy again.*

John: *I don't treat you like a tomboy.*

She stared at him.

John: *Okay. I'll do it. Now, are there any other surprises, or is that it? Because if there are....*

Joanne: *No other surprises.*

John: *You promise?*

Joanne: *I promise.*

And that was how it was left.

The few weeks between Thanksgiving and Christmas passed too quickly, as they always do. Joanne and her uncles were trying to make headway with the infectious disease which the government had tasked them with investigating. As a result, Joanne continued to visit the lab frequently, and Susie was always quick to remind her about their bet.

John was enjoying the European tour much more than he had anticipated. The concerts and the press grind remained the same, but he was often surprised at how differently Christmas was celebrated in the countries where he performed. And European fans were wildly enthusiastic. Also, it was nice to be away from the glad handers, butt sniffers, and hangers-on entourage back in "The States." The only complication occurred on his return flight. There was a minor mechanical issue with their plane which led to an unexpected diversion to an airport in Gander, Newfoundland, a beautiful airport, (if you can call an airport beautiful), in the middle of nowhere. Passengers were disembarked while the repair was carried out, and the plane took on additional fuel. The delay stretched to six interminable hours. The plane finally landed in New York around 1 a.m. John collected his baggage, rented a car, and pulled into his garage at around 4 a.m. He climbed into bed and fell sound asleep. He awoke six hours later feeling still sleep deprived and disoriented by jet lag. He checked his answering machine and started to work his way through a series of messages, most of which were inconsequential. However, the last two were important.

The first was a message from Ben to remind John that he had promised, before leaving on the tour, to pay an afternoon visit to a Boston Hospital's Children's Cancer Center where he would be the guest of honor at a combination fundraising auction/Christmas party. Ben said that the event had been moved to Friday afternoon, so John might as well stay over in a Boston hotel after his plane landed on Thursday. John's first reaction was that he wished he had gotten word sooner. Here he'd just driven home from Boston, and now he'd have to drive back up there tomorrow. Oh well, he concluded, another two-hour drive was a minor inconvenience.

The second was a call from Joanne, saying that she had his tree and wanted to bring it over. He called Joanne first, and she arrived with the tree shortly thereafter. He scrambled a couple of eggs for breakfast. He had helped her with the tree. It was only slightly larger than last year's, but still large enough to be awkward for one person to manage. They attached the stand, and John fetched the boxes of lights and ornaments from Joanne's car, while she made more coffee. He made note of the fact that there were two light strings this year and twice as many ornaments, but he decided not to mention the additions.

They made small talk, mostly about John's tour, while they strung the lights. John casually commented that it was a good thing that he had arrived home on Thursday, so that he had time to put up the tree and wrap the presents he'd brought back before driving to Boston tomorrow.

Joanne: *Your jet lag must be catching up with you.*

John: *Why?*

Joanne: *Today's Friday.*

John: *Yeah, right. Don't make me more confused than I already am.*

Joanne: *I'm not. Today's Friday.*

John: *What?*

Joanne: *Today's Friday.*

John: *Oh my God.*

Joanne: *Are you serious? I thought you were kidding. Did you really think it was still Thursday?*

John: *Oh shit. I lost a day when we got held up in Newfoundland.*

Joanne: *What?*

John: *The plane got delayed. I have to be in Boston at a fundraiser in a few hours.*

Joanne: *A fundraiser? In Boston? Today?*

John: *Yeah, I'm the guest of honor. That's all right. I still have an hour before I have to leave.*

Joanne: *But what about the party?*

John: *What party?*

Joanne: *The Christmas party at the base. Remember?*

John: *But that's Friday.*

Joanne: *And today's Friday.*

John: *Shit, shit, shit, shit, shit.*

Joanne: *Oh, John. You promised.*

John: *Okay. What time does the party start?*

Joanne: *At seven.*

John: *Okay, so if I leave Boston at 5:00, I can drive straight to the party and still get there around seven.*

Joanne: *You can't drive there. You have to be driven there, remember?*

John: *Oh, yeah. I forgot. Okay, so how about you have your guys pick me up here at 7:00 and they drive me there.*

Joanne: *But that means you won't even get there until around 8:00, and I'll have to walk in alone.*

John: *Well, I can try to leave Boston earlier, but they're doing some kind of Christmas auction to raise money for the cancer center, and that doesn't start until 2:00, so I don't know how much earlier I can get out of there. I'll try, Joey, I'll tell them that I'm jet lagged or sick or something. I'll really try.*

Joanne: *Oh, forget it. I'll just go alone.*

John: *No, you won't. I'll be there. I promise. Just explain what happened.*

Joanne: *Well, I suppose that getting held up at a fundraiser for a children's cancer center is a pretty good excuse. Everybody knows that this cause is important to you. I was just hoping to knock Susie out of her socks by walking in with you. I suppose I can keep her in suspense for an hour.*

John: *Oh yeah, the bet. I'd forgotten about that.*

Joanne: *She won't have.*

John: *Okay. Like Ruth always says: "Desperate times, desperate measures."*

John reached around to the back of his neck and undid one of the two drumstick necklaces. He then stepped behind Joanne, placed the necklace around her neck, and reclasped it. He did it so quickly that Joanne didn't really register what had taken place at first.

Joanne: *What are you doing?*

John: *Pranking your friend.*

Joanne: *What?*

John: *If this doesn't convince her, nothing will.*

Joanne: *When's the last time you took this off?*

John: *My memory doesn't go back that far.*

Joanne: *But what if somebody notices that it's missing this afternoon?*

John: *I'll wear a turtleneck.*

Joanne: *But won't you need it for Scarlett? You said Christmas weekend.*

John: *Scarlett? Why? Oh yeah. I forgot.*

Joanne: *I'll take it off after we leave the party, okay?*

John: *Fair enough.*

Joanne: *Wait. Does that mean I'll turn into a pumpkin at midnight?*

John: *Probably. You are a silly goose, Joey.*

Joanne: *Wow. When's the last time you called me a silly goose? I haven't heard that in years.*

John: *It must be the drugs I took in London. I'm reverting back to my childhood. Hey, listen, do you mind if I jump in the shower and change?*

Joanne: *No. Go ahead. It's almost done anyway. I added a few things.*

John: *I noticed.*

Joanne: *I've got some last-minute running around to do, so I'll probably be gone when you come back down.*

John: *Okay, just tell your FBI guys to be here at about 6:30 in case I can cut out early. Oh, and listen, please hide that until the party, just to be safe.*

Joanne: *Of course. I don't know why you're concerned. There are thousands of teeny boppers walking around with fake ones.*

John: *Yeah, but those are plastic, and these are platinum.*

Joanne: *Great. I'll sell it to the highest bidder.*

John: *See you tonight, silly goose.*

Joanne: *Don't be late. Honk!*

Joanne had left by the time John started for Boston. He couldn't get over losing a day, but he'd heard of it happening to others. He was still on European time, so when he arrived at the hospital around two o'clock, it felt like early evening. He walked in sporting a "Santa beard" and toting a huge bag of candy canes, Christmas ribbon candy, Johnny Domino promotional tchotchkes (buttons, pins, plastic drumstick necklaces, etc.) and lots of 45 rpm singles of his latest hit, "Second to None." The kids were thrilled to see him. Many had drawn signs of welcome with crayons the staff had distributed. John had a fleeting thought image of a little Patsy who would probably have eaten some by now. Joanne had told him that Patsy wouldn't be home this Christmas, so the Russo's had decided to suspend their epic annual gathering until he returned safely. Angelo had told Spike, and Spike had told Joanne that he was in a place called Da Nang Province.

Many had drawn signs of welcome with crayons the staff had distributed. John had a fleeting thought image of a little Patsy who would probably have eaten some by now.

The Christmas auction was a great success. The grand prize was four front row seats at Johnny's next Boston concert, along with "All Access" passes for his personal guests, which would allow them to visit with him backstage, both before and after the concert. Some Brookline dad bid $3,500 for those. Johnny had expected that someone with deep pockets from one of Boston's tonier neighborhoods would do that, so he asked the nurses, on the sly, to identify the patient they thought would probably be least able to afford that kind of extravagance, and Johnny presented a little girl from Roxbury with four additional tickets. Around 4:30, the staff passed the word that the kids would have to start cleaning up for dinner. Most of them had already eaten dinner in the form of cake, candy, and ice cream, but they were also due for their evening meds, so John saw his opportunity to leave. After saying his goodbyes, he started back for Connecticut at what was still 10 pm "his" time. He cracked the window to let in some cold air and cranked up the radio to keep himself awake. When he arrived back home, the black sedan was idling in front of his house. He ran inside, took a quick shower to revive himself, changed, jumped into the car's back seat, and fell asleep almost immediately. The last vision he had was of a driver who still wore dark glasses.

THE BALLAD OF JOHNNY AND JOEY: Part 10
Joanne's Christmas Party

John slept soundly during the 45-minute ride and even through the several security stops required to access the base. In fact, the driver had to lower the partition to rouse him. John reoriented himself as he awakened. He stepped out of the car to find himself surrounded on all sides by tall, modern buildings. His first impression was of a futuristic college campus, all steel and glass. The country club, however, stood in architectural contrast. It was situated on a knoll, probably the reservation's highest point, and it was decidedly and intentionally out of place. It was old-school faux colonial, with a white clapboard exterior, multiple chimneys, and double hung windows with shutters. It had an expansive lawn, now covered with snow, and was surrounded by trees and shrubs which were festooned with multi-colored Christmas lights. A golf course stretched out behind the main building which glowed from within. He could hear music coming from inside.

He stepped into the foyer as his ride pulled away. It was a beautiful paneled room lit by a huge chandelier and matching sconces. He noticed that every light bulb was clear, not frosted, which gave the room a particularly warm, cozy feeling, despite its size. Several Christmas trees, each with wrapped presents at its base, dotted the room, along with comfortable furniture arranged for conversational groups. A few couples, drinks in hand, strolled from tree to tree taking in the atmosphere, foursomes sat and chatted, staff hurried here and there proffering hors d'oeuvres or refilling wine glasses. The few men in military uniform served to remind John of where he was. Three oversized sets of French doors led into the main dining/ballroom area. He saw people seated at tables, some still eating, while others were up on the dance floor. A five-or six-piece band on a raised platform was cranking out a respectable cover version of "Put Your Head on My Shoulder," a recent Paul Anka hit. He saw no sign of Joanne, so he decided to head to the bar before he started searching. He noticed some people casting "Where do I know you from?" glances his way, while others nudged their partners and gestured toward him. Life in a goldfish bowl, he thought.

John surveyed the room as he waited for the bartender to head his way. He estimated that there were a couple of hundred people in the room, an eclectic mix of young and old, military and non. Most people seemed to know each other. Given the nature and location of their work, John wasn't surprised that the guests would be socially insular. He noticed also that some wore traditional clothing of foreign countries; Africans and Arabs, for example. Asians were also well represented. No sooner had the bartender taken his order for a vodka and tonic, than John noticed an attractive young woman elbowing her way toward him.

Susie: *Hi Johnny, I'm Susie, Joanne's friend. I hope you don't mind me calling you that, Johnny I mean, because you're him—boy, do I sound stupid or what?*

John: *You don't sound stupid at all. Hi Susie, it's nice to meet you. I think Joanne might have mentioned you at some point.*

Susie: *Yeah, we work together, and we're friends outside of work, too. She's powdering her nose. Why don't you come over to our table and wait for her there?*

John: *Yes, that would be good. I'm feeling a little conspicuous right now.*

Susie: *I'm not surprised. You should have heard the buzz that went around this room when one of the waitresses started spreading the word that Johnny Domino was in the reception hall. We don't get many celebrities visiting our campus. In fact, I think you're the first.*

John: *Well, I'm honored then.*

John retrieved his drink from the bartender and let Susie lead him through the crowd. Whispering and sidelong glances marked their progress across the room. Several people, all women, said, "Hi Johnny," as he passed their tables. He nodded and said "Hello" in return. Susie introduced John to her date, Ron, and to her colleagues, Paul and Lucie. She pointed out Joanne's uncles, all of whom were on the dance floor with their wives except for Uncle Maurice who was dancing with a gaudily attired African lady whom Susie identified as a biomed researcher. They'd just about run out of small talk when Susie looked over John's shoulder and said, "About time," and John felt two hands rest on his shoulders. He recognized Joanne's voice immediately when she said, *"Mind if I join the party?"*

He stood to greet her and was flummoxed by the woman he saw. Actually, "flummoxed" is inadequate to describe what he felt at first sight of Joanne; "poleaxed" might be a more accurate description. Joanne's long, blond hair was up in a twist. She wore a classic L.B.D., a little black dress that showcased ample cleavage and long, long legs in dark, patterned hose with sky-high heels. Her jewelry was minimal, silver drop earrings perfectly complimenting a neck chain which terminated in a miniature drumstick, identical to the one around John's own neck. He was so stunned by her transformation that he stood mute and motionless, until she finally kissed him lightly on the lips and sat herself. *"Still jet-lagged I see,"* she quipped.

He retorted, *"It must be that dress you're almost wearing."*

The exchange drew laughter from the others. John and Joanne did their best to suggest a persuasive level of intimacy; they sat close together and held hands under the table, while he fielded questions about his European tour, which Joanne pretended to know about already, and about his trip to Boston earlier in the day. They deferred more personal questions from Susie about their future plans. When she asked about their plans over the holiday, John said that he'd barely seen or spoken to Joanne since arriving home on account of his disrupted schedule, so they hadn't made arrangements yet. He sensed that Susie was skeptical. Joanne, sensing the same, suggested that she introduce John to her uncles. The band was taking a break and the dancing uncles were headed back to their table.

At the sound of the opening riff, Uncle Maurice jumped to his feet, exclaimed, "I love this song," grabbed Joanne's hand and literally dragged her to the dance floor.

Joanne made the introductions, and Uncle Ward brought over a couple of vacant chairs. The band started a tape recorder which played pre-recorded music during its break. The first song on the tape was "Get Ready" by The Temptations. At the sound of the opening riff, Uncle Maurice jumped to his feet, exclaimed, "*I love this song,*" grabbed Joanne's hand and literally dragged her to the dance floor, where he began to gyrate wildly. She did her best to keep up. Meanwhile, the conversation back at the table was comparatively low key. Ward, Andrew, and Ming wanted to hear about how John and Joanne had come to know each other. John was surprised that Joanne had divulged so little about the history of the original Fab Four + One. They hadn't even heard of The Shades, so John proceeded to give them a capsule version of his and Joanne's friendship.

The talk then turned to Joanne, herself. They were unanimous in their praise for her contributions thus far. Uncle Andrew commented about how her youthful energy had breathed new life into "this team of geriatrics." Uncle Ward said that he would find it difficult to go back to seeing her in oversized sweats or a lab coat after tonight.

This brought an elbow from his wife, which he countered by saying, "*Well, look at her, Mother; there isn't a man in this room who hasn't eyed her up and down, and not a woman who isn't jealous of what her man is thinking. I have a feeling that, starting Monday, a lot of male staff is going to find a reason to visit our department. You wait and see.*"

Uncle Ming, always the least demonstrative member of the group, quietly dubbed her, "A genius, possibly the greatest mind of her generation."

Joanne and Uncle Maurice returned to the table somewhat breathless. He scooped up Uncle Ming's wife with, "C'mon Toshiko. Shake a leg." And they were off to celebrate Tommy James and The Shondells singing "Mony, Mony." Uncle Andrew reached across the table and tapped the back of John's hand, "Best escape while you can. He'll probably be after you next." Everyone at the table laughed knowingly but not unkindly.

John and Joanne said their goodbyes, wished everyone Happy Holidays and headed back to their table. On the way there, Joanne mentioned that she'd like another glass of chardonnay, and John commented that he could use a Drambuie on the rocks before facing more of Susie's interrogation, so they detoured to the bar.

Joanne asked him if he thought Susie was convinced. He ducked her question by saying that she (Joanne) was more qualified to answer that question than he was. She thought for a moment and then said that she didn't think Susie was sold yet, but she couldn't think of how to dispel Susie's lingering doubt. At that moment who should join them at the bar but the subject of their speculation, fresh from the ladies' lounge.

Susie: *So, are you two coming back to the younger generation's table?*

Joanne: *Yes, we're just waiting for our drinks; then we'll head over.*

Susie: *Great, we're all dying to know how and when you started wearing Johnny's necklace and what it means; as much as you're willing to say, of course. You know what I mean. I didn't even know that you and Joanne even grew up together.*

John: *Well, you know, Susie, I live a lot of my life in the public eye now, but I like to keep what's really important to me private. That's why you'll never see Joey on the cover of National Enquirer. Most of the women in those photos are like ornaments on the trees out in the lobby, pretty to look at, but hollow on the inside.*

Susie: *Wow, Joanne! That's quite an endorsement.*

John: *And that's our song, so if you'll excuse us, I want to dance with my date.*

The song John referred to was "Whoever You Are," sung by newcomer Chrissie Gardner. It wasn't his and Joanne's song at all, but Susie wouldn't know that, and John saw an opportunity to put some distance between them and her; besides which, he did genuinely like the song.

Arriving on the dance floor, Joanne raised her right hand so that John could take it in his left to hold against his shoulder. Instead, he took both of her hands and raised them to the back of his neck.

John: ***Both hands behind my neck in a hug and your head resting on my chest. You want to win that bet? This is the first step.***

Joanne: ***Okay. What's the second?***

John: ***In a minute. See if you can sneak a glance over at the table. Tell me when your friend is looking at us.***

They danced without speaking for a minute during while Chrissie Gardner transitioned from the second verse to the bridge.

Joanne: ***She's watching us now.***

John: ***Good. Raise your head and kiss me.***

The word "what?" started to form on Joanne's lips, but they were already otherwise engaged. Still, her eyes remained wide open in surprise. When the kiss ended, they returned to their original posture: her hands joined behind his neck, and his hands clasped behind her waist.

Joanne: ***I'll assume that was step two.***

John: ***It was.***

Joanne: ***Have you practiced it on Scarlett?***

John didn't comment. They danced for another minute or so. Meanwhile, Chrissie Gardner was through the verse for the second time and starting on the bridge again.

John: ***Is she still watching?***

Joanne: ***Move to your right a little. There's a couple blocking my view. Yeah, she's glued to us right now.***

John: ***Good. Kiss me again, but this time, don't kiss me like you're kissing your brother.***

Where the first kiss could best be described as "chaste," this kiss was anything but. Tongues met, grips tightened, bodies pressed, and everything changed.

Where the first kiss could best be described as "chaste," this kiss was anything but. Tongues met, grips tightened, bodies pressed, and everything changed.

The kiss and the song ended more or less at the same time. The band had returned, this time opening their set with "My Baby Does the Hanky

Panky" which brought Uncle Maurice back to the floor dragging Uncle Ward's wife, a true Southern Belle, behind.

John and Joanne detoured to the bar to reclaim their drinks without exchanging any words. When they arrived back at their table, Susie greeted their return with, "Get a room, you two!" which brought embarrassed laughter from John and Joanne. John decided to avoid the line of interrogation he fully expected to follow by asking Joanne if she would mind if he retrieved their coats so that they could start the 45-minute drive back home. He explained that he'd only had a few hours of sleep since getting off the plane, and that he still felt pretty jet-lagged, because, while it was 10 p.m. for them, it was 4 a.m. for him.

Joanne said, *"No, that's fine. I'll come with you. You probably won't recognize my coat. Susie and I can settle up after New Year's. Right, Susie?"*

Susie held her glass up as if to toast Joanne in wordless congratulation. Everyone wished everyone else a Merry Christmas and a Happy New Year. Their ride was waiting nearby when they exited the country club, and they climbed into the back seat. No sooner had the car started to pull away, when Joanne turned to John and said, *"What just happened back there?*

But Johnny Domino was already fast asleep.

The After Party

What followed was three-quarters of an hour of much-needed sleep for John and confused speculation for Joanne. The driver assumed that John would get out first, since he'd been picked up last and pulled into John's driveway after a quiet ride home from the base. Joanne roused John, whose first words were, *"Have we landed?"*

She responded, *"Yes, O sleeping superstar. Out you get."*

As she was exiting, she said to the driver, *"Won't be long."* He just nodded.

Once inside, they tossed their coats on the sofa. Joanne immediately started to unclasp the necklace.

Joanne: *This won't come undone. Is there a trick to it?*

John: *Yeah, actually there is. Let me pour us a nightcap, and then I'll do it.*

Joanne: *Okay, I just don't want to keep Scarlett the Starlett waiting. Are you calling her tomorrow, or are you two meeting up somewhere? By the way, have you personally autographed her copy of your poster?*

John: *Why? Want me to sign the one you have in your apartment bedroom?*

Joanne: *Who told you? Was it Susie?*

John: *No, it was you.*

Joanne: *Me? When?*

John: *Just now.*

Joanne: *Touche.*

He handed her a drink and sat facing her.

John: *Listen, I want to ask you something.*

Joanne: *Oh, Oh. Sounds serious. Make it quick. At midnight I turn back into a pumpkin.*

John: *Do you remember a conversation we had in my hot tub about a year ago?*

Joanne: *I remember being very upset and driving here because I didn't want to go home and have to explain why I'd been crying. And I remember that I was really hoping that you'd be here, but I certainly didn't expect to find you naked in a hot tub, outside, on a cold winter night.*

John: *I wasn't exactly expecting visitors. Do you remember what we talked about?*

Joanne: *You mean after I told you that I'd broken up with Richie?*

John: *Yeah.*

Joanne: *We talked about what qualities we'd want to find in someone else, someone special, I mean.*

John: *The list.*

Joanne: *I remember we made a list, but I don't remember what was on it—especially at the end. I think I was pretty out of it by then.*

John: *We both were.*

Joanne: *Me more than you. Let's see, I remember good looking and sexy, and smart. I remember smart.*

John: *Those are the easy ones.*

Joanne: *Yeah, well, a lot of what we said turned into a fog after another drink or two. I don't even remember when you helped me upstairs to the guest room.*

John: *Creative. And kind; kindness was important.*

Joanne: *And empathetic. I remember that, because you couldn't think of the word at first.*

John: *Yes, empathetic, how many is that?*

Joanne: *Let's see.* (She counts on her fingers.) *Six, that's six. We got to ten, didn't we?*

John: *Yeah, ten. A good friend.*

Joanne: *Right! A good friend is more important than a lover. Boy, that's rich, coming from America's heartthrob.*

John: *Now, now.*

Joanne: *Oh, wait, I know one we missed.*

John: *What?*

Joanne: *Style. Somebody with style.*

John: *Style, right. See, you remember more than you thought.*

Joanne: *Don't ask me how. What does that make?*

John: *Let's see. Good looks, smart, sexy, stylish, sympathetic.*

Joanne*:* *Empathetic.*

John: *That, too. Kind. A good friend.*

Joanne: *Creative.*

John: *Creative. That's eight. And interesting. We said they'd have to be interesting.*

Joanne: *I don't remember that. Are you sure?*

John: *Yep. We said interesting.*

Joanne: *Okay, I believe you, but that still leaves one to go.*

John: *The most important one: personal intimacy.*

Joanne: *Yeah? So that's it then? That's ten.*

John*:* *Good looking, sexy, intelligent, stylish, interesting, empathetic, creative, kind, a good friend, and someone you could trust with personal intimacy. That's it. That's the list.*

Joanne: *You remembered better than I did.*

John: *There's a reason. Joey, I've thought about that list every day since.*

Joanne: *Really?*

John: *Really. Sometimes, several times a day, in fact.*

Joanne: *Huh? Why?*

John: *Because I'm tired of being my own best company.*

Joanne: *So, you've been taking inventory.*

John: *I guess that's one way to put it.*

Joanne: *And?*

John: *Several people have come close. But there's only one person who measures up.*

Joanne: *Oh my God. What time is it?*

John: *Why?*

Joanne: *Because if it's after twelve, then it's Christmas Eve day, and I have to get this jewelry off, so you can give it to Scarlett. Help me get it off.*

John: *No.*

Joanne: *I don't think I can do it alone.*

John: *No. That necklace is right where it belongs.*

Joanne: *What?*

John: *It's you, silly goose.*

Joanne: *Me?*

John: *It's been you since that night a year ago. It just took me six months to admit it to myself.*

Joanne: *Six months? I'm missing something here.*

John: *I needed to convince myself that I was ready.*

Joanne: *But Scarlett....*

John: *Convinced me that I was ready to commit. I mean, not her, that relationship, or whatever it was.*

Joanne: *Commit how?*

John: *Look, Joey, I'm not proposing or anything. It's not like that. But I would like us to be exclusive to each other. That was your word, "exclusive," remember?*

Joanne: *You mean like going steady?*

John: *I hate that, but, yeah, I guess it's sort of a grown-up version of that, isn't it?*

Joanne: *Are you sure about this? Because with your track record....*

John: *Yeah, I know. That's why I didn't say anything for six months. I had to be sure I could do this.*

Joanne: *You mean you haven't….*

John: *I've been a monk.*

Joanne: *But Scarlett….*

John: *Has only been in the picture for the last 6 or 7 weeks.*

Joanne: *Still….*

John: *I told her I had contracted something, so we had to wait.*

Joanne: *Wow.*

John: *Yeah. Wow.*

Joanne: *John, I really didn't expect….*

John: *I know.*

Joanne: *And love….*

John: *Wasn't on the list.*

Joanne: *Right.*

John: *I know where you're going here. I have no expectations, Joey. I want to see you. I want us to spend time together, whenever we can. I want us to be a couple. I want to have other people think of us as a couple. If it doesn't work, that's okay. Whoever has had enough contacts the other, and that ends it. We're no longer exclusive. On the other hand, if it works, then let's see where it will take us.*

Joanne: *You really have thought this through, haven't you?*

John: *I've had six months.*

Joanne: *But I haven't, and I'm going to need some time. So, can I say I'll think it over?*

John: *For as long as you'd like…with one condition.*

Joanne: *Which is?*

John: *Wear the necklace.*

Joanne: *But if I do that, everyone will know….*

John: *So hide it. You don't have to fill your closet with turtlenecks. Wear it somewhere else.*

Joanne: *Well, I suppose I could do that. But what about you?*

John: *I don't have to reveal who I gave it to. The press will go crazy. It'll be great publicity.*

Joanne: *So, I become a woman of mystery.*

John: *Until you decide. And if you decide that we should make it public....*

Joanne: *I go from being a woman of mystery to being one of the most hated women in America.*

John: *Your security team will protect you from assassination attempts.*

Joanne: *Very funny. Okay. I'll think about it. Don't expect a quick response.*

John: *No pressure. You play lead.*

The grandfather clock in John's foyer sounded.

Joanne: *What time is it?*

John: *It sounds on the quarters.*

He looked at his watch.

John: *11:45.*

Joanne: *And I didn't even turn into a pumpkin.*

John: *Not yet, anyway.*

Joanne: *Well, I think I'll see if I can catch up with my parents at midnight mass.*

John: *You'll be late.*

Joanne: *It won't be the first time*

She prepared to leave. He gestured toward the necklace.

John: *You might want to... Oh, right. It's going to take a little getting used to.*

He helped her remove it.

John: *See. It's got a security clasp.*

He shows her how it worked.

John: *I'm sure that one of the great minds of her generation can figure it out.*

She looks at him, puzzled.

John: *Your Uncle Ming.*

Joanne: *He said that?*

John: *He did.*

Joanne: *Wow. This night has been one for the books. I'm going to head over to Saint Patrick's before something else happens.*

John: *It's not midnight yet. You still have time to turn into a pumpkin.*

Joanne: *You must be exhausted.*

John: *The nap in the car helped, but I'm headed up.*

Joanne: *Call me when you're awake.*

John: *Okay.*

They kissed, rather awkwardly at first.

John: *Sleep well.*

Joanne: *No chance.*

She headed out to the waiting car, then turned and gave him a little wave as she climbed in. He gave her a little wave back and watched the car as it pulled away, its tail lights disappearing as it turned off Hummingbird Lane and onto Battle Street. Just as he was about to head back inside, he noticed the stars. The sky was clear, and there was no moon, so the panoply of stars was on full show. All of his friends were there; Orion and the Great Dog, Taurus the Bull and Auriga, the charioteer.

He remembered back to almost exactly one year ago when he'd also looked out on another clear, silent night. Suddenly, his mind swam with memories; memories of unsold Christmas trees, of pet store dogs in empty malls, and of a vigil light burning in an empty factory warehouse. It saddened him to think that they were still part of the world, and probably always would be. His heart went out to them. But somehow he felt that they were no longer part of his world, and that was a good thing. He turned away and closed the front door behind him.

Epilogue

On Frenchtown and Me

Have you missed me? Hopefully you wondered where I had gone and what had become of me. On the other hand, perhaps I flatter myself in thinking so. I believe that the last time you saw me was when I dismissed the idea of becoming The Shades' leader. So, what happened to me? Not much, and that's the point. My life was unremarkable when compared to the others. I didn't choose to share it simply because I didn't deem it interesting enough to share.

Although I was a charter member of the late, great Fab Four + One, I lived on the periphery of Frenchtown, where that culture started to mix with the Main Street mainstream. The others, Tommy and Patsy and Joanne and John, lived in close proximity to each other in the very heart of Frenchtown. I always walked, or later biked, to where they were; they rarely walked or biked to where I was, unless they had cause to do some downtown Thompsonville shopping or to see a film at The Strand Theater, which, as I mentioned, I could see from my house. North School was the common denominator for us in the early years, then Higgins School, which was really just a junior high extension of North School.

High School, Friendly Fullerton, started a change which lasts to this day. Our weltanschauungs began to redefine our identities and our relationships. I suppose those changes were inevitable. We were growing up. Santa Claus wasn't coming down the chimney anymore, and Joanne was no longer "one of the guys." I still had the drums, Tommy still blew things up, and Patsy was still Patsy. But John left to follow his dream, and then Joanne left to follow hers. The three of us who remained still hung out together, but it just wasn't the same. Carlene gradually became Yoko Ono to Tommy's John Lennon; Spike married Ray and moved away from the river into a new development in Scitico. Then we graduated. I went off to college downstate, Tommy went off to college out of state, and Patsy went off to boot camp, and eventually to Vietnam.

And that, as they say, was that. We'd see each other periodically. Patsy's Christmas party was always a sure bet. We even talked about a one-night-only Shades' reunion in Patsy's rec room, but it never got past the talking stage. It was probably just as well. Anticipation always trumps reality when it comes to events like that. Johnny Domino's itinerary would probably have made it impossible anyway. The last time we were together as a group was Patsy's funeral. Angelo bought a plot for four, by the way; two for himself and Patsy's mom, one for Patsy, and one for… well, I don't think I need to tell you who the fourth plot was for, do I? I thought that was a beautiful and well-deserved gesture.

So there you are. Tommy and I gradually faded from the narrative because we were the closest to normal. And who wants to read about normal? That leaves just one circumstance worth mentioning. Joanne and I started writing to each other. It came about from a suggestion she made at the funeral. She told us that she had written to Patsy regularly. He answered sporadically, but she understood why. She suggested that we, who remained, stay connected via letters. I don't think that any of us expected that to happen, but, somehow, it did; in fact, it does to this day, now via e-mail of course. The point is that she kept me up to date on what was happening between her and John. Obviously, I had to invent a lot of the detail, and most of the dialog, but both she and John have read this manuscript and approved of its overall accuracy, allowing for the writer's artistic license, of course. They're fine by the way, as are Tommy and Carlene, Spike and Ray, and yours truly.

As for Frenchtown, well, it will come as no surprise that it, too, has changed. I no longer live in Connecticut, but I still have cause to visit two or three times a year. And once every few years I make time to drive down those streets. I wend my way through those neighborhoods, just as John did on that lonely Christmas Eve so many years ago. The houses are still there; the street names haven't changed. Most everything else has. The principal mill buildings still exist, but they've been converted into upscale condos. From what I understand, some of The Mill's industrial features have been incorporated into the architecture; brick walls left exposed in some apartments, and segments of the overhead belt system that once powered those huge, noisy looms are still extant in public areas. I've never been inside. Most of the smaller, satellite mill buildings are now gone, along with the businesses that once serviced the workers. Chick's is gone, but I'll bet that urban archaeologists will someday marvel at all the fossilized bubblegum they find near what once was the store's entrance.

North School is still there, but it's now some sort of social services facility. I'm sure it's been totally reconfigured on the inside; I prefer the version I hold in my memory of a huge central staircase in the center of the building that progressed up to a landing where it split into two smaller staircases on opposing walls that reached the second floor. There you were greeted by paintings of Washington or Lincoln, depending on which stairway you took. Still, I'd like to see what they've done with the space where Miss Sullivan once pounded out "I'm a Little Teapot" on that archaic piano before taking her last breath. I'll bet those tall windows are still there, hopefully with the draughty single glass panes now replaced by something more energy efficient. Higgins Junior High is still there, too, but it's now an elementary school. I doubt that it has changed much. I'd like to see the cafetorium where I played the drum solo and Patsy held court as King Neptune.

St Partrick's Church is still there, the austere interior probably the same. The life size crucified Jesus probably still hangs above and behind the altar reminding us of how He gave His life for us, and scaring the shit out of little children as He always has. The Catholic Church still uses the fear of our own eventual destinies to make us walk life's straight and narrow, much as politicians use fear to get reelected. The church school where Sister Kerosina ruled with an iron fist is a parking lot now, but the Sisters of Mercy Convent, which nuns disapperated into and out of, is still there. The Strand Theatre is still there too; it's been shuttered for decades now. There's a weathered "for lease" sign on the building with a number to call. I've been tempted, just to see the interior, or what's left of it, again, but I think I'd just come away depressed.

Most of the smaller, satellite mill buildings are now gone, along with the businesses that once serviced the workers; Chick's is gone, but I'll bet that urban archaeologists will someday marvel at all the fossilized bubblegum they find near what once was the store's entrance.

What's changed most about Frenchtown is the population. When The Mill moved to South Carolina in search of cheaper non-unionized labor, Frenchtown lost its reason to exist. The Italian and Polish families gradually moved away or died off, or first moved away and then died off. I'll bet some of my grandparents' generation stuck it out to the end, but they're all gone now, too. The Thompsonville commercial center is gone, too, except for a liquor store, a Good Will store, a Cumberland Farms and a head shop. Our house, the house my sister and I grew up in, is still there, but it's in sad shape. Factory workers didn't have much, but they took pride in what they did have. Everything was kept tidy inside and out. The peer pressure to do so was formidable. If your house was dirty or your lawn was untended, then you must have come from Sicily.

A good percentage of the people who live in Frenchtown are now renters, not owners. Many of the two-story houses are divided into first floor and second floor apartments. Two story duplexes are now four-unit apartment houses. The landlords are often corporations, some of them foreign. All of the pathologies associated with a struggling population are on show. Every few years, an opportunistic politician will make a case for urban renewal; flowers will be planted in open spaces, the Enfield Library will host a display of photos and related Frenchtown memorabilia, but another stabbing or overdose death always steals the spotlight. Our Yankee Stadium miniature Louisville Sluggers have morphed into 45 calibers and 9 millimeters.

So, why do I bother to return, you might ask. Why feed depression? Well, I did mention the attraction that melancholia has for some people, didn't I? Oh, you thought I was talking about John? Only in part. But mainly it's because I see those buildings: the church, the schools, The Mill, the houses, and The Strand through the filter of childhood. Did you notice that I put "The Strand" last in that list, even after "the houses?" I didn't do that consciously. I just did it. But it should tell you something about me. It certainly tells me something about myself. The Mill might have been the heart of Frenchtown, but The Strand was always its soul, to me anyhow. If Hollywood was America's dream factory, The Strand was Frenchtown's.

Frenchtown, my Frenchtown anyway, doesn't exist anymore; and, before long, I, and people like me who grew up there, won't exist either.

There are many positives to living in an insular community like Frenchtown: friendship, trust, safety, communication, similar tastes, similar beliefs, similar values, yadda, yadda, yadda. Florida has made an art form of insular living. Are those "gated community" gates walling people out or walling people in? Let's just say that if most of "The Villages" residents weren't too old to reproduce, they'd probably be rife with inbreeding. After all, human beings are herd animals by nature, but we want to choose our own herds. Most of us prefer the company of others, as long as they're more or less like us. The problem, of course, occurs when we cross over the line from insular to tribal, and Frenchtown certainly was that, tribal to a fault. When that happens, insular positives turn to tribal negatives. So maybe it's a good thing that if you were to ask anyone living there now about "Frenchtown," you'd probably be greeted with a blank stare, because Frenchtown, my Frenchtown anyway, doesn't exist anymore, and, before long, I, and people like me who grew up there, won't exist either.

I don't know if I'll travel there again. I'm getting older and travel has become difficult; my world is shrinking. I guess that happens to all of us as we age, but that's okay, because being in one place most of the time allows for memory and for reflection.

Lately, I've been thinking a lot about change. They say that the only constant is change. But some things never change, do they? The stars never change. They've been unchanged for centuries, millennia, for millions of years even. Think about all the people who have come before us... before you. Every step you take on dirt, on sand, on your lawn, or in a field is on someone else's grave. Every time you turn a spade of earth, you're disturbing someone's rest. That'll make you think the next time you plant a petunia, won't it?

But I take comfort that the stars, the real stars, won't ever change. I need only step outside and look up, and I'm back in The Strand. I'm back in Frenchtown.

Stars never change. Orion still hunts, The Great Bear still stalks, The Scorpion still stings, Taurus still charges, Sagittarius still draws his bow, and Hercules still wields his club. If you could get inside The Strand and shine a flashlight up into the ceiling roundel, they'd still be there, all of them and more, still there, staring down at you. I'll bet they still hear the long-ago music and dialog that once pumped through the speakers, that they still bear witness to the phantom black and white, and sometimes Technicolor, images that flickered across the screen, and that they still watch over the ghosts of five children, who found a second home, a place of safety, of friendship, of acceptance and of wonder in there. The lights that marked the principal shapes of those painted constellations are long ago burnt out, never to be replaced. More change. But I take comfort that the stars, the real stars, won't ever change. I need only step outside and look up, and I'm back in The Strand.

I'm back in Frenchtown.

Frenchtown started off as a podcast. If, after reading this version, you'd also like to listen to it, you'll find that it's available on all major podcast platforms. *Frenchtown* will also be released as an audiobook in the near future.

As neither podcasts nor audio book versions include biographies of the voice actors, I'll take this opportunity to salute my talented cast.

***Daina Schatz** (Reader) is grateful to have been a part of this project! Daina received a BA in Psychology with a concentration in Law and Society from Cornell University, and has worked with such regional theatres as Yale Rep, Seven Angels, The Schwartz Center for Performing Arts, and the River Rep at Ivoryton. She also has various commercial, TV and film credits, and is enjoying her newest and most important role: Mom. Love to Mom, Dad, Jeff and Isaac, and special thanks to Mr. G and the entire* Frenchtown *team!*

***Jeffrey Anbinder** (Reader) is a Cornell and Yeshiva University educated attorney and writer living in Brooklyn, New York, who has at various times been a professional fundraiser, a rock musician, and a cab driver. Many years ago he was also dubbed "The Sexiest Man in Ithaca Radio" (which is a bit like being the toughest kid in second grade), and he is grateful to have had the opportunity to pick up a microphone again as part of* Frenchtown, *especially working alongside someone as talented as Daina Schatz. Love to Dad, Daina, and Isaac; much gratitude to Mr. G and the Frenchtown crew; and I miss you, Mom.*

Made in the USA
Middletown, DE
01 August 2024

58352402R00126